TheCentury
for Young People

PETER JENNINGS
TODD BREWSTER

Adapted by Jennifer Armstrong
Photographs edited by Katherine Bourbeau

TheCentury
for Young People

A Doubleday Book for Young Readers

A Doubleday Book for Young Readers

Published by
Random House, Inc.
1540 Broadway
New York, New York 10036

Doubleday and the portrayal of an anchor
with a dolphin are trademarks of Random
House, Inc.

**Library of Congress Cataloging-in-
Publication Data**
ISBN 0-385-32708-0

Book design by Elton Robinson
Manufactured in the United States of America
October 1999
10 9 8 7 6 5 4 3 2 1
RRD

Acknowledgments

This book was the idea of the people who run
Random House Children's Books—chiefly Craig
Virden, Beverly Horowitz, Karen Wojtyla, and
Candice Chaplin—and its existence is a testament
to their expert work at adapting a very large volume (the original *The Century*) in a very short
time. We are also indebted to Jennifer Armstrong,
who reconceived the text. And we owe thanks to
members of the ABC staff who helped to make
this version of *The Century* possible: Terry
Carnes, Zahava Mahlab, and Shari Rothseid, who
secured permissions to reproduce the photographs, and Elisabeth King, who checked the
adapted text against her extensive research on the
original volume to ensure that no mistakes or
errors of historical judgment crept in. Thanks for
their special efforts go to Susan Warga, Barbara
Perris, Fiona Simpson, Janet Parker, Gabriel X.
Ashkenazi, Patrice Sheridan, and Elton Robinson
at Random House Children's Books. We would
be remiss to publish this—yet another volume
called *The Century*—without noting, yet again,
the extraordinary work of *The Century* television
series staff, especially those producers who found
the eyewitnesses we include here and interviewed
them. And we owe much, of course, to the original
The Century book staff: photography editor
Katherine Bourbeau and her assistant, Audrey
Landreth, and the text and research staff that
included Amy Faust, Tim Frew, and Elisabeth
King. As always, we hope our work makes our colleagues proud.

For our children: Elizabeth, Christopher, and Jack

Contents

Introduction

Left: In 1900 Oliver Lippincott's Locomobile became the first horseless carriage to edge out onto the top of Yosemite Park's Glacier Point, illustrating one of the thorniest conflicts of the century: technology versus nature.

Introduction

How do you tell the story of the past hundred years? When we took on that task a few years ago, it was with great excitement . . . and a little nervousness. Both of us had worked as journalists—Peter with ABC News, Todd with *Life* magazine—covering some of the major events of the past quarter century. And we understood that the stories we covered each day were usually only the most recent chapters in long-running dramas that stretched back to the beginning of the twentieth century; indeed, well beyond that.

The stories we watch on the TV news or read about in newspapers or magazines often have complex histories. Why did the Balkan states erupt in such turmoil? Why did America go to war in the Persian Gulf? Why did the verdict on the Rodney King beating set off such intense violence? Why did people so mourn a princess who never would have been queen? The answers to these questions, and so many others that became important in the 1990s, have roots in the story of the twentieth century.

Still, we were frustrated, in the way that journalists are on any assignment: How were we to get at that story? How were we to find a fresh perspective on the way life was lived in this amazing period? Only when we realized that the twentieth century was a time when the lives of ordinary people became the focus of history—as they reaped the benefits of the new technologies, enjoyed new political freedoms in the spread of democracy, and, sadly, became ever more the target of war—did we land on our answer: We would tell the *people's* story. And we would do that in part by interviewing hundreds of men and women who were distinctive only in their ability to recall what the world had been like in their lifetimes. Edited versions of those interviews are an essential part of this book, the memories that keep history fresh.

For example, we knew about Orville and Wilbur Wright's dream of flight. But Mabel Griep, whose father used to hitch up the horse and wagon and take her out to a field in Dayton, Ohio, to watch the Wright "boys" tinker with their machines in the early 1900s, gets us so much closer to what it felt like to see the miracle of flight for the first time. "When that plane took off," she told us, "I think I held my breath the entire time."

Griep is just one of dozens of people you will meet in these pages. Betty Broyles is another. She remembers what it was like to go on a joy ride in the 1920s, when cars were new. Albert Sindlinger recalls the early days of radio, when programming provided more static than anything else. Edward Francis gives a vivid account of the horror of trench life in World War I, when the stench of death competed with the lice and the mud and the sniper fire. Sheila Black remembers the London blitz of World War II, when she gave birth by the light of the bombs. Diane Nash describes the power of nonviolent protest in the civil rights movement in America in the 1960s. And Larry Gwin recalls the distinctively American misery of Vietnam. Long after we had completed this book, we heard the voices of Griep and Francis and Nash and Gwin as we thought back on the twentieth century.

If there was one theme common to the recollections of nearly all our witnesses, it was the inevitability of change. There have been so many momentous events in this century—and so much change at speeds that people who lived in earlier centuries would have thought impossible. As one historian told us, a citizen of the nineteenth century could be pretty sure that the life he would lead would be very similar to that led by his parents. There would be some important changes, but none so radical that the entire society would be remade. In the twentieth century, however, we faced radical changes over and over again—with scientific theory, medical advances, the personal computer, air travel, nearly instantaneous communication, and, of course, the ability to destroy the entire world.

Our witnesses spoke often of the difference America has made in this century. At the beginning of the 1900s, the young, quite innocent United States was very reluctant to be dragged into Europe's bloody affairs. But it happened. And over the decades America emerged as the preeminent world power, particularly after the collapse of the Soviet Union and the end of the Cold War. The story of the triumph of freedom and democracy is part of the legacy of the twentieth century.

This was the century of popular culture. In the 1800s, people played music at home on the piano in the parlor and families gathered to sing together. Higher culture was something that was reserved for the rich. In the twentieth century, however, technology helped to create a new kind of culture available to the general public. Music was mass-produced on recordings. Movies opened in theaters across the country. And radio and television created new, popular dramas that tens of millions of people experienced together, at the same time, in their homes.

Finally, this was the century of race. That seems an odd thing to say. How can "race" have a century? But from the earliest days of the 1900s straight through to the 1990s, Americans were challenged to create a just and equitable society that respected the rights and dignity of minority populations. At the beginning of the century, African Americans in the South were forced to use separate facilities. By midcentury, African American men were among those fighting in Europe to defeat Germany, whose leader had advanced a sinister belief in the racial superiority of the German people, even as the American armed forces remained segregated. And as late as the 1960s, many black Americans were still being denied the right to vote. We have come far, but we have much farther to go.

Of course, that's a statement that can apply to many of the themes of the twentieth century. Indeed, after reading these pages you may conclude, as we have, that these past hundred years have brought amazing advances, yes, but that the central questions of human existence remain the same. We still need to seek the just and the morally right thing to do—and we will face that challenge in the next hundred years, your century.

1 Seeds of Change

1901–1914

For generations, people have looked forward to a new century with both hope and nervousness: What will the new age bring? Faced with a mysterious future, they feel both the thrill of possibility and the fear of the unknown. The end of the 1800s carried even more tension than usual because it witnessed the end of many ideas that had ruled people's lives for a long time. Charles Darwin's theories of evolution and natural selection had challenged religion, shaking up people's understanding of their own origins. At the same time, the political ideas of socialism and democracy began to dominate a world that had long been ruled by kings and queens. While vastly different political ideas, both socialism and democracy argued that power should be taken from the elite few and given to the masses. Finally, the growth of science and industry began to change the way people related to the natural environment. More and more, people were leaving the farm to live in a machine-made world, the world of cities. They knew that the city was where the new century would take shape.

In America, these advances in technology promised a bright future. It was American inventors who thrilled the world with new machines, American factory owners who made these new machines for the world's use. Design by design, object by object, they promised to establish a new way of life—not just for a few privileged people, but for all humanity.

Left: More than any other, this was the century of the city. And more than any other city, New York would become the steel-and-concrete emblem of the modern era. It was at the turn of the century that the New York we know today began to be built. Here a worker helps to top off the new Woolworth Building, c. 1912, one of the first of many skyscrapers that by the 1920s would make old New York into *new* New York.

Mabel Griep was born in 1896 in Dayton, Ohio, just a few doors down from the Wright Brothers' bicycle shop. She witnessed a landmark event in the history of technology in 1904.

When I was growing up, we didn't have electricity. We used a lot of candles for light, and of course we had gas fixtures. And then outside in the streets, we had street lamps. Every evening at sundown the lamp boys would light the lamps one by one. All the little kids would rejoice when the lamp boys would come, because it meant we could still play outside, even though it was dark.

My father, who was an architect with an office in downtown Dayton, Ohio, was designing and building a new house for us in the country, and it was to be fully equipped with electricity, which was pretty modern back then. There was just so much change going on those early years of the century. I remember when we got our first telephone. You would have to stand at the wall and talk into this contraption, and we shared the line with four or five different neighbors who would all come on the line at the same time. Sometimes you didn't know who was

Above: Griep (right) and her sister Lorine Hyer, c. 1905.

Below: The 1904 Wright Flyer during a test flight at Huffman Prairie.

talking to who. Still, it was all very exciting. Life was changing so much and so quickly that it made some people anxious. But not my father; he was extremely interested and excited by what was going on.

One day he came home from work early and said, "Get your things ready. Our boys are going to try a flight today!" My father always referred to the Wright brothers as "our boys." He said, "We'll go out, and if it's successful, we'll be there to see it. It'll make history." Then he hitched our horse, Old Nip, up to the surrey and we headed out to Huffman Prairie, where the flight was to take place. We were good friends with the Wright family. Their bicycle shop was down the street from our home. And when they started working on their flying machine, the word spread pretty quickly around town. Some of the neighbors were pretty skeptical about what they were trying to do. They were always saying, "They're back in that bicycle shop again. I don't know what they think they're going to do. They'll never make a machine that can fly." The Wright brothers were so sold on building a flying machine that none of the negative talk bothered them at all. They just kept working.

Our father had driven us out to Huffman Prairie a number of times. That's the place that Orville and Wilbur used as a testing ground. All the other times we were out there, there was no flying going on. They would just be testing their machine: working on the propeller, or motorizing something, or making it move here or there. But this time my father had heard that they were actually going to make it fly. Now, the Wright brothers had already had a successful flight down in Kitty Hawk, North Carolina, but none of the newspapers really reported on it, and most people didn't believe it actually happened. So as far as we were concerned, they were attempting the impossible that day.

Dad knew of a place at Huffman Prairie that was on an incline, and it offered us a pretty good view of what was going on. There was much activity going on down in that field, and we had the bird's-eye view of it. Dad was so excited, he turned to us, shaking his fist, and said, "Are you all paying attention to this? Now listen to me, you're going to remember this to your last day." Every time either Orville or Wilbur did something the crowd would inch a little closer to try and see what was going on.

When that plane took off the ground, I just can't describe how I felt. I think I held my breath the entire time, and I'm sure an awful lot of people said a prayer. It was spectacular—just unbelievable. That's all I can say. The plane lifted sort of level at first and then started to rise up. I don't know just how far they went. The whole flight couldn't have lasted longer than a minute, but it proved that it could be done. When the plane landed, the whole field just exploded with applause. And then it got strangely quiet. Nobody could believe what they had just seen. People stood around kind of dumbstruck. Not many people were even talking about it. I couldn't help but think about all of those mouthy people who said it would never happen. I was just exhausted when it was all over. It was like witnessing a miracle.

On an almost daily basis, it seemed, Americans were witnessing miracles of new technology. They were eagerly making way for the future even as they asked themselves these difficult questions: How could this new machine age be made to reflect American values and character? Just what would it mean to *be* American in the frightening and thrilling future that was about to unfold?

If the future had a shape at the start of the 1900s, it was the skyscraper. The architectural wonder of the new era had risen from the ashes of Chicago, which had burned in 1871. When that city was rebuilt, it was not with wood, but with steel, glass, and reinforced concrete. These modern materials were used to create buildings that rose higher than ever toward the clouds. Since exploration and settlement of the western frontier had been completed, it was time to start building upward, into the air itself.

New York built skyward as did few other cities. And as the main port of entry into the United States, it made its skyscrapers a picture of upward mobility to the millions of immigrants who now began pushing toward America. From 1890 to 1910 nearly thirteen million immigrants came to the United States. They came from many countries, all in search of the land of opportunity. Their vastly different backgrounds, their diverse religious beliefs and customs, would pose a challenge to the very idea of what it meant to be an American.

The cover of this song sheet paid tribute to the era's fascination with technology.

Alfred Levitt, born in 1894, emigrated with his family to New York City in 1911. He described what the experience of coming to America was like.

Levitt in 1914.

I was born in a small Russian town of about ten thousand people. We were a poor family. My father made the horse-drawn carriages that the bourgeoisie used on Sundays to promenade down the street. It would take him about six months to build each carriage because he couldn't afford any tools and he had to build each one with his own ten fingers. During the six months it took my father to finish a carriage, the family starved. We had no money, and the rich people wouldn't pay my father until he finished his carriage. It was a very hard life.

My family was part of a population of about two thousand Jews in our city. People yelled out "bad Jew" and "Christ-killer," and they said that we shouldn't be allowed to live. There was a pogrom [a massacre] in 1905 where the Russians looted every store that was either owned or operated by a Jew. I remember my mother pulling me into a hiding place for fear that I would be hurt. It was this abuse against the Jews that made my two brothers decide to go to the United States. In Russia, everyone thought that America was such a rich country that you could literally find gold in the streets. At home there were no jobs for Jews, but in America surely my brothers would find work. They went to New York, worked hard as house painters, and accumulated enough money to buy passage for the rest of the family.

I had never seen an ocean before we got on the boat for America. I looked out onto the sea and saw these huge waves crashing up against the rocks. It was a frightening experience. But then I saw the openness of the ocean, and that great body of water opened my mind to a world that I never knew existed. As we approached New York Harbor I saw

The Woolworth Building—shown here in 1912, just before it was finished—held the honor of being the world's tallest building for seventeen years.

"Not yet Americanized. Still eating Italian food."

—*Early-twentieth-century social work report*

the Statue of Liberty, and I was overwhelmed with a feeling of hope for a beautiful life in a new nation. Then we headed toward Ellis Island and I could see the big buildings of New York. It was an amazing sight. The city I came from only had little shacks made of wood and stone. Here everything was big and new. At Ellis Island they looked in my eyes to see if I was healthy and they checked my hair for lice. When they determined that my family and I were not sick, they put us on another boat and we were finally admitted to the United States.

At first I was afraid to go in the subway. I didn't want to climb down into that dark hole. In Russia the only means of transportation that I knew about were horses and bicycles. When I did go in, I discovered a whole new world. There were advertisements that told me what to buy. And I saw people—blacks, yellows, all sorts of different facial looks and ethnic groups, people like I had never seen before. Most of all, I was amazed that I could go anywhere for five cents. I was able to go all the way down to Battery Park, and then, if I chose, I could transfer and turn around and go all the way up to Yonkers for the same nickel.

My first school was on 103rd Street near Third Avenue, but when I discovered that there were too many foreign boys in the same class, I left it, because I wasn't learning the American language fast enough. I wanted to learn the American language because I wanted to understand the American people, the American mind, and the American culture. I wanted to be completely American, and that couldn't happen in a school full of foreign boys. Mostly I wanted to get a good job somewhere, and I knew if I didn't speak English, I couldn't get a good job. So I walked down to another high school in Harlem on 116th Street and asked the supervisor to give me an audience. I told him I wanted to learn the American language and I wasn't getting it on 103rd Street. He said, "I will give you two questions. If you pass them, you are admitted." He asked me to spell *accident* for him, and I did right away, with two *c*'s. Then he asked me what two-thirds of fifteen was, and I said, "Ten," so he admitted me to high school. In Russia, only a small percentage of Jewish children could go to school, and then it had to be a special Jewish school. In America, I could go to school with everyone else.

For Americans whose ancestors had arrived in earlier centuries, these new immigrants and the new age showed up together—and both required some adjustments. Many Americans were meeting the problems of big-city life for the first time, seeing the grime, disease, overcrowding, and crime that came with rapid growth. Many of them saw these ills as the fault of the foreigners who pressed into the cities. The character of the city was changing so rapidly that some Americans complained that the new immigrants were carrying all the flaws and failures of the Old World to American shores. Called "nativists" for their insistence that people native born in America were inherently superior to those arriving now, these people feared that much was at stake in the new

Although they enjoyed greater freedom and opportunity in the United States, many immigrants were dismayed by the squalid living conditions in overcrowded urban ghettos such as New York's Lower East Side. "Was this the America we had sought?" asked a Jewish immigrant. "Or was it only, after all, a circle that we had traveled, with a Jewish ghetto at its beginning and its end?"

Many workers faced appalling conditions in mines and factories across the United States, including nearly two million child laborers. Reformers now pushed for the establishment of laws curbing such abuse. "Breaker boys," such as these at a Pennsylvania coal mine, were often injured as they worked ten-hour shifts in the dangerous mines.

At the 1904 St. Louis World's Fair, two thousand "primitive peoples" were on display. The exhibition was a kind of zoo for *human* animals, demonstrating to the millions who came to St. Louis the superiority of "enlightened" white Americans to all other peoples. Shown here is the man who designed the display, anthropologist W. J. McGee, in the Maricopa Indians exhibit.

era. If the nation was reshaping itself in the machine age, they wanted to guarantee that the new nation looked like the old one: white, English-speaking, and Christian.

After all, in 1900 America had been a largely homogeneous farm society of only seventy-six million citizens, a nation of dirt roads and horse-drawn carriages, of kerosene lamps and outhouses. And it was a place where many people felt confident of two things: that America was heaven on earth, and that Americans were God's chosen people. The new age, with its teeming cities and smoky factories, challenged such certainties.

Charles Rohleder, born in 1905, described some of the conditions that shaped his childhood in Pittsburgh, Pennsylvania.

Rohleder in 1908.

When I was growing up at the beginning of the century, times were very hard for the poor. Very tough. There was no welfare to help you out. If you were hungry, the only places you could go to were the missions.

My mother rolled tobacco into cigars at home to try and raise a little extra money. Actually, we all pitched in and helped—my father, my grandfather, me—everybody who was in the house. Back then, very few cigars were actually made in a factory; most were made in people's homes. We would spread out these big leaves of tobacco on the kitchen table and just roll and roll and talk and talk. And then my mother would take them in and sell them to a cigar company, which paid her according to how many she rolled. Of course, she didn't get very much money for them. Cigars at the store only cost about three or four for a dime, so you can imagine what the cigar company paid my mother for them. One time when I was a little boy I got into a box of tobacco clippings and just started chewing. I had seen all of these other people chewing on tobacco, and I thought, "Oh, boy, I'd like to try that!" I couldn't even go to school that afternoon. I was sicker than two dogs.

At that time there were a lot of foreigners moving to Pittsburgh—a lot of immigrants. There were also a lot of blacks moving up from the South. People came from all over because they could get a job right away. People used to say that if you couldn't get a job anywhere else, you could get one in Pittsburgh. There was a Greek family next door to us, and we used to make fun of them because they were immigrants and they spoke a language that we didn't understand. And even though they were really hard workers and were making a go of it, we used to look down on them. I guess it was just ignorance on our part. But back then we just thought that all immigrants were no better than the dirt under our feet. Despite what we thought about them, they worked very hard to try and get ahead—twelve-hour days, six days a week.

As far as the immigrants were concerned, I didn't want to have anything to do with them. I just didn't concern myself with them. I was too busy trying to make a living to fuss with them. I started working when I was six years old, selling newspapers out on the streets.

Pittsburgh was very dirty back then. Everyone burned coal for heat, and it was soft coal, which emits a lot of sulfur and black fumes. Some days you couldn't see the sun at noontime because of the thick smoke from the factories. There were steamboats on the river, and they had these big smokestacks. When the boats went under low bridges, the smoke would come right up and cover the whole bridge. There were times when I walked across a bridge and went in clean on one side, but by the time I reached the other side, I needed a new shirt.

And the rivers themselves were even worse. They put these big sewers in, so that everybody could have flush toilets. The sewers just dumped right into the river. I used to see just awful stuff coming out of there. There was a hospital nearby, and if they had an operation and they chopped off a few pieces of that person—cancer or anything else—they just threw it right in the sewer. Before you knew it, it would come out in the river. And of course, there was the sewage from all the toilets. The worst of it was that kids used to fish right where that sewer came out because that's where the catfish were. I tried it a few times, but luckily I never caught anything.

There were also all of these factories and slaughterhouses and steel mills along the river. You could always tell when the canning factory was processing tomatoes or making chili sauce, because the river would run red with tomato skins. And you would see chunks of fat floating down from the slaughterhouses. At night the sky above the river would look like it was on fire from the open hearths at the steel mills. It was lit just like it was daytime. What a beautiful sight that was; it looked as if the whole city had burst into flames.

The Suwanee, Georgia, train depot with separate facilities for "colored" and "white" passengers, c. 1915.

At a time when immigrants were looked down on with suspicion, and when city life meant rubbing shoulders with all kinds of different people, it was only natural that the continuing separation between white and black people should be examined with fresh eyes. It *was* examined again at the start of the century, but not to the benefit of black America. It is hard to look back and contemplate the nation's level of bigotry at that time. This was an era when popular magazines described blacks as "coons," "darkies," or "pickaninnies." This was a time when lynchings of black men were considered entertainment in some places in the South.

For a short time after the Civil War it had looked as though the South might advance toward racial equality. But in the last years of the nineteenth century southern whites' power over blacks was strengthened. As long as blacks had been slaves, they were seen as no great threat to white power, even while living and working in the heart of the white community. But now that African Americans were free, they were seen as a threat to the established white community, to be kept at a distance and under control. In the South, new laws robbed blacks of the right to vote, and a new system of segregation was born: Jim Crow laws.

Jim Crow laws meant separate schools, buses, restaurants, rest rooms, and swimming pools. Oklahoma had separate telephone booths. Others had separate school textbooks. This segregation was made legal by the Supreme Court in a case called *Plessy v. Ferguson*. It declared that the U.S. Constitution allowed public facilities to be "separate but equal."

Jim Crow laws penetrated so many aspects of southern black life in the early years of the century that it is hard to believe the forces of slavery had been defeated a generation before. Signs separating black areas from white areas were often barely needed; people just understood. Here a Florida tobacco farmer and his farmhands stand for a portrait, c. 1910.

Marjorie Stewart Joyner, an African American, was born in 1896 and grew up with Jim Crow laws in the South.

Even though my grandparents had been born slaves, I was born long enough after slavery that the slave element didn't really exist in my world, or even in my thinking. The beginning of the century was a time when we dreamed that things were going to get better for blacks: better housing and neighborhoods, better schools, better jobs. As a little girl, my dream was to grow up, get married, and have a big house on a large farm with horses and cattle and people working for me. As a people, we had high hopes. But we also knew that to get there we would need an education.

My father was an itinerant teacher. He traveled from one village to another, and would hold classes for children—or adults, for that matter—that had never been to school but still wanted to learn. He would go from village to village after harvesting time or planting time—the times when children didn't have to be in the fields working—and they would hold classes either in a church or at the village hall or even in a clearing out in the woods. Parents wanted their children to have an education. They wanted them to learn to read, write, and do arithmetic, so that they would have the opportunities to make a good living and have a better life.

We were coming out of a time where people actually belonged to other people. And while we no longer belonged to the white man, the white man was still saying, "I don't want my white child seated beside a black boy or a black girl. I want my child to go to a school where there are whites only." It was that kind of prejudice that separated the races. Of course, black people worked with white people all the time. Black people cooked for white people; black people took care of white children; they took care of the white people's houses. Even so, people at that time thought that there must be a separation of the races in order to get along. In the South, we had Jim Crow laws. There were separate facilities for white, and separate facilities for blacks. Out in public, we were always separated from the white people. When people traveled, I mean when *white* people traveled, they didn't want to sit in the same coach or car with black people. So the black people had to sit in a designated Jim Crow car, which was either up in the front of the train, right in back of where they shoveled coal into the furnace of the engine, and cinders would fly all over you, or in the caboose, the last little car on the end of the train.

George Kimbley was also born in 1896 and recalled some of his experiences growing up as an African American in the Jim Crow South.

One day I was walking down the road outside Frankfort, Kentucky, on my way to a white person's house where I was doing some work, when I saw this dance pavilion over across a field. It looked really nice, and even though I was in a white part of town, I got off the road and cut through this field just to get a better look at this pretty pavilion. But then when I turned around to head back, there was a white man standing there with his rifle pointed right straight at my head. Now, I was scared, but I didn't show it. I just walked right up to him and as I passed him I told him that all I did was stop to look at the pavilion on my way to work. I showed no fear whatsoever, and he just let me pass.

I was born at a time when they still did things the old slave-time way. They felt that you had to lynch a black man every so often to keep him in his place. And that was the general idea. When I was very young they lynched a black man right here in Frankfort. He was accused of robbing someone, and they strung him up right out in the open. My dad took me down there to see that dead man. He even lifted me up so I could get a good look at him. When I turned around and looked at my dad, there were tears rolling down his face. And he said to me, "George, when you grow up, I want you to do something about the way these white people are treating us black people." I promised my dad that I would, and I'm still trying to do something about it.

Booker T. Washington, 1856-1915.

W.E.B. Du Bois, 1868-1963.

Segregation posed a crucial question for black Americans: What path to black progress should they follow? Two influential black leaders offered two differing opinions. W.E.B. Du Bois was the voice of protest. He wanted blacks to push for greater freedom, and for laws that would guarantee equality for black citizens. Booker T. Washington wanted black Americans to improve their own lives apart from mainstream white society, more gradually advancing toward equality. In the end, Du Bois's philosophy won the day and led to the great civil rights movement later in the century.

Everyone, it seemed, was looking for greater opportunity as the century got under way. Now women began to demand an equal share of opportunity, too. Progressive thinkers were split on the issue of women's rights. On one side were the suffragists, who insisted that nothing could be improved unless women had the right to vote. These activists demanded the vote as one of the foundations of democracy. Some suffragists even made their case for the vote by joining a racist argument: If white women were given the right to vote, white votes would instantly double.

Other progressives saw votes for women as *harmful* for women. They feared that if women were given the right to vote, it would suggest that men and women should be treated equally under all aspects of the law. That would make it harder to push for special laws to protect women and children in the workplaces of the new industrial cities.

Suffragists were also attacked by both women and men who were afraid that the vote would destroy families, or at least the traditional division of family responsibilities, with women keeping house and men earning the paycheck. What sort of next generation would evolve, they asked, if all women considered their first duty to be to themselves?

By the early 1910s suffragists had decided to put all their energy into changing the U.S. Constitution to give women the vote. They carried out acts of civil disobedience in an attempt to force the nation's leaders to give in.

Lucy Haessler, born in 1904, grew up in a family of political activists. She first marched for the right to vote when she was ten years old.

Haessler's parents, Celia and Charles Whitaker.

Haessler as a teenager.

I came from a long line of New Englanders. One of my ancestors was on the *Mayflower*, and others fought in the Revolutionary War. My more recent ancestors had been abolitionists in the Civil War. So I grew up with this tradition of public interest and public service. When I was still a young girl, my family moved to Washington, D.C. For me, Washington was an incredibly exciting place. There was the Washington Monument, the Capitol, and the White House. Occasionally my mother would take me out of school to go see Congress in session. We would sit up in the gallery and watch all of these men giving speeches and debating issues. It was very exciting for a little girl.

On Sunday afternoons my parents would invite their friends to our house. These were people who worked for Congress or who worked in government offices, or sometimes they were just enlightened people who were interested in the progressive issues of the day. This was where I first heard talk about women's suffrage—about women's rights and about women getting the vote. It wasn't just that women didn't have the right to vote; they didn't really have the right to own property, they didn't have the right to custody of their children, there were just all kinds of ways in which they didn't have rights. Even at my school, girls weren't noticed as much as boys were. If a teacher asked a question, and the hands went up, it was always a boy that was called on to answer.

I hardly ever heard the suffrage issue discussed outside my home. In school I think only a few of my girlfriends even knew what the word meant, and even they knew very little about the issue. It was at home that I really learned about suffrage. You see, my mother was very involved in the issue. And being the only girl in the family, it was just natural for me to listen to her and to do things with her.

The suffragettes had a big headquarters in downtown Washington. My mother would take me up there on Saturdays when she volunteered to help out with mailings. The backbone of the suffrage movement was composed of well-to-do, middle-class women, both Republicans and Democrats. There weren't many working-class women in the movement. Most of them were too busy working to get involved.

The suffragettes organized pickets and marches and rallies. I was only ten years old the first time I went to a march with my mother. She told me, "Oh, you're too young, you can't go." But I said, "I *am* going, because you're going to win the right to vote and I'm going to vote when I'm grown-up." So she let me march. It wasn't a particularly large parade. We had permission for a group of about fifty women to march from the Capitol to the White House. Everyone there was much older and bigger than me, and they took longer steps than I did. So I had to really hustle to keep up with my mother, but I managed to do it. The more marches that were held, the more you could feel the movement just building and building. In my heart, I knew that this movement was going to go somewhere, and it was going to help with the struggles of women.

Suffragists faced fierce opposition when they marched for women's right to vote. At parades such as this one in Washington, D.C., in 1914, they were often "spat upon, slapped in the face, tripped up, pelted with burning cigar stubs, and insulted by jeers and obscene language," reported one government official.

"You go into Roosevelt's presence, you feel his eyes upon you, you listen to him, and you go home and wring the personality out of your clothes."

—Author Richard Washburn Child describing TR after a visit to the White House

What kind of president could lead a country with so many voices cry-ing out for so many things? Theodore Roosevelt became president when an anarchist shot President William McKinley in 1901. Roosevelt, the vice president, was climbing mountains in the Adirondacks of upstate New York when he got the news. At forty-two, Theodore Roosevelt, or TR, as he was affectionately known, was sworn in as the youngest president in the country's history. Physically strong and filled with enthusiasm, he was an enormous inspiration to the nation's young people. In the spirit of the new machine age, TR was sometimes described in technological terms. "A steam engine in trousers" and "a wonderful little machine" were two descriptions of him.

Even though America was busy with its own growing pains, TR pushed Americans to look outward, beyond the country's borders. He believed that as a great nation the United States had duties toward the rest of the world. Roosevelt felt that Americans were ignorant about foreign policy and were too confident in the protection offered by the oceans on its east and west coasts. He believed that developments in transportation and communication had created a more connected world. Most important, he believed that this new, connected world should be guided by the United States, as if by a father. He flexed America's muscles for all nations to see by parading the U.S. Navy fleet around the world in 1908.

Teddy Roosevelt had been out of office for nearly two years when he appeared at Grant's Tomb on Decoration Day in 1910. TR's strong will and enthusiastic spirit kept him in the public eye. "He brought in a stream of fresh, pure, bracing air from the mountains," said literary critic Harry Thurston Peck, "to clear the fetid atmosphere of the national capital."

Anne Freeman, born in 1901, recalled what a hero TR was to people at the time.

Above: Freeman in 1903. Right: Her father, Carl Pederson, in his navy uniform.

EQUALITY

Roosevelt had purposely issued the press release announcing his 1901 dinner with Booker T. Washington (depicted in the drawing above) in time to make the morning papers. As historian Edmund Morris described it, he caused "white supremacists all over the South to gag on their grits."

I feel like I've heard about Teddy Roosevelt practically from the time I was born. My father was such an admirer of the man that it felt as though he was just part of my life. Teddy Roosevelt represented just about everything that my father admired. He had fought valiantly in the war; he had been an assistant secretary of the navy; he was gregarious and forthright. And although he had come from a very rich family, he fought hard for the common man. Teddy Roosevelt had this sense of adventure and spontaneity that my father respected. My father could find no wrong in TR.

I remember him laughing and telling me about how TR was such an independent and headstrong man that people had a hard time keeping track of him, even when he was in the White House. He would get up early in the morning and just take off and leave the White House, unbeknownst to anyone. They didn't have the Secret Service or things like that to keep an eye on him, so he would just take off and go for a walk around Washington before coming back to work. You'd think he would have been a little more careful, seeing as he originally got into office when President McKinley was shot.

One day when my father was working at the Brooklyn Navy Yard, there was this strange man walking around and looking at things. He must have come in as part of a tour group or something, because they had gates and fences to keep people from just walking in. But here was this short man with thick glasses and a mustache walking around as if he owned the place. And then all of a sudden he pulled out a camera and started taking pictures. Well, this one guard immediately went up to the man and told him that he was not allowed to take pictures in the Navy Yard.

"Oh, I can take a couple of pictures," the man replied. "It's okay. I'm not a spy."

"Oh, no," the guard said, "you are not allowed to do that. And if you do, I'm going to have to take you in."

After a gentlemanly argument, the man agreed not to take any more pictures. Well, what this guard did not know was that the man with the camera was actually Teddy Roosevelt. Somehow he had gotten into the Navy Yard and decided he wanted to take some pictures. Even when the guard approached him, he didn't say, "I'm Teddy Roosevelt." He just acted like he was a normal citizen. I think he was trying to test the guard. It wasn't really that odd that the guard didn't recognize TR. You see, back then, before television, the president wasn't as recognizable as he is today. You might see his picture in the paper, but you just didn't see his face all that often. And you certainly wouldn't expect to see him by himself, with a camera, walking through Brooklyn!

Nobody found out that day that it had been Teddy Roosevelt snooping around. But a little while after the episode, the guard received a letter saying that he had been accepted to the Naval Academy—and he hadn't even applied. I guess Teddy was so impressed by the young man's persistence that he pulled some strings to see to it that he got ahead.

To my father, America was a young country full of promise. And Teddy Roosevelt was a president who typified that. He too was young, and he wanted America to be noticed and to be a leader around the world. Teddy Roosevelt had an incredible strength of will that really appealed to new Americans who were trying to make their way. Once he set his mind upon something, he felt he could accomplish it.

Theodore Roosevelt sitting atop one of the gigantic steam shovels used to dig the Panama Canal. In November 1906, when he visited Panama, Roosevelt became the first American president to travel outside the country.

One of the goals TR was determined to accomplish was to unite the Atlantic Ocean with the Pacific: to build a canal across the thin strip of land that connected North America to South America. This dream dated back to the sixteenth century. But as the nineteenth century ended, a canal across Colombia's Isthmus of Panama still seemed to be an unreachable goal. A French engineering company had tried and failed miserably. Malaria and yellow fever had crippled or killed twenty thousand laborers. Equatorial rainstorms were another problem, and workers reported seeing tree trunks black with tarantulas. Nature itself seemed to be against the project. After all, no one had ever attempted such a massive reshaping of the earth, a fifty-mile gash from one ocean to the other.

But no president loved a challenge more than Teddy Roosevelt. TR wanted America—and American technology—to be the first to succeed. America would dig the "Big Ditch." Roosevelt himself bullied the nation of Colombia for the rights to dig the canal at Panama. When the government wouldn't agree, he gave unofficial support to the revolt that led to Panama's independence from Colombia. The new nation of Panama quickly agreed to let TR's engineers get to work.

Like Roosevelt himself, the canal was a bridge between two eras. The idea belonged to the 1800s, but the work itself would have been impossible without the technology of the 1900s. The canal's loudest statement about the modern age was the way in which it would be used. TR believed that his nation's chance for world leadership was tied to a bold presence on the seas. It was America's destiny to use the two oceans to guide the world safely into the new century. Easy movement between the Atlantic and the Pacific through the Panama Canal would be key to that plan. To demonstrate their new naval power with flair, officials planned an elaborate opening-day ceremony for the canal.

But it was not to be. Almost at the precise moment when America's great technological challenge was achieved, events in Europe plunged the world into darkness.

The Gatun Locks alone made the Panama Canal an engineering wonder. "The impression," wrote historian David McCullough, "was of looking down a broad, level street nearly five blocks long with a solid wall of six-story buildings on either side; only here there were no windows or doorways, nothing to give human scale."

2 Shell Shock
1914–1919

World War I was the bloodiest conflict the world had yet known. Nearly ten million people died and twenty million more were wounded—many of them maimed for life—on three continents. During its biggest battles, the same pieces of land were traded back and forth a dozen times. It left countless widows and orphans, ruined economies, and robbed the world of a generation of young men. Did a scientist die who might have found a cure for cancer? Did we lose a great poet, a wonderful artist? The answers lie buried in the soil of the battlefields.

World War I completely changed the old political order in Europe. When it began, Europe was controlled by a small circle of men drawn from the upper middle class and the aristocracy. Five empires—the Austro-Hungarian, Russian, German, French, and British—dominated the map, and each one (except for France's) was governed by royalty. From Austria, Emperor Franz Josef ruled an empire of fifty million Czechs, Austrians, Magyars, Slovaks, Croats, Serbs, Turks, Transylvanians, Slovenes, Gypsies, Jews, and Poles. In Germany, Kaiser Wilhelm II had the most powerful army in the world and was building a navy to match it. From England, King George V ruled an empire that stretched across more than a quarter of the globe, and in Russia, Tsar Nicholas II controlled a vast nation. Three of these monarchs were related: King George and Kaiser Wilhelm both were descendants of Queen Victoria, and Tsar Nicholas was a cousin by marriage.

Democracy hardly existed in Europe. Politicians and government officials were almost always members of the privileged classes. They were ignorant of the problems of their own poorer countrymen. Though there had been social reforms, most Europeans still led hard lives, toiling in factories, in mines, and on farms. Unhappy with their situations, they had begun to listen to the people who were calling for socialism and self-government.

On Sunday, June 28, 1914, a young Serb named Gavilo Princip fired two shots that would change Europe forever. Frustrated with the treatment of his people under the Austro-Hungarian Empire, Princip longed for the day when Serbia would be a separate nation. The emperor's son and heir to the throne, Archduke Franz Ferdinand, was visiting Sarajevo that day in June. When the archduke's motorcade passed Princip, the young Serb stepped up to the car and shot Franz Ferdinand and his wife.

Gavilo Princip (right, with two of his coconspirators) would not see the war's end. He died of tuberculosis in a prison hospital in Austria in 1918.

This murder triggered a feud between Austria-Hungary and Serbia. Russia came to the aid of the Serbs; Germany supported Austria. Then France gave its backing to Russia, and England rushed to defend Belgium, which Germany had invaded on its way to attack France.

The elite classes saw the assassination in Sarajevo as a chance to compete for a larger say in world affairs. They may also have seen it as an opportunity to distract the working classes from their dissatisfaction at home. There were some feeble attempts at diplomacy, but on August 2, 1914, the Great War began. Europe would never be the same.

Many men saw battle as a test of manly virtue and patriotism. War was exciting. War was an adventure. War was honorable. War was a rite of passage. War was a way to sacrifice for one's country. In short, war was good.

But while these men did not realize it at first, modern technology had changed war forever. For centuries, men had thought of war as a competition won by the side with the most grit and determination. But what good was grit in an age of sophisticated war machinery? Modern weapons had put an end to hand-to-hand combat. Machine guns and heavy artillery made an assault on enemy lines nothing more than a suicide run. All a soldier could do was dig in and wait. The long stalemate had begun.

The trenches of the First World War were like graves for the living. Across Belgium and France there were thousands of miles of them, zigzagging this way and that.

As German citizens sent their smiling, confident soldiers off to battle, few people realized the devastation the war would cause. By the end of 1914, four hundred thousand German soldiers lay dead on the western front.

There were frontline trenches and support trenches, reserve trenches and communication trenches, all tied together to form huge underground cities.

Inside, soldiers lived like rats. The combination of boredom and sudden danger was overwhelming. The trench conditions were so miserable and so new to warfare that they caused a strange psychological illness called "shell shock." Constantly surrounded by dead bodies, listening for the faintest sound of danger, always on the alert for an attack, shooting at an enemy so far away that he was almost invisible, men just shut down. Some went temporarily blind or deaf, or lost the power of speech. Some suddenly shook uncontrollably, lost their memory, or became paralyzed.

The fighting went on for what seemed forever, each side caught up in the illusion that it could just wait the other out. Week after week, month after month, desperate generals prayed that the next day's raid would bring the knockout punch. It never did. One of the most disastrous battles of the war took place in France in 1916, when British troops attacked German trenches in the valley of the river Somme. More than twenty-two thousand men died on the first day of fighting. By the end of the battle five months later, more than half a million British, French, and German soldiers were dead. Yet the Allies never advanced more than seven miles. In fact, from 1914 to the spring of 1918 the line of the western front moved less than ten miles in either direction.

Edward Francis, who was born in 1896, served as a private in the British army from the start of the war until its end and became accustomed to living in the trenches.

Francis (seated) at age eighteen, with his brother Harry, twenty, in late 1914, just before going to France.

The mood among all of us young men was that we couldn't get to be a soldier quick enough. In Birmingham, where I enlisted, they expected to make one battalion, which would be made up of about a thousand men. But within the first few days of war they had forty-five hundred. We had a wonderful time training. I was in a section of about fourteen men, all from the same area. We were like one big family. And then came the great day when they issued us a rifle—the newest Lee-Enfield rifle. You should have seen some of the lads looking at it, those who had never held a gun in their life. We were so itchy to get to France we couldn't stand it. All we were thinking was, "We must get to France before the war's over."

The men training us had never experienced a war where you're in trenches facing each other, with shells coming at you every minute. So we had no idea what it would be like when we got there. We crossed over to France after we finished our training, and we walked fifteen miles to our base camp. When it was our turn to go up into the trenches, the regiment coming out had been there almost since the start, and they looked at us as if to say, "Heh, you're smiling now, but you won't be later."

We learned all about the trenches and their risks and what we had to do to fight the Germans. And of course the morning came when we had to "go over the top"—which meant you'd leap over the trench and cover three, four, five hundred yards toward the enemy lines. So when the officers blew their whistle, we were to dash out of the trenches and make our way toward the German trenches. And it was then that we looked at each other and wondered if we'd ever get through it. Some were visibly shaking. Some were crying. Some were almost shell-shocked before they started. But of course when the whistle went, we had to scramble over. There was always an officer a few yards behind you with a loaded revolver in his hand. Anyone who was a bit slow to go would receive a shot in the foot just to remind him that he was there.

We would only learn later what happened. If we took the trench we went over to capture, then we'd have time to rest and talk. And one would say to the other, "Where's Bill So-and-so?" And someone else would say, "Oh, he's got it. He's killed." And then you see that friends of yours or people you know are missing—some are wounded, some are killed. And you could be talking to a man in the trench, and while you're talking he accidentally looks over the top of it, and in that few seconds he might get it in the head.

We spent a lot of time walking from one trench to the next, and when the weather changed to rain and mud, well, it's almost impossible to describe what that was like. If you've seen pictures of the surface of the moon, it was something like that, only worse—all dug up and wet through with mud. Impossible to walk. To get two miles would take seven or eight hours. Sometimes you were in water up to your waist, and had to walk in it for a week to get to the firing line. And under those conditions, they couldn't bring food or water up to us—all the people bringing it were shot down or shelled. So we were hungry and thirsty most of the time. When we'd been there about six or eight months, covered in mud, wet through practically all day, absolutely chewed up by lice, we used to say, "And to think we wanted to come to this hole."

In our first month there, we could smell the dead bodies. But after a while we took no notice of it. For a person just arriving there, it would stink. But to us, who were used to it every day, we didn't think a lot of it. The noise was always on. And when you'd been as long in the trenches as I was, you could almost say for sure if a shell was going to drop by you by the sound it made.

British soldiers rest in a reserve trench during the Battle of the Somme, 1916.

Practically everyone had shell shock, but there were two kinds: one for the privates and one for the officers. With an officer, at the slightest trembling of the lips, they would be sent to the hospital for a week, and then to England to recover. But privates would get a dose of medicine and be sent back onto the line. That was the difference. You could easily see when a man had shell shock. He was crying, shaking; his face was absolutely a different color. It was all we could do in the trenches to hold him back. Sometimes we'd even sit on him. Because once he got out of the trenches, he was a dead man. Some couldn't stand it and walked out. And inevitably they got shot for deserting.

In the later years of the war we got used to the dead bodies and treated them as nothing, like pieces of wood. Everything had a use. We'd even put the bodies in the bottom of the trench and stand on them to keep dry. Of course, these bodies were recovered later, but if they were left too long, they became skeletons, because the rats chewed on them. Some of them had food which had been sent by relatives from England, and that was a godsend, because other than that we could not have stood up to the conditions we were forced to fight in.

Almost from the moment the war began in Europe, America started its own debate about it. Many German Americans sided with Kaiser Wilhelm. But supporters of the Allies far outnumbered them, especially after one of the kaiser's submarines sank the British ocean liner *Lusitania* on May 7, 1915, killing more than a thousand people—including 128 Americans.

·PEACE·HAS·HER·CONQUESTS·GREATER·FAR·THAN·WAR·

R.M.S. LUSITANIA
QUEEN of the SEAS.

The luxury liner *Lusitania* is shown here on a souvenir postcard. When it was sunk by a German submarine, it carried more than twelve hundred passengers and a cargo that included ammunition and small arms.

To the growing number of American socialists, the war in Europe was simply a battle between Germany and Britain to see which country could become the greatest commercial power. Other Americans saw the war as a symptom of Europe's decay. If Europe wants to commit suicide, they asked, why should we help? President Woodrow Wilson declared that America would remain neutral.

In Europe, the enormous casualties created doubts about the war among soldiers and civilians. Men returning from the front wondered why they had been fighting. A willingness to question authority took hold: Just who were these people in control of this horrible war? And why should we fight so that they can stay in power?

Many people began to see more clearly the huge gap between the rich and the poor, the powerful and the powerless, the few and the many. As they did, the enemy in uniform seemed less responsible for their pain than the "enemy" sitting on their own country's throne.

In Russia, soldiers had begun the war with the same enthusiasm as the English and the French, and had the same fantasy of a quick end. But, of course, it *was* a fantasy. Russia's war minister had thought machine guns and other modern weapons were cowardly, and sent his soldiers up against the torrent of enemy artillery. Russia lost four million men in just the first year of fighting. By 1916, with an unprepared Tsar Nicholas himself commanding the army, the troops were losing the will to fight.

"Colorless, expressionless, endless regiments marching through dead cold. . . . They were not individual Russians anymore; they were not men who were going to die for their country, they were just men who were going to die."

—Russian soldier, describing the scene on the eastern front, 1916

Both the war and an unusually harsh winter had forced enormous sacrifices back home in Russia. Short of fuel, factories closed. Breadlines stretched around the block. Amid the chaos, the cries of the nation's downtrodden peasants for their own land now merged with the demands of the rest of the population for peace. Russia was ripe for revolution.

The revolt began on February 23, 1917, when a parade of female textile workers erupted in protest against food shortages in Petrograd (St. Petersburg). The next day two hundred thousand workers went on strike. Soon the entire city was shut down. Trams were overturned, and bakeries were looted. Artillery depots were taken over, and the weapons and ammunition were distributed to the rioters.

Hearing of the revolt, Tsar Nicholas rushed back home from the front, but he was stopped a hundred miles from his capital and forced to give up his throne. The February Revolution had overthrown the powerful monarchy of Russia in only a few short days.

Vladimir Ilyich Ulyanov, better known as Lenin, saw the revolt as an opportunity. Lenin was the leader of the Bolsheviks, a small political

Revolutionary troops occupied the
Winter Palace soon after the February
uprising. More than seventeen thousand soldiers from the Petrograd gar-
rison joined the crowds in the streets
rather than defend the tsar.

party that had been calling for an uprising of industrial workers, and was in exile in Switzerland. News of the revolt brought him back to Petrograd, where he was greeted by a crowd of admirers. Most were surprised at the radical reforms he suggested. But they all cheered when he announced he wanted Russia out of the war. The cheers grew even louder when he declared he was in favor of land for the peasants.

Lenin's message dramatically increased membership in the Bolshevik Party, and more than a million soldiers abandoned their duties and returned home to get their share of land. In October Lenin rose to power in an almost bloodless takeover.

Alexander Bryansky, who was born in 1882, witnessed the Bolshevik Revolution firsthand.

Bryansky (with beard and hat, second row, right) stands behind Lenin (front row, right).

I had been a revolutionary from the time I was a child, because growing up in poverty under the tsar's regime had taught me very early about exploitation. My father worked as a tailor, and I had a very hard childhood—sometimes we were starving. I went to work at a very young age and then educated myself. In 1905 I learned about Lenin, how he wanted to change life so that everyone would be equal, so that there would be no poverty and exploitation. This affected me greatly.

In 1914 I was sent off to fight in World War I. I was awarded the St. George's Cross, and then ended up in the Petrograd Reserve Regiment after some time in the hospital. That's how I happened to be in Petrograd in 1917 when the February Revolution happened. Of course, I wanted to take an active part in it. I joined a crowd of workers moving toward Nevsky Avenue. The Cossacks [peasant soldiers loyal to the tsar] were deployed at Znamenskii Square. There was a police officer in charge of the Cossacks, and he shouted into the crowd, "Move back, or I'll shoot!" A woman ran up to him and got his horse by the bridle. She wanted to take him aside. He shot her dead right away. Then the crowd shouted, "Cossacks! Why do you keep silent? Cossacks, go home!" And all the Cossacks rode away.

Then the demonstration moved on along Nevsky Avenue. People shouted, "Down with the war! Down with autocracy!" Machine guns rattled from the roofs where policemen were stationed, and several people were wounded. The crowd hesitated. Then a student, a small man with both hands amputated, cried out: "Soldiers, come on! Defend the revolution! Take them down!" A bunch of people broke into the building, went up to the roof, and took the machine gunners down. Soon all the policemen disappeared from the streets to avoid being beaten.

After the February Revolution we saw that nothing had really changed. The new leaders were not going to put a stop to the war. At home capitalism remained, and life for the poor did not change. There were rallies when Bolsheviks were beaten up by crowds of thugs. But

Vladimir Ilyich Lenin,
1870–1924.

worst of all, there was no bread! Bakeries and shops were stormed to provide the people with food. The starvation was universal.

One morning in April Lenin's sister said that he would be arriving that day. Because it was the second day of Easter, all soldiers were on leave, and all workers had the day off, so we called them all to a rally at the station. Finally the train was coming. And then we saw Lenin, standing in a third-class car. When he came off the train he gave a small speech, saying, "Long live the social revolution!"

I met him a few days later, and my impression was that he was just an ordinary man. He seemed to me just like one of the comrades. I thought such a man could not be bloodthirsty, and he wasn't; he made sure the October Revolution was bloodless.

When that moment arrived, one hundred sailors crept into the palace through a back door and convinced some of the guards to give up fighting against the Bolsheviks. I was outside the palace waiting, and when the sailors opened the gates, I ran up the carpeted stairway. In the very first room I saw cadets standing with their rifles ready. I shouted, "Put down your weapons or you'll get it!" When they saw a big crowd of soldiers behind me, they dropped their rifles and raised their hands. I said, "No one will shoot you. We will let you go free if you promise not to raise arms against the Soviet power." Then all the soldiers left, and only the government members remained. They were all arrested without any violence and released, even the worst enemies of the people. So in this way, Lenin was able to accomplish a revolution that turned the whole world upside down.

Germany's own desperate shortages forced it to target American merchant ships delivering supplies to the Allies in early 1917. Germany knew that this might draw the United States into the conflict but decided that it was worth the risk. After enduring several months of submarine attacks, the United States declared war on Germany.

Still, it wasn't easy convincing Americans to join up without making the country's goals quite clear. Many Americans wondered why the United States should join in Europe's war. President Wilson himself had resisted getting America involved. But as the conflict deepened, he believed that it threatened all of Western civilization. And in that he discovered a reason to spur Americans on to fight. He began to refer to the war as a fight for democracy, a chance to rescue Europe with *American* ideas.

The United States was poorly prepared for a major military conflict. The army had a grand total of 208,034 men. The air force was made up of about fifty-five dilapidated airplanes. In spite of this, the very idea of Americans participating in the war was a powerful boost for the Allies. The strong, healthy, confident Yankees arriving in Paris in the middle of 1917 brought fresh hope to the war-weary people of France. The Americans had an enthusiasm that hadn't been seen at the front in years. And they were fighting for ideas that had become important to the average European soldier and his family, too: democracy, self-government, and freedom.

Corneal Davis, born in 1900, answered President Wilson's call to fight for democracy.

Davis in 1919, just after leaving the service.

When I was in my last year of high school down in Mississippi, I read this great speech coming from Woodrow Wilson, who was president at the time. I was so excited by it that I clipped it out of the newspaper and sat down and remembered it by heart. He said, "It is a fearful thing for me to try to lead a great peaceful people into war. It could be one of the most terrible and disastrous of all wars. Because civilization itself could hang in the balance." But here is the thing I appreciated and got excited over. He then said, "Right is more precious than peace. We will fight for the things that we carry nearest our heart. For a universal dominion of rights, by a concert of free people, that is going to bring peace and happiness to all of this world."

That's what he said: "We will fight for the things that we carry nearest our heart." And I read that stuff and went crazy over it. Don't you think that an African American boy listening to that sort of speech would get excited? Wouldn't you, if you couldn't drink out of the same water fountain that white people drank out of? It excited me, really, that's the truth. Oh, yeah, I said, that's the thing, a universal dominion of rights, where everybody is going to have the same rights. "A concert of free people": If you read that speech, you will find those words in there. And I thought I ought to get in there and help to bring about this universal dominion of rights, this concert of free people, because it sure wasn't free down where I was.

So that was one of the reasons I wanted to go off to war, but I also wanted to make some money so I could go to college. So I went down and joined. But the question being debated at that time was whether or not they should really train black officers for the war. There was quite a controversy about whether or not blacks should really go over there and whether they would be, I guess, accepted by the French. They only had about ten thousand African Americans in the armies back in those days, but the number went up to about fifty thousand by the end of the war.

I went over to France in a convoy of black soldiers, led by a black colonel who was highly educated and had all the military knowledge that we needed. We picked up more ships in New York City, an infantry outfit they called the Buffalo Soldiers. There were also a lot of Creoles out of New Orleans who could speak French.

I think we made a great hit with the French. I guess back home they thought the French were going to object to us, but we rounded up two or three French generals, and they gave us ammunition and everything else they had. There were plenty of American marines who didn't want us to go into certain places in Paris—there was no "universal dominion of rights" so far as the marines were concerned, I can tell you. They used to say the nastiest things about us, telling the French women that we weren't even human. But the French people didn't feel that way. I don't know of anyplace where a black person couldn't go in France; if there was such a place, I didn't know of it.

With Americans fighting the Germans in France, patriotism ran high at home—and so did suspicion. Anyone with a German last name was suspected of being a spy. A wild anti-German mood spread across the country. Schools banned German classes. German words were changed: Sauerkraut was called "Liberty cabbage," dachshunds were called "Liberty pups," and hamburgers became "Liberty steak." The Post Office even refused to mail magazines and newspapers that printed articles against the war.

Leon Despres, who was born in 1908, shared the patriotic mood of the country during the First World War.

Despres with his sister Claire, 1917.

A group of boys from Cooperstown, New York, knitting warm clothes for American soldiers.

When America entered the war I was nine years old and completely caught up in the superpatriotism of the times. It seemed to me that the United States had been patient and neutral for a long time, but that they had to get involved because the Germans were cruelly killing people and sinking our ships with their torpedoes. I felt that our soldiers going over were tremendously brave.

This was a time of great bitterness towards the Germans. There was no feeling that the war was the result of long economic rivalries or anything of that sort. It was purely an evil thing, perpetrated solely by the kaiser. Since part of my family was German, we had been accustomed to speaking German around the house, but once the war began we stopped speaking it. We turned our backs on anything German— literature, music, history. A German name was a great liability during World War I. Families changed their names. There was a boy in my class whose last name was Kirshberger, and his family changed it to Churchill. It seemed downright unpatriotic to keep a German name and very patriotic to change your name. In fact, anyone who was known to talk positively about Germany was thought to be a spy.

I was totally caught up in the righteousness of the war, and I wanted to do my bit. I wrote letters to the soldiers and learned to knit scarves for them, though I never really caught on to it, so I don't think my scarves amounted to anything. I had a victory garden, and that was very exciting, though I don't think I ever grew anything more than radishes. We collected salvage for the Red Cross; I was very conscientious in collecting and tying up newspapers, collecting as much metal as I could. They would give you coupons, which you would paste on a card, and when you filled the card, then you could put the card in your window. It was an exciting time, and everything we did—knitting, gardening, rolling bandages, walking in parades—we felt was part of winning the war.

It was a wonderful time to be a young boy. I remember going to see the war games on the lakefront in Chicago. They had rifles and terribly loud explosions and flashes, and I thought it was glorious. That was my idea of war. You know, it didn't occur to me that people were getting their faces blown off, that they were losing limbs, that they were being wounded forever, that young men were being killed. I was aware that young men died in the war, but to me it was kind of a beautiful sacrifice, sad but very beautiful.

American civilians proudly bid their soldiers good-bye at a parade down New York's Fifth Avenue in 1917. This scene mirrored similar ones all over Europe at the beginning of the war, three years earlier.

American troops march through London in August 1917. Rested, well fed, and confident, they injected new energy and enthusiasm into the war-weary Allied forces.

Most Americans wanted to "do their bit" to help in the war effort. For the most part American women helped the war cause on the home front, but many responded to the nation's call for service in Europe.

Laura Smith, who was born in 1893, described her life as a war nurse.

Smith (right) with fellow nurse Marion Jones in Paris, 1918.

The day that the war was declared, my boyfriend went to enlist, and the line was so long they couldn't receive everyone who showed up. I was just finishing nursing school in 1917, and our whole class enlisted with the Red Cross as soon as we graduated. We were sent down to New York, where we marched in a parade wearing our nurse uniforms. Everyone waved their flags and applauded as we went by; there was so much enthusiasm for the war. I don't think we knew what we were getting ourselves into. I wasn't scared at all. I didn't know enough to be scared.

I got my first dose of the real war when they put me on duty in the amputation ward of a hospital in Paris. I had to help a doctor amputate a young man's leg. It was very difficult to look at. That's when I learned what I was going to be up against. I think they put us there just to prepare us for what we would be doing on the front. And what made me so sad was that the boys in the ward were all so full of fun—happy and joking. I just cried all day. I told myself I was going to forget everything, and deliberately closed my mind to a lot of things that even now I can't remember. I can still recall the sound of a leg being sawed off, though, and that's the one thing I wanted to forget.

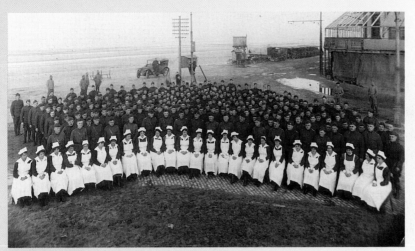

Smith's nurse corps with American soldiers at Dunkirk, shortly before returning home in 1919.

They sent us out to our evacuation hospital, which was a group of tents about twenty miles from the front lines. Each tent held twenty cots, and the boys were sent down from the front in ambulances. We cleaned them up, dressed their wounds, and let them sleep, but there wasn't too much we could do for them. They came in so dirty, with fleas and all, that some of them had to be deloused, and they were just glad to be clean and out of those trenches. Sometimes they came in so many at a time that we had them lying on the ground outside our tent because there wasn't room for them.

We tried not to attach ourselves to anyone, but my friend and I became so fond of one of the boys that was injured. He had a hole right in his forehead and he couldn't speak except for one word, which was *glass*. One day one of the nurses sang "Over There" to him, and he sang and sang, every word. For whatever reason, the music triggered something in his brain that allowed him, at that moment, to sing. My friend and I wanted to get him to talk again, so we kept him for two or three days, which was something we'd never done with any of the other patients. But we never got him to talk. He was so young, and he smiled all the time and didn't seem to be in any pain, but it was so sad to think that it was his brain that was affected in that way.

The European conflict had a dramatic effect on American society. American businesses took advantage of the European need for food, raw materials, and weapons, and the increased business activity boosted America into a period of prosperity. At the same time, the flow of immigrants into the United States from Europe had dropped off, cutting back on the availability of cheap industrial labor.

These wartime labor shortages helped open many nontraditional jobs to women. Women worked on the railroads, in metalworking and munitions jobs, and as streetcar conductors. This helped change social attitudes and made people more willing to grant women the right to vote.

But perhaps the most enduring effect of the war on American life occurred in the African American community. In 1910 four out of five African Americans lived in the South, where most were tenant farmers. As America's wartime economy took hold, thousands of these men and women made their way to the big cities in the industrial North, looking for jobs in the steel, auto, and mining industries. Black southerners, urged on by visions of freedom and jobs, hoped they would find the promised land. The population shift was so large that this phenomenon was called the Great Migration.

Milt Hinton, who was born in 1910, was part of the Great Migration. He described his journey from Mississippi to Illinois.

Hinton in Chicago in 1922, four years after he moved north with his grandmother.

Left: By the end of the Great Migration, Harlem was the cultural, artistic, and intellectual hub of the African American community. Here residents dance at a block party in 1915.

When I was growing up in Vicksburg, Mississippi, the South seemed like a happy place to me. My mother had gone to Chicago, so I lived with my grandmother, who was born a slave. I didn't know what the word *segregation* meant. I knew that black people had to do all the dirty work and weren't allowed to go into certain places. Nobody ever had to explain all of this to me; I just knew it. But by the time I was eight years old I had seen my first lynching. I was on my way home from school, and I saw a black man who'd been hung up on a tree. A bunch of white men were standing around him—they had poured gasoline on him and set him on fire, and now they were shooting at his body. I didn't really understand what was happening.

I knew people were leaving Mississippi and going north. It was no problem for a black woman to leave town, but a black man couldn't go to the railroad station and buy a ticket out of Mississippi because the white people didn't want to lose all of that cheap, unskilled labor. In 1910, the year I was born, my uncle was working at a white barbershop in Vicksburg. His friends who had gone up north would write back and tell him what a wonderful place Chicago was.

My uncle wanted to get up there, so he faked a letter from somebody in Memphis and told his boss that he had an aunt who was dying and wanted to see her nephew. His boss read the letter, took him down to the railroad station, and used my uncle's money to buy him a round-trip ticket. He said, "Now, you go up to Memphis and you come on back here, you hear?" My uncle said, "Yes, sir." But of course when he got to Memphis he sold the other half of that ticket and kept on going to Chicago. My mother joined him after I was born. From 1910 to 1917 my uncle and my mother worked and saved up enough money to rent an apartment and bring the old folks and the children up to Chicago.

I was eight years old when we left, and all it was to me was a wonderful train ride. It was all happiness to me—you know, "I'm going to Chicago to see my momma!" And my grandmother really felt good because she had made great progress from where she had started out, being born a slave and all.

We didn't make the morning train, because by this time my grandmother was a pretty old lady, slow getting around. It poured down rain as we waited for the evening train, and the nice little cap my mother had bought me got all wrinkled up. We boarded the train, and the coach we were allowed to sit in was right next to the coal engine, so the smoke and soot were horrible. My grandmother had made her hard-boiled eggs and fried chicken, and we sat back there brushing the coal soot off the chicken and eating it and enjoying every morsel of it. My mother used to love to tell the story of when they met us at the railroad station in Chicago, because we looked so very bad! Totally disheveled. They threw coats around us and took us home to clean us up so we would look presentable.

With America's entry into the war, a new feeling of hope had taken hold in Europe. The stalemate was ready to break. True to his word, Lenin and his Bolsheviks negotiated an end to the war on the eastern front. But even with the Russians out of the fighting, Germany still struggled. American soldiers were pouring into Europe, and the kaiser had to push for victory or give up. In March 1918 the Germans made their last huge effort, but it was not enough. In July the Allies turned the tide and sent the kaiser's forces into retreat.

Flowers poured from the windows and band music filled the air as Parisians jammed the streets to greet President Woodrow Wilson when he arrived in France to attend the international peace conference. His triumphant welcome demonstrated Europe's appreciation for America's participation in the war as well as the hopes its people placed in the ideals of American democracy.

The "Spanish flu" (so named after eight million Spaniards fell ill in May and June 1918) brought fear and death around the globe at the end of World War I. Approximately 550,000 people died in the United States, six million in India. This sign appeared in a Chicago theater in 1919.

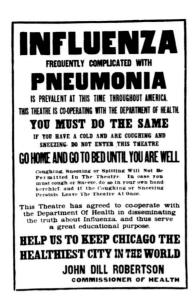

INFLUENZA
FREQUENTLY COMPLICATED WITH
PNEUMONIA
IS PREVALENT AT THIS TIME THROUGHOUT AMERICA.
THIS THEATRE IS CO-OPERATING WITH THE DEPARTMENT OF HEALTH.
YOU MUST DO THE SAME
IF YOU HAVE A COLD AND ARE COUGHING AND SNEEZING. DO NOT ENTER THIS THEATRE
GO HOME AND GO TO BED UNTIL YOU ARE WELL

Coughing, Sneezing or Spitting Will Not Be Permitted In The Theatre. In case you must cough or Sneeze, do so in your own handkerchief, and if the Coughing or Sneezing Persists Leave The Theatre At Once.

This Theatre has agreed to co-operate with the Department Of Health in disseminating the truth about Influenza. and thus serve a great educational purpose.

HELP US TO KEEP CHICAGO THE HEALTHIEST CITY IN THE WORLD
JOHN DILL ROBERTSON
COMMISSIONER OF HEALTH

The treaty ending the First World War was signed five years to the day after the assassination of Archduke Franz Ferdinand. But instead of ending the hostilities, it continued them by other means. The Allies used the peace treaty to punish the Germans. They demanded that Germany accept all the blame for the war and pay the Allies back all the money the fighting had cost them. The Germans felt stunned. When they heard the terms of the peace treaty, masses of people protested in the streets. What should have been the end of a terrible story became the start of another, for many believe it was Germany's attempt to regain power and avenge its harsh treatment that sowed the seeds of World War II.

Still, some good came out of the war. It toppled cruel dynasties in Austria-Hungary, Germany, and Russia. In their places newly independent countries such as Poland and Czechoslovakia were formed. And it helped make societies all over Europe more democratic. The days of the ruling aristocracy were over. A new spirit of equality spread throughout Europe. Women were given new rights, and in Britain and the United States these included the right to vote.

The old Europe, the continent of kings and queens, was gone forever. Ready to fill the gap were two systems, democracy and socialism, both of which aimed to take power from the elite and give it to the people. World War I truly had destroyed a world. The challenge to the survivors was to create a better world in its place.

A Canadian transport struggles through the rubble of the French countryside in August 1918. After years of warfare, Europe lay in ruins.

3 Boom to Bust

1920–1929

The 1920s were the decade when modern society began. Americans were excited by the technological advances that were becoming a part of their lives—the movies, the automobile, and the airplane. But they were also a little frightened, for technology was changing the world faster than it ever had before. For many Americans, it was a time when they felt torn between the simple, traditional life as lived on the farm, for example, and the new, exciting Jazz Age that beckoned from the city.

Europe, too, was changing and restructuring itself after the First World War. But the spirit of this decade belonged to America and its thirst for the new. Businesses advertised new mass-produced products. New mass-audience media, such as radio, reached right into people's homes. Women, who could now vote, were showing a new spirit of independence. And new, cheap cars could carry Americans farther from home than ever before.

For some, especially the white citizens of small-town America, these developments set off alarm bells. Some hoped for a return to old-fashioned values. But there was no going back. Americans were busting loose, and the inventions of the age were driving them into the future.

Automobiles had been around for a long time. Henry Ford had built his first car in 1893, and his first Model T was completed in 1908. In 1920 there were already eight million horseless carriages rattling around the muddy, rutted roads of the American countryside. Most of those eight million cars were Model Ts, which cost only $300. Now that the automobile was affordable for so many people, and the engine of America's robust twenties economy, it was beginning to reshape everyday life and thought.

The automobile age created a new sense of freedom and individuality. People could decide for themselves when to travel, instead of having to rely on train schedules. It also brought communities closer together, now that motorists could drive from one town to the next in a fraction of the time it had once taken to go by horse or on foot.

Even the countryside began to change to make way for cars. Road building went into high gear. With each new mile of highway, it seemed, something new popped up: the first traffic light in 1922, the first shopping center in 1924, the first national road atlas in 1924, the first motel ("*mo*tor ho*tel*") in 1925, and the first public parking garage in 1929.

Left: Traffic jams, such as this one in St. Louis's Forest Park, became increasingly common during the prosperous 1920s. At the beginning of the decade, there were nearly eight million cars on American roads; by 1930, there were more than twenty-six million.

Henry Ford, 1863–1947.

The joy of the automobile was the car itself and the places it could take you. Whether you were going from a small town to a bigger one or from a bigger town to a city, cars were literally the vehicle of escape. Betty Broyles, who was born in 1919, described how the car changed her family's life.

Broyles in 1928, before her car trip to New York.

In the days before the car and the radio, we found ways to amuse ourselves. I always loved to read, and that was a very important source of entertainment, particularly in the winter.

Then, when I was quite young, my aunt bought her first car, a two-toned brown Dodge. The salesman gave her the driving lessons. And I got to ride along in the backseat, which was a big thrill for me because I learned as much as she did. I watched all the things he told her to do. And that was how I learned to drive. At that time we didn't have to have a driver's license, so I really did quite a bit of driving by the time I was thirteen. And got along fine.

Then in the summer we were able to get out and really have some good trips. We saw all of the Indiana state parks, for instance, in the first year or two. It was such fun driving.

My aunt liked to stop before it was dark. So by four o'clock or so we'd start watching for a tourist court or a tourist home. Many people would rent rooms in their homes to tourists. And they'd have a sign in the yard advertising tourist rooms, usually about a dollar a night. There were many tourist courts available, too. They featured separate little cabins, and they would rent for maybe two or three dollars a night.

The roads were sometimes surprisingly good. From Warsaw to Fort Wayne we'd drive on Highway 30, which was a cement road. Of course, it was narrower than it is now, and just two lanes. If you had a breakdown—and there were plenty of breakdowns—you'd hope you'd find a gas station soon. But even if you couldn't, there were always plenty of people glad to help you. There was no concern as far as being robbed or mugged. You felt very safe.

In the late twenties my father was stationed at Charleston, South Carolina, in the navy. So we decided that the three of us, my aunt and my grandmother and I, would go down and visit him. That involved, of course, going from Indiana to South Carolina. And we took several days to do it. I can remember driving into the area of the Smoky Mountains, on a gravel road from Gatlinburg into the Smokies. A gravel road! But we made it fine to Charleston.

On that same trip, after we left Charleston, we drove on to New York City. I remember going through the Holland Tunnel. I never had been in such a large tunnel before. And to go under a river, it just seemed incredible. And the lights impressed me so. We had a wonderful time in New York City.

We stayed with a relative who was a housemother for a musical sorority. We went to Central Park, and she took us down to watch the sailing of a ship, the *Europa*. We got to go on board the ship and see all the tourists getting ready to leave for Europe that night. We enjoyed New York, stayed for a few days, and then drove home, stopping at our little tourist courts along the way.

With the gradual improvements in the nation's highway network, "auto camping" became the rage during the 1920s. Here two families enjoy an afternoon picnicking on the banks of the Stewart River in Minnesota, 1922.

"I am careful and I am thrifty. At least I was until I became a motorist."

—*William Ashdown,*
Confessions of an
Automobilist *(1925)*

The car was so attractive it even altered how people thought about money. While Ford continued to produce the plain black "Tin Lizzies," the new General Motors company manufactured cars that had style. With hydraulic brakes, chrome plating, and six cylinders, the GM cars were more expensive, but people ached to get their hands on them. So GM offered a new way to buy them: the installment plan.

Installment buying, or buying on credit, was a slightly shameful idea for most middle-class Americans at the time. It was something that only poor people did. But the lure of the new cars and the spirit of excitement that filled the 1920s began to change this attitude. People wanted new cars, and they wanted them *now*. The auto age paved the way for an era of buy now, pay later.

Now that people felt comfortable buying cars on the installment plan, they began buying other things on credit, too. By the end of the 1920s more than 60 percent of all sewing machines, washing machines, vacuum cleaners, refrigerators, and furniture were bought on credit. And one of the most popular items was the newest communications technology: the radio.

Amateurs had been fooling around with makeshift radio sets since the first years of the century. As early as 1911 instructions for building a radio receiver were listed in the Boy Scout manual. Radio had a quality of adventure, especially when it involved listening in on signals from navy stations. During World War I all civilian radio broadcasters were ordered to be silent, to keep the airwaves open for military use. But even when the war was over, most people still thought of radio broadcasting as an odd-ball hobby.

With the licensing of the first stations in the early twenties, that began to change. Now there was actually something to listen to between the static, even if families still had to build their own receivers. It was a thrill to see how a few wires and tubes could make a voice come out of thin air. A radio, like a car, could take you to faraway places.

In 1922 radio really took off. At the beginning of that year there were 28 stations; by the end of the year there were 570. Albert Sindlinger, who was born in 1907, was like many young boys of the time, tinkering with a homemade radio, trying to catch an echo of the future from out of the air.

Sindlinger (left) with his brother, Walter, and dog, Tippy, outside their house in Ohio.

When I was about seven years old, in 1913, my uncle gave me a book by Marconi on how to build a wireless [radio]. The Marconi book prompted me to build my first radio, which utilized a Ford motor. At that time, the Model T was the Ford car. And if you took the spark system out of an old Model T, you could build a wireless spark transmitter. I had a cousin about five miles away, and we used to talk to each other by the spark radio.

A few years later I read about the invention of the vacuum tube and discovered someone in Marion, Ohio, who had one that he wanted to sell. I think the price was fifty-three dollars, which was a lot of money. But I had a newspaper route and had saved up. And so in the summer of 1920 my uncle drove me to Marion. It happened that Warren Harding, the presidential candidate, was passing through Marion that day in a train heading for New York. So I got to meet him and [future president] Herbert Hoover, who was fascinated by my vacuum tube. The next day we drove back home. We had to wait overnight because car [head]lights weren't powerful enough for true darkness then.

About four or five days after I had gotten the vacuum tube hooked up, I started to hear music coming across the wires. Music! And then, between the music, I could hear somebody talking. It took me five or six evenings to put together what was being said, but I finally determined that it was "I am Dr. Conrad. I am experimenting with radio station eight-XK. If anybody can hear me beyond Steubenville, Ohio, to the west please call me long distance." And he gave his telephone number.

Now, there were only three telephones in our system. My father, as school superintendent, had one, the mayor had another, and the minister had the third. But none of us had ever called long distance. So I ran across the street and knocked on the door of our local telephone operator and told her that I wanted to make a call to Pittsburgh, which was about a hundred miles away. It took her about forty-five minutes to go through the manual and figure out how to make the long-distance call. But when we finally got through, I don't know who was more excited,

Conrad or me. His signal was getting out a hundred miles! For the next three weeks he would go on the air and I would go on the telephone and tell him whether his signal was better or worse.

Soon I got a letter from him, and he said that on the night of the presidential election of 1920 he was going to broadcast the election returns in what would be the first official radio broadcast, and he wanted me to come celebrate the moment with him at the station. My family went to Pittsburgh with me, and when he met my father, Conrad thought he was the guy he had been speaking to these many months, not some thirteen-year-old kid!

Announcers at KDKA in Pittsburgh report the results of the Harding-Cox presidential election in the first official radio broadcast on November 2, 1920.

The transmitting station was at the top of a tall building, and I went in and took an elevator to the top. It was my first elevator ride, and I was impressed that there were so many elevators in the building. Then I found out that this was known as the K Building of the Westinghouse Company, where they tested elevators. So it was a building of elevators. And on the top floor they had built this little shack. There were two men in there doing the transmitting. They had two microphones. One was held with rubber bands in front of a Quaker Oats box that had been propped in front of the speaker of a Victrola. This was the mike they used to transmit music. And then the other microphone was used for voice.

Now, by January of 1921 I had decided to build my own broadcast station. I built a hundred-watter and then applied for an experimental broadcast license. In March I got a letter saying, "One of my first official duties as Secretary of Commerce is to award you this license. Aren't you that young fellow I met back on the railroad platform in Marion, Ohio, with that vacuum tube? What's a fourteen-year-old kid going to do with a broadcast station? Signed, Herbert Hoover."

"[From movies] we learned how tennis was played and golf, what a swimming pool was . . . and of course we learned about Love, a very foreign country like maybe China or Connecticut."

—*Writer Kate Simon, recalling the 1920s thrill of movie-watching*

Another new entertainment form was on the rise, one that was pure magic: the movies. By the mid-1920s there were twenty thousand movie theaters across the country, in small towns and big cities alike. Every place that was anyplace had a movie palace, and everybody who was anybody went at least once a week.

Like radio, movies helped create a shared national culture. Teenagers from Maine to California looked to the movies to see the latest fashions and hear hit songs. Charlie Chaplin was the biggest star, but moviegoers flocked to see screen idols such as Rudolph Valentino, Clara Bow, and Douglas Fairbanks.

Even more than cars or radio, movies let people escape to exotic places. In big cities the theaters were designed to be the fanciest places in town. Because the earliest films were silent, many of these movie palaces had enormous pipe organs, or a full orchestra, to provide the soundtrack. The moment people walked through the doors of these extravagant theaters, with their plush velvet curtains and crystal chandeliers, their imaginations soared.

In the 1920s, the theater itself was part of the show. Here a New York movie house's "human billboard," featuring live showgirls on the marquee, attracts viewers to the premiere of *Hollywood Revue* (1929).

Pete Pascale, who was born in 1914, grew up in New York City. When he stepped into a movie theater he felt the same thrill people all across the country felt.

When I was a kid in East Harlem, there were a lot of movie palaces with names like the Cosmo, the Beaumont, and the Stadium. And then we had the Liberty Theater, which was smaller and showed the older movies. We used to go to the Liberty because it was easy to sneak into. Sunday was the big day there. A lot of people would come and bring their food with them in a pail. They would sit in the theater, watch the movie, and eat their Sunday afternoon dinner. The place was always a mess. And you had to be careful where you sat because the guys in the balcony eating their dinner would set their pails on the railing and forget about them and then some macaroni would end up falling on your head. We kids would watch it happen and then laugh like hell. It was crazy, but we had a great time.

Back then, many of the studios were in New York, and we could go to them and watch movies being made. We got to see many of our favorite stars—Harold Lloyd, Douglas Fairbanks, Tom Mix. We got to see Harold Lloyd making a movie on 116th Street, hopping onto a bus and hanging out of the window. And then *The Jazz Singer* came out, and it was all anyone could talk about: "Did you see the talking picture?" It was a big topic, this new step in the movie industry, because this was our main means of recreation, just going from one theater to the next, and suddenly after years of watching the silents, we had sound!

The 1920s were energized by yet another magical machine, the airplane. Aviation had grown slowly since the Wright brothers had flown the first crude machine in 1903. By the mid-1920s the airplane seemed more likely to become a thrilling toy than a means of transportation. Carnivals and country fairs featured daredevil fliers. They performed stunts such as wing walking and parachute jumping, and people could buy a ride for $5—if they dared! While the flying machines were exciting, the general feeling was, "You'll never get me up in one of those things." Then came Lindy.

In May 1927 Charles Augustus Lindbergh flew his single-engine *Spirit of St. Louis* from New York to Paris. It was four hundred miles farther than anyone had ever flown before, and he did it solo. Few people thought he could make it. Less than a month before, two French pilots trying the same route had been killed in a crash. But Lindbergh was determined to succeed.

The weather and visibility over the Atlantic Ocean were so poor that sometimes Lindy flew only ten feet above the waves. After seventeen hours he was so exhausted that he slipped into hallucinations. He slapped his face, opened the window for air, and forced himself to stay awake. Twenty-six hours into his flight he saw a bird, and then a fishing boat. "Which way to Ireland?" he called out to the surprised fishermen. At last, thirty-three and a half hours after leaving New York, he landed in Paris. The whole world cheered.

The Sheik (1921) made Rudolph Valentino the Hollywood heartthrob of the 1920s.

Charles Lindbergh and *The Spirit of St. Louis* take off from Roosevelt Field, Long Island, on the way to Paris, May 20, 1927. The plane, built to his specifications, was financed by Missouri businessmen and $2,000 of Lindbergh's own savings.

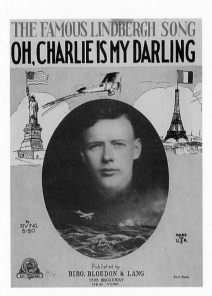

Hundreds of songs were written in honor of Charles Lindbergh, but the man himself quickly grew tired of the hero worship. After receiving an ecstatic welcome in St. Louis, he said, "I was so filled up with this hero guff, I was ready to shout murder."

When Lindbergh returned to New York after his heroic flight, he was welcomed with a Congressional Medal of Honor and a parade up Broadway that attracted an estimated 4.5 million people.

Lindbergh's flight made the world smaller, easier to reach. An aviator who flew with Lindy in air shows was Elinor Smith Sullivan, born in 1911, who went on to train pilots for the air force.

I was seven years old when I took my first ride in an airplane. It was just after World War I. There was a man out on Long Island who sold rides in a plane he had designed. He would sit there in the middle of this potato field with a big sign: Rides for $5 and $10. I was strapped in on my father's lap, while my little brother sat on the pilot's lap. As we went up over Long Island the clouds parted and we looked out over the fields. It was like a fairyland. The streaks of sun came down all around us and changed colors. And from that moment on, I knew I wanted to fly planes.

When people saw that little children like us were willing to go up in the plane, they felt it must be safe after all, and they lined up for rides. We brought in so much business, the pilot began to give us free rides week after week. By the age of twelve I felt that I knew all there was to know about flying, but my father told me I'd have to be eighteen before he'd let me go up alone. I cried on my mother's shoulder and begged until finally, when I was fifteen, she let me take lessons. After two and a half flying hours my instructor told me it was time to do my solo. I was terrified, but I told myself, "You've always wanted to do this, and now you've got to do it." And once I got up there around one thousand feet, it was like I was home. That's the only way I can describe it.

At the age of fifteen I was flying and hanging around with some of the best pilots in the world. We were having so much fun flying around in those primitive planes. And they were primitive! If your engine didn't give out, that was considered a great flying day. We got to be experts at crash landings because you'd be flying along and suddenly have no engine. You'd look down and find an open field and think, "Well, gee, I can probably make it down there," and make a sudden landing.

We had no radar, and no way of communicating with the ground once we took off, because radios were still too heavy. We navigated by using railroads or by just looking for landmarks.

When I was seventeen I pulled my first major stunt—in order to prove myself to the male pilots. There was one who had just lost his license for crashing a plane while trying to fly under the Hell Gate Bridge on the East River. He was hanging around and griping about being grounded while "this little girl" was allowed to fly, and I decided to show him by trying the stunt myself. When I told my family, my father said, "Well, I don't like the idea of you doing it, but if you were to fly under all four East River bridges, they'd certainly never forget that." So I did. Because of my age, it was supposed to be a secret, but a whole gang of newspaper reporters and newsreel photographers showed up. The Brooklyn Bridge turned out to be the only tricky part of the stunt— I had to fly through it sideways to avoid a big destroyer ship coming upstream. This was the shot they showed in theaters all over the country. The Department of Commerce sent me a letter reprimanding me, but enclosed in the envelope was a note from the secretary asking for my autograph!

Everyone thought of us as daredevils. Many people also thought we were all crazy. I still have letters from people who seemed to think we were from outer space or something. But after Charles Lindbergh's flight, we could do no wrong. It's hard to describe the impact Lindbergh had on people. Even the first walk on the moon doesn't come close. After Lindbergh, suddenly everyone wanted to fly, and there weren't enough planes to carry them.

There weren't too many women fliers in the twenties, so I was kind of an oddity. But I was lucky in that no one ever gave me a hard time about it or harassed me. Strangely enough, though, when I would lecture to women's groups there would always be someone saying, "Well, she really belongs at home. A girl her age should be married. What right has she got to be out there wearing pants?"

Elinor Smith at Roosevelt Field, Long Island, April 28, 1929, just before her attempt to break the world's flight endurance record for women.

the Bambino
the Sultan of Swat
the Mauling Mastodon
the Behemoth of Bust
the Mammoth of Maul
the Colossus of Clout
the Prince of Powders
the Mauling Monarch
the Blunderbuss
the Rajah of Rap
the Wazir of Wham

—Nicknames for Babe Ruth, as coined by the tabloids

George Herman "Babe" Ruth was the most famous sports figure of the 1920s. He transformed baseball from a pitcher's game of defense to a thrilling hitter's game. His celebrity was so great that newspapers ran columns entitled "What Babe Ruth Did Today," and businessmen paid him to endorse everything from cigars to underwear.

More and more women were stretching their wings in the 1920s. They ventured beyond their traditional role as housewives, cutting their hair, wearing shorter dresses, and even aspiring to careers of their own. But this new freedom came at a price. By the late 1920s, there was one divorce for every six marriages—up from one in seventeen in 1890. In spite of new opportunities, women's options in the workplace were still limited.

Lillian Hall Gerdau was born in 1913. She described her attempt to move up the corporate ladder.

Policewomen confront four women for disobeying a law banning short bathing suits at Balboa Beach, California, 1922.

Florence Arnold, born in 1918, watched the conflict between her conservative mother and her daring older sister.

Since money was scarce in my family, it was very important for me to start working as soon as I could. And I was very fortunate to get a job with a publishing company, which I liked a great deal. After about one week in the business world I was absolutely in love with the corporate structure. But it was hard for women to get ahead, and we weren't encouraged to do very much. After two years with the company I was promoted and became a correspondent in the distribution department. But I was told, "When you correspond, be sure you don't sign your letters 'Lillian Hall.' You must write 'L. M. Hall,' because we do not want the news dealers to know that they are dealing with a woman." This didn't really bother me, because I was so thrilled that they were letting me do it; I was the only woman doing something at that level. Of course there were two men doing my same job, and they were making $35 a week to my $22.50 a week. But after that promotion, I was so excited, I thought, "Oh boy, I can just see myself becoming circulation director here." So I asked my boss what I should do. And he said, "Why, Miss Hall, you can't be a circulation director, you're a woman. The best thing for you to do is to train yourself so that you can be a good secretary." I was terribly disappointed.

My mother was not very contemporary. She was very rigid and so my older sister and I were brought up according to very strict lines of deportment. We were not to flirt with anyone or wear too much make-up. We were to dress modestly, and we were never to be seen anywhere that ladies did not belong, which was just about everywhere. But my sister defied all of that. She was a flapper. She worked at the phone company, and she wore beautiful short dresses, fur coats, coach-style hats that covered up her head like a turban, and—of course—the galoshes, always unbuckled. That's where the term "flapper" came from because these things flapped, flapped, flapped. The day my sister came home with bobbed hair, my mother took one look at her and retired to the couch with her "aromatics"—her smelling salts that kept her from fainting. When my sister decided she wanted her own apartment, you can imagine how my mother reacted. She refused to let her move out until she was married, so my sister lived at home until she was forty-one years old!

Langston Hughes,
poet, 1902–1967.

The vibrant national culture of the 1920s found its voice in a new kind of music—jazz. Jazz began in New Orleans during the previous century. Then it traveled north with the Great Migration of African Americans and settled in Chicago. There it took on a new sound. Now it had "swing," a danceable sound that pointed to the influence of white musical styles as well. In the 1920s jazz became America's music.

Night after night, jazz lit up cafés and clubs, especially in the New York City neighborhood of Harlem. Many African Americans had moved out of the agricultural South and become city people. From 1920 to 1929 New York City's black community grew six times larger. By the middle of the decade Harlem was almost entirely black, and it was a national center of entertainment featuring the new, truly American sound.

With so much attention focused on black entertainers, African American culture thrived. Harlem poets, playwrights, and essayists produced powerful work dramatizing the African American experience. This "Harlem Renaissance" helped broaden people's understanding and appreciation of black life.

Howard "Stretch" Johnson was born in 1915. He described what jazz and the Harlem Renaissance meant to him.

Johnson onstage at the Cotton Club.

As a young boy, growing up in Orange, New Jersey, I had the opportunity to meet Willie "The Lion" Smith and J. P. Johnson, two of the great piano players of the time, who also happened to be friends with my mother. They would commute from Harlem to Orange to record piano rolls at a local music studio. At the end of the day they would get together with my mother and her sisters and cousins, and it would be party time in the community. It was exposure to musicians like these that led me to read about and appreciate what was being called the Harlem Renaissance, where artists, musicians, and writers were beginning to come forward.

The time was ripe for a renaissance back then. After the defeat of the kaiser in Germany, a spirit of optimism and positive expectation swept across Harlem. The Allies won the war for democracy, so now it was time for something to happen in America to change the system of segregation and lynching that was going on. In Europe, the black troops were welcomed as liberators; so when they came back to America, they were determined to create a situation that would approximate the slogans they had been fighting for. They wanted democracy at home in the United States. And this general idea helped feed the concept of the renaissance.

A lot of people wonder how there could be joy and optimism in a community under the conditions of segregation and discrimination. But the black community had two very important forces that enabled it to survive and grow. One was the church, and the other was the entertainment world, where you had jazz.

The first time I was truly seized by jazz was in 1927, when I heard Duke Ellington broadcast from the Cotton Club. When I heard that music, that sound that Ellington created, it just went through me: *rah . . . rah . . . dah . . . dom . . . bah.* I still love that music today.

Fire-and-brimstone preachers like Billy Sunday rocked churches with their colorful sermons. Sunday was known for his athletic style, in which he stomped, pounded, jumped, and slid back and forth across the platform.

Not everyone shared this enthusiasm for the Jazz Age. If there was one attitude that matched the excitement about the new in the 1920s, it was nostalgia for the "good old days." Hadn't America once been a place where your neighbor looked like you, talked like you, thought like you? In the 1920s people who thought like this began to glorify a past that was mostly white, Anglo-Saxon, and Protestant. Many traditionalists looked for comfort by embracing a literal interpretation of the Bible. They called themselves "fundamentalists," and the subject they hated most was evolution. They worked hard to make the teaching of evolution a crime. In Tennessee, they succeeded, leading to a sensational trial in 1925. Called the Monkey Trial, it featured two famous lawyers: William Jennings Bryan, who argued for the state against the teaching of evolution, and Clarence Darrow, who defended John Scopes, the high-school biology teacher who had taught evolution.

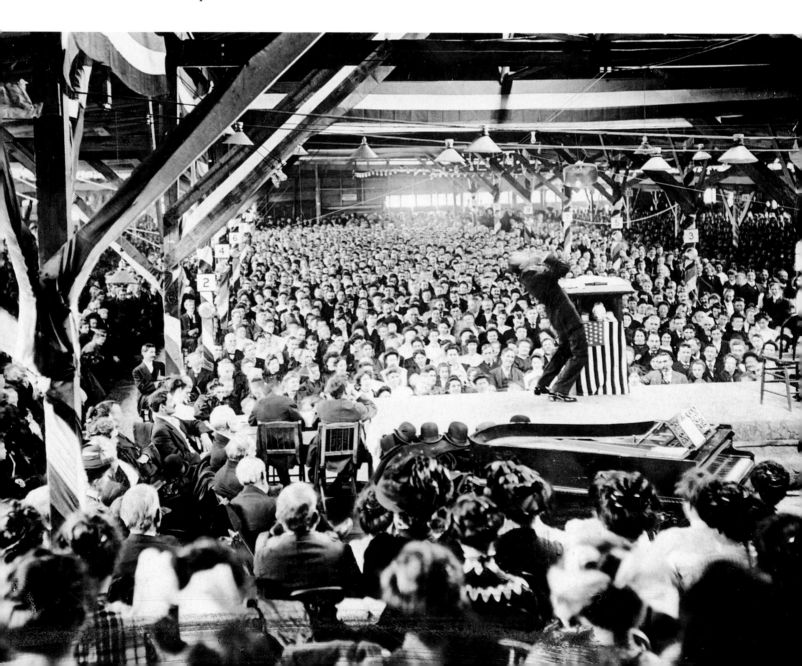

Students being sworn in as witnesses during the Scopes trial in Dayton, Tennessee.

People across the country eagerly followed this dramatic fight between the traditionalists and the modernists. In the end Scopes was found guilty of teaching evolution (though he was only fined $100). But it was Clarence Darrow's defense of science and truth that left a more lasting impression on Americans.

Some traditionalists who wanted to restore old-fashioned morality turned to the Ku Klux Klan. In 1921 the Klan had more than a million members spread across the North and South. By 1924 it boasted four million members. Earlier in the century the nativists had spoken out against new immigrants. Now the Klan revived those feelings. It stirred up hatred of Asians in California, Mexicans in Texas, Jews in New York, and Catholics in the Deep South. The Klan appealed to people who believed that their jobs and their very way of life were threatened by "modern" life and the increasing numbers of nonwhite, non-Protestant, and non-Anglo-Saxon immigrants.

Many people cheered the Klan on and put members in powerful positions. By 1924 the Klan had become so powerful that it had members in the governments of at least six states. Future president Harry Truman almost joined the Klan himself. Tempted by the political benefits it would bring him in Missouri, Truman gave $10 to a Klan organizer. Then he was told that if he won the election, he wouldn't be allowed to hire Catholics. Truman took his $10 back.

A Klan parade in Anderson, Indiana, 1922.

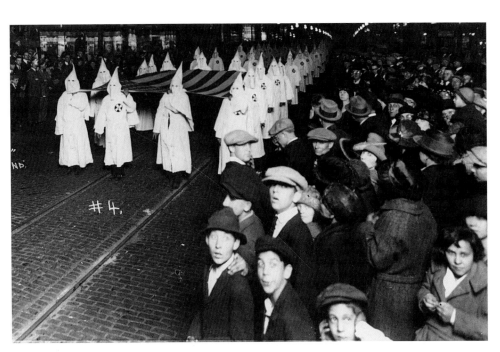

Carl Leisure, who was born in 1913 on his grandparents' farm in Indiana, had firsthand experience with the Klan—and so did almost everyone he knew.

A great many people think of the Klan as simply a hate organization, and that it was. Hate is probably the easiest emotion to teach. It's very easy to be "us" against "them," and that, really, was a large part of what the Klan was about. My parents both belonged to the Klan, and so did my sister and I.

But the Klan was also a natural outgrowth of the time, and movements like it were all over the world. We were changing from an agrarian society to a manufacturing society, and the Klan was a reaction to it. People in Indiana had always been farming people. The land was there, and that was your life. It was stable and renewable. But suddenly, in the twenties, the farming went sour and we changed over to a manufacturing existence.

Anything that fought against the changing world was welcomed in these quarters, and the Klan was certainly that even if it was trying to preserve a society that was no longer preservable. The Klan taught the sanctity of the home. They wanted prayer in school. They wanted you to follow the Bible as long as you didn't admit that any part of it was Jewish.

Every businessman who was not Jewish belonged to the Klan, not necessarily because they believed in what the Klan said but because it was good business. Most ministers belonged to the Klan. Many teachers belonged to the Klan. In this state, we even had a governor who belonged to the Klan.

The hatred was big. All new immigrants, regardless of where they came from, were bad. If they happened to be from England, that was pretty much acceptable. Some immigrants from Germany were acceptable. But Irish immigrants were more "them" than "us," because they tended to be Catholic and all Catholics, of course, were "them." Jews, of course, tried to control all the wealth. That was what the Klan claimed. Jews were international, and anything international was suspect. And Negroes were unacceptable, of course. Even Chinese were a no-no, but we didn't have very many, so we didn't hate them much. You can only hate what you have. We felt like we were just engulfed in a sea of people who were not us, and had to fight back.

Then it all collapsed. After some scandals, people lost the faith in it. When the power started to dissolve, the whole thing disintegrated. And it was a good riddance.

If there was one issue that united traditionalists with modern reformers in the twenties, it was the Eighteenth Amendment to the Constitution. That amendment prohibited the sale of alcohol, and the period after it became law in 1920 is called Prohibition. Some supporters felt that alcohol was immoral. Others hoped that Prohibition would put a stop to the destructive influence of alcohol on family life. The Klan saw Prohibition as a way of rejecting the wine-drinking immigrants from countries such as Italy and Greece. But Prohibition had unexpected results.

What Prohibition actually did was to encourage crime on a scale never seen before in America. Smuggling alcohol into the country (bootlegging) became a big business. But it wasn't just big-time bootleggers who were breaking the law. Average citizens carried hip flasks, visited "speakeasies," and brewed their own alcohol in stills they bought at the hardware store. Meanwhile, many of the so-called law enforcers were getting rich off bribes. And organized crime, which controlled most of the illegal liquor trade, was booming. Al Capone ruled Chicago, and gangsters controlled other cities, too. Gangland murders filled the newspapers.

By the late 1920s there were thirty-two thousand speakeasies in New York City alone—twice the number of bars before Prohibition. In many places around the country liquor was sold publicly in open defiance of the police. The Eighteenth Amendment had made society less law-abiding, not more moral.

Al Capone, 1899–1947.

Neighborhood children frantically try to salvage wine after federal agents dumped several barrels into a gutter in Brooklyn, New York, 1926.

John Morahan, who was born in 1915, helped his family run a typical speakeasy in New York City.

My mother was Irish, from county Sligo, and for her making booze was a family tradition. In Ireland everyone makes their own stuff. So when she got here to New York, she and my father bought some rooming houses, and when Prohibition hit, she just started making booze in the kitchen and selling it from the ground floor. She was a real businesswoman, my mother, and I guess I took after her. As a teenager, I was already driving around in a Nash convertible making deliveries and running four speakeasies.

The way it worked was we'd make some of our own stuff, and the rest we'd bring in from Scotland or Canada. Our speakeasies were just like a regular bar you'd see today except for the door with the peephole in it. We had to be careful who we let in, and we knew our customers on a first-name basis—they were like family. If a stranger were to come in

Patrons enjoying illegal brew at a speakeasy.

and he turned out to be a government agent and you sold him anything, you'd be finished. The minute you asked him for the money, he'd pull out the badge and pow! They would put a big lock on your door and close your joint down.

We had to watch out for cops, too, but we knew quite a few of them. Some of the best customers we had were cops. Sometimes they'd pay for their drinks, but mostly we'd take care of them, you know, if they were working the beat. When we'd bring in barrels of beer, we'd give the beat cop a dollar a barrel if he was watching. This kind of thing was going on across every level. If the Prohibition agents were going to raid us, we would usually get a call from the police captain at the desk telling us ahead of time. So we'd move everything next door, and they'd come in and look around and there'd be nothing. Everyone was on the take back then, all the way up to the mayor, Jimmy Walker. In fact, we used to make deliveries to his house every week.

We couldn't always know when they were coming, though. Once, when I was about fifteen, the Prohibition agents came and broke down our door with an axe. I grabbed a broom and made like I was sweeping the joint. And when the guys came in they said, "Get the hell out of here. You're too young to be working at a place like this." Meanwhile I was running the joint! So they locked up the bartender and, boy, were they surprised when I was the one who came to bail him out. This kind of thing didn't happen to us too often, though, because we ran a respectable joint. As long as your joint was respectable, you were generally okay.

In spite of nostalgia and the Klan, in spite of Prohibition, the 1920s drove ahead with wild excitement. Radio, movies, airplanes, automobiles, jazz—everything screamed, *Go, go, go! Faster! Louder! Richer!* Americans were buying on credit, living it up, and expecting that their prosperity would go on and on. So when the stock market crashed in October 1929, few people were paying attention, and few people realized that the party was about to end.

A solemn crowd gathers outside the New York Stock Exchange on October 24, 1929—Black Thursday, the day the market crashed.

4 Stormy Weather
1929–1936

The stock market crash of 1929 was a catastrophe. But it was just one part of a much bigger picture of pain and suffering in the 1930s. Suddenly the bright lights of the Jazz Age went dark. It was as if America had gone from a carefree summer into a freezing winter.

Only a small percentage of the country was directly affected by the stock market crash in October 1929, when almost $30 billion went down the drain in a matter of days. And many of those involved thought the situation would change for the better quite soon. But by the early months of 1930 it was clear that more than just the stock market was in trouble. Businesses were closing, jobs were scarce, and banks were shutting down, wiping out the life savings of millions of people. The nation, and the whole Western world, sank into what is called the Great Depression.

Left: Desperate for jobs and searching for answers, unemployed men march on Boston's city hall, February 1934.

Right: In a scene that was all too common during the Great Depression, a family has been evicted from their Brooklyn apartment and turned out on the street with their furniture. The homeless took shelter where they could find it: in doorways, under bridges, in packing crates, in abandoned cars, or in crude shacks made of discarded wood and cardboard.

In 1930 some twenty-six thousand American businesses collapsed. The next year even more went out of business. By 1932 almost thirty-five hundred banks had closed. Twelve million people were out of work (almost 25 percent of the workforce). Still, it is hard to understand what that means without imagining the scenes people saw every day. Lines for free meals at soup kitchens stretched for blocks; fathers knocked on their neighbors' doors to ask for a piece of bread so their children could eat; people fought over garbage cans behind restaurants, looking for scraps of food; families sat on the sidewalks surrounded by their furniture after being thrown out of their homes. America had once been the land of possibility; now it was the land of despair. Americans looked back longingly at the happy-go-lucky twenties, wondering what had gone wrong.

To this day, economists debate the causes of the Great Depression. One common explanation for this disaster is that wages had not kept up with the growth of industry in the twenties. Factories had been churning out more products than ever before. But because the owners of the industries were keeping most of the profits, fewer and fewer people could afford to buy what the factories were making. For a little while the buy-now-pay-later shopping spree had disguised the problem. But eventually people had to pay their bills. When their wallets got emptier, they stopped buying new cars and radios and furniture. In turn, the factories had to slow down production. That meant laying people off from their jobs, which meant that people had even less money to spend.

Clara Hancox, born in 1918, grew up during the Great Depression, and her experience was shared by millions.

Hancox in 1923 with her parents, Solomon and Sarah.

My parents migrated to New York from the Ukraine in 1916, and when I was a young girl we lived in the slums of the Lower East Side. During the 1920s we didn't know there was going to be a depression—we were just building ourselves up and struggling along. We lived in a poor place, but we were never desperate. My father started working in the flooring business, and as the building trade boomed he really started making money. This allowed us to move uptown to the Bronx, which to us was like living out in the country.

My father was doing very well, and he got this marvelous order to do the floors in a building that could be called a skyscraper in those days. He went to the bank and borrowed a huge sum of money to buy the materials. And just as the work was about to begin, the market crashed. We weren't even paying attention to the stock market, so we didn't really know what was happening at the time. But almost overnight it was like a bomb had fallen. All of a sudden faces were tragic, and people were walking around in the hallways of our building and in the streets with inquiring eyes, saying, "Has it happened to you?" It was awful. It was like a domino effect: Everything that happened to one person gradually happened to other people who were connected with them, until everything just shut down. The people who had given my father the contract lost all their money, and since my father had borrowed all of that money, he was wiped out. Psychologically, he never recovered.

Weary, dejected farmers in Spotsylvania, Virginia, look on as their land is sold at public auction. Crop prices fell sharply, and farmers did not have enough income to keep up the payments on their heavily mortgaged farms. In 1933 a quarter of the farmland in Spotsylvania County was sold at auction, for as little as thirty cents an acre.

People jumped off the George Washington Bridge. We heard about it. People we knew who were involved with Wall Street couldn't meet their debts. They were so disgraced that they killed themselves in order to get their families the insurance money. It was incredible and horrible what happened in those years. Respectable businesspeople would walk around in the streets of downtown Manhattan with a tray of bright red apples, and they would ask you to buy an apple for five cents. And horrible as that was, it was even more horrible that we didn't even have five cents!

For about five years I had been saving money in a piggy bank. If I even had a penny or two, I would put it in the piggy bank, and I loved to shake it and feel the weight. One day I came home and grabbed hold of my piggy bank, just to give it a shake, and discovered that there was nothing in it. The bank was empty!

My mother was standing in the doorway, looking at me, and she said, "Your father borrowed the money. He has to go out to look for work and he needed the money to go downtown. When your father comes home don't say anything. It's bad for him." And he came home and I didn't say anything but my face was swollen with tears. And my father took me in his arms and he said, "I'm sorry. I had to have money. But it's a loan. I'll pay it back to you." He never did. But it was so embarrassing for me and so painful, even then in my childish years, to have to see my father in this terrible state. That's what was bad. My father walked the streets every day and found something to do. My mother went to work, and I even worked. My mother would find a few pennies and we would go to the greengrocer and wait until he threw out the stuff that was beginning to rot. We would pick out the best rotted potato and greens and carrots that were already soft. Then we would go to the butcher and beg a marrow bone. And then with the few pennies we would buy a box of barley, and we'd have soup to last us for three or four days.

Then one day I came home from school and saw furniture on the sidewalk that looked familiar. We had been evicted. What hurt me most about it was the look of pain on my mother's and father's face. I couldn't bear to look at them.

The Great Plains were nicknamed the Dust Bowl in the mid-1930s. A combination of land mismanagement and three years of drought destroyed farmland as the soil literally dried up and blew away. So many farmers from Oklahoma moved to California that the word *Okie* came to mean "migrant." Here a family takes to the road in Pittsburg County, Oklahoma.

When the Depression began, most people in positions of power thought that the government should not tamper with the economy. They viewed the economy as though it were the weather: When it's bad, there's not much you can do but wait until it's good again. But the Great Depression wasn't just bad weather, it was a hurricane.

People had expected that the good times of the 1920s would go on forever. They never dreamed that the economy could collapse so completely. While President Herbert Hoover promoted the idea that the crisis would be over soon, ordinary people watched bizarre things happen. Unemployed lumberjacks set fires so that they could earn a few dollars as firefighters, putting out the same fires they had started. Farmers who could not get a fair price for their crops let fruit and vegetables rot in their fields, even as millions of people went hungry. In the spring of 1931 the people of Cameroon, a country in West Africa, sent New York City a check for $3.77 to help the "starving." American harbors were filled with ships carrying immigrants back home to Europe, where they hoped things would be better.

With factories and farms closing all over the country and no jobs to be found, some Americans left home and, in search of a solution to their troubles, began to drift across the landscape. People crammed their belongings into rusting Fords or Chevrolets or hopped freight trains to find work, to find a meal, to find a decent way to keep their lives together.

Bill Bailey, who was born in the 1910s, was one of those whose life became a scene of desperation.

I hit the road to look for work, but as the Depression got deeper, things just got worse and worse. And while people may have wanted to help you, with a loaf of bread or a sandwich or something like that, they had to start getting selective: Should they give it to a thirty-five-year-old man or to a woman with two kids? So bit by bit you began to see yourself getting less taken care of. There was this horrible law across the whole United States, called the vagrancy law. Any cop could come up to you and say, "Hey, you got a job?" "No." "Where do you live?" "Oh, I'm from another state." "You got any money with you?" "No." And then they'd have you for vagrancy. So I just minded my own business and tried to avoid all that by moving on.

Soon I discovered that the best way to travel was by railroad boxcars. Of course, the railroad companies were opposed to the idea originally. But in towns where things were really bad, the people were going to the sheriff and saying, "You've got to do something about all of these people bumming on the streets." Then the sheriffs would call up the railroads and say, "We want your train to slow down in this little town

Bailey (right) and friends, when he was working as a longshoreman.

every now and then to pick up all these hoboes." So because of the pressure from the sheriffs, these trains would slow down and we'd jump on and ride. It wasn't so bad. Some days if the weather was nice, you could sit up on the roof of the cars and sun yourself.

Heading westward into California, we joined masses of people, because everyone was under the illusion that there was work out there. But who needed a hundred guys picking oranges anymore when there was no market for the oranges? It was a very sad type of deal. But I will say this: As bad as things were, there was no violence. You'd never hear of a woman being attacked or beaten. And all the mothers on the road with families, they got the preference in the boxcars. When you were making a grab for a freight car and you were just getting ready to jump in, somebody might be there at the door and say, "Sorry, fella, family car." That meant there was a whole family in there, and you respected that and you stayed out. That's just the way it was. As things got worse there were more and more families out there. Sad, but that's the way the country was.

So you'd just have to learn to survive—somehow. I'd go to the undertaker and say, "Anybody leave a good coat here?" Because often they'd take the clothes off the dead people and bury them in their Sunday suits. And the undertakers were pretty good guys, so they'd say, "Well, why not? He don't need it anymore. Good luck." And if that stiff lying there was your size, then you were in luck.

Bumming was easy for me, because I was young and had a schoolboy face and I'd always say "madam" or "mister," and "I'm willing to work if you will give me a meal." I've been in places where I was bumming at the front door and while I was trying to get their attention, I could hear a knock on the back door—someone else looking for a handout. Some people even put up signs saying, "Please do not knock. We have nothing for ourselves." And you always had to be careful that you weren't thrown in jail for asking for food.

Roosevelt: 22.8 million votes
Hoover: 15.7 million votes

—Results of the 1932 American presidential election

Most of all, during the early years of the Great Depression, people looked for a leader, someone to point the way out of this crisis. America's wish for a savior would be answered by an energetic aristocrat from New York.

It's hard to imagine the hope and expectation that greeted Franklin Delano Roosevelt when he became the thirty-second president of the United States in 1933. He was the wealthy governor of New York and a distant cousin of Teddy Roosevelt. His legs were so crippled by polio that he couldn't even stand without awkward leg braces. But the task ahead of him was the greatest challenge for any president since Lincoln. Within days of his inauguration, half a million people had written letters to the White House to wish him well.

"The only thing we have to fear is fear itself," Roosevelt claimed. And with the help of radio, which allowed him to talk directly to Americans in their own homes, the new president led the country into a series

"He's honest, he's strong and he's steady, a chip off the block that gave us Teddy," read part of the chorus of this 1932 campaign song.

of drastic reforms. In his first hundred days in office, the government passed new laws to help farmers, set up a federal relief program, establish a minimum wage, regulate the stock market, insure bank accounts, and employ millions of people. These programs, and others that came later, became known as the New Deal. Roosevelt believed that the federal government had a right to play a more active role in managing the national economy. He also believed it had an obligation to actively help ordinary people.

For most Americans, Roosevelt was exactly the leader they needed. In what were desperate times, FDR offered hope and inspiration. With his legendary "fireside chats," as he called his radio talks, President Roosevelt asked the country to give his plans for economic recovery a chance to work.

Marty Glickman, born in 1917, described the effect Roosevelt had on people when he became president.

When Roosevelt came to power in 1933, there was an almost immediate change in attitude. By that time Herbert Hoover was the losing president. He rarely smiled. When Roosevelt came to power, that voice . . . that brilliant, ringing, uplifting voice which we all heard on the radio made an almost immediate philosophical difference. We felt better about things. We felt we could win, we could get ahead, we could come out of the Depression. This feeling was certainly reflected in the activities of the adults around me. And I even felt it as a kid. I liked Roosevelt. I liked his smile. Herbert Hoover was a dour individual, but Roosevelt, with that smile and that lift in his voice, he was a leader, a true leader. Perhaps the greatest leader we ever had.

Roosevelt, en route to a Democratic rally in Sea Girt, New Jersey, in 1932, greets Jersey City mayor Frank Hague.

Enthusiastic supporters welcome New York governor and presidential candidate Franklin Roosevelt to Pittsburgh in 1932. Audiences loved Roosevelt, whose charm was a refreshing break from his stuffy opponent, President Herbert Hoover.

In traditional black culture, the church minister is the divinely appointed storyteller. He gives meaning to existence. So for the black community of the 1930s, the use of the voice to affect us was nothing new. It was just that of all the voices that I heard and respected and loved, Roosevelt was the master. He could reach out and touch everybody and sort of bring us all together. He made us feel that all we needed to do to resolve our problems was to come together, work out a plan, and do it. And me, a little black boy down in Georgia, hearing that voice over the radio, I felt it. It wasn't that he told it to Daddy and then Daddy told me. He was talking to little Ossie sitting there listening to him. He engaged my support and my sympathy. It was very much one of the reasons why we Americans never gave in to despair. He was always there to spur the troops on: "Come on, fellas! One more time, and you're going to get it done! It's going to be wonderful." And you know, you felt better about yourself.

Like an actor preparing for his big moment onstage, Hitler posed for this series of photographs in the 1920s. He hoped that by studying them he could learn the gestures that would be most effective in public speaking.

The same winter Roosevelt became president of the United States, a new figure came to power in Germany. Like Roosevelt, Adolf Hitler became a leader at a time of economic collapse. Along with America and most of Europe, Germany was also suffering from a depression, with unemployment as high as 25 percent. But Germany might have followed a different path if its people had been merely hungry. Unfortunately for the world, Hitler's enormous popularity was also a product of Germany's lingering desire for revenge.

Despite Germany's surrender in 1918, few Germans accepted that they had been defeated in World War I. Hitler had been a corporal in the army, and he believed that the peace treaty, which was meant to punish Germany, was a crime. He blamed the Jews and the Bolsheviks for the collapse of the German "fatherland." At first the Nazi movement was dominated by people from the fringes of society. After the complete breakdown of the economy in 1930, Hitler's message of anger and revenge found willing listeners among the broader public.

Hitler's speeches on the radio and at massive Nazi rallies struck a chord in German hearts. With his finely tuned oratorical skills, he could hold a crowd of half a million people spellbound. Many people now believe that it was the emotional appeal of the Nazi movement, more than its political ideas, that made it so popular. Germans, suffering from economic despair, heard Hitler pledge that their lives would improve and that those responsible for their pain would be punished. Hitler promised to restore German pride and claim for Germany what he felt was rightfully its own: more land.

While Germany was cheering, Hitler ordered the arms industry to go into full production. If he intended to expand Germany's borders to the east, he would need to lead a powerful nation. Hitler also began to "punish" those he felt were responsible for Germany's collapse. The group Hitler targeted from the start was the Jews. Within weeks of becoming chancellor of Germany, Hitler had barred Jews from public service. By the end of 1933 Jews were excluded from universities and from professional occupations.

Like Roosevelt, Hitler used the radio to speak directly to his nation. Margrit Fischer, born in 1918, shared the optimism that Germans felt when he came to power.

Fischer (second from left, wearing head scarf) at the moment when she met Hitler, 1936.

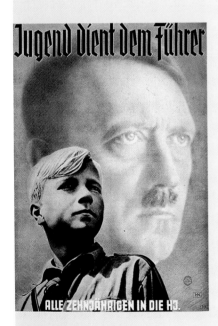

This 1935 poster reads, "Youth serves the führer! All ten-year-olds into the Hitler Youth."

I was born in the last year of the First World War, and from earliest infancy I was aware of Germany's hatred for the Treaty of Versailles. I remember very clearly my mother's grief over her fallen brothers and cousins, and my family's very strong antiwar feelings. The early 1930s was a catastrophic time for Germany. In Bremen, where I grew up, there were lines in front of the employment offices, lines in front of the food distribution centers, longer and longer lines every day. There was a great sense of uneasiness everywhere. So when this odd Hitler came along with his slogans that captured the essence of what was in the hearts of the German nationalists, then it became clear, even to a child, that things would change very soon.

At that time he never spoke of war. He promised us that unemployment would end, and that Germany would once again take its place in the world as a state worthy of respect. And I think that was probably the key thing, for the Treaty of Versailles had cut to the root of Germany's self-respect, and a people cannot survive long without self-respect. So this man was not only admired but welcomed, longed for.

As a young woman, I pinned all of my hopes on this new personality—the hope that now everything would be entirely different and better. I still remember January 30, 1933 [the day that Hitler became chancellor], very clearly. It wasn't a revolution in the real sense of the word, but rather a relatively peaceful transition. Now, suddenly, there were brown-shirted troops who marched around and made a very orderly and cheerful impression. The sidewalks were lined with people, there were nice marching bands, and there was a festival-like atmosphere everywhere. There wasn't any jubilation yet, but there was expectation.

The jubilation came one or two years later, after unemployment had really been fought and the streets were clean. At that time there was still no mention of war, and no mention of persecuting Jews, either, at least not publicly.

We had no television then, only radio and newsreels, and of course everything we saw and heard was terribly slanted. Before every radio news announcement the government played a beautiful fanfare that struck you to the very core. When you heard the fanfare, you went running to the radio thinking, "What has happened now?" It was very cleverly done, and very exciting. Whenever Hitler's voice came on the air, you felt a kind of inner attentiveness. It was always something special to hear him speak.

We were never allowed to see anything that would tarnish Hitler or the image of his leadership. Of course, we didn't see everything as positive. We were certainly not thrilled about the characters who worked with Hitler, for example. But we couldn't publicly rebel against the state. That was the price we paid, and we said to ourselves, "Well, we are really well off, and we have climbed so far." Basically people were satisfied. The fact that we had to keep our mouths shut and to guard against being too critical, that we were not entirely free, that was the price that we paid for this positive feeling, this positive, upward movement of our nation.

A triumphant Hitler arrives at a youth rally in Berlin in 1934. No matter how spontaneous he may have seemed, Hitler carefully prepared every word and every gesture. Everything about the Nazi movement reeked of manipulation. The parades, the banners, the singing, and the lighting were all arranged for the greatest dramatic effect.

For the human race to be punished by a Hitler in the twentieth century was bad enough. But he wasn't the only tyrant who darkened civilization in the middle of the century. In the Soviet Union, the ideals and hopes of the Russian revolution were crushed by the dictatorship of Joseph Stalin.

Stalin had inherited his position as leader of the Soviet Union from Lenin. After the bloody civil war that put the Bolsheviks in power (at the cost of fifteen million lives) and a famine in 1921 that caused the deaths of more Russians than had died in World War I, the Soviet Union's leaders faced a dilemma. The revolution had been a struggle for the rights of industrial workers. But more than 80 percent of the nation's people were peasants whose lives had nothing to do with industry.

Russian peasants had eagerly taken the farmland from the large estate owners during the 1917 revolution. But that was as far as their loyalty to the Communist Party went. When Stalin took charge, he pushed for collective farms. Instead of individuals owning farmland, the land would be owned communally by the state. Peasants would work the land on these collective farms, handing over their quotas of grain or milk or potatoes. In return, the Communist state would distribute these agricultural products "fairly" to all citizens. However, few peasants wanted to give their newly acquired land back to the state. They resisted violently.

Over the first few years of Stalin's regime, millions of farmers were forced into collectives. This created chaos for Soviet agriculture. Peasants who refused were deported to labor camps in Siberia or were shot. During this period more than fourteen million people either died of starvation or were executed. Whole villages were destroyed, and millions of children were orphaned, set loose to wander the countryside scavenging for food like lost animals. But the peasants found ways to rebel. People killed their own livestock and destroyed their farm machinery rather than give them to the Communists. In 1930 alone they slaughtered a quarter of the nation's cattle, sheep, and goats, and a third of the pigs, feasting on them in defiance of the government. But this form of rebellion had tragic consequences. With experienced farmers murdered or sent to labor camps, livestock nearly wiped out, and farmland left untilled, Russian agriculture slipped backward, becoming even less productive.

Stalin (wearing hat) poses with delegates at the Sixteenth Party Congress in Moscow in 1930. The two party officials standing to his right were eventually killed in one of the Soviet leader's many purges.

The part of the Soviet Union where collectivization was most difficult and where treatment of the peasants was harshest was the Ukraine. Stalin pushed the Ukrainian farmers to the limit and still insisted that they were hiding grain from the government. In fact, the Ukrainians were starving, forced to hand over so much of their harvest that they had nothing left for themselves.

Death began on a giant scale in 1933. Five million peasants starved to death even as Stalin demanded more grain. Dead bodies littered the countryside. Millions tried to flee, but they were refused train tickets or arrested if they tried to escape on foot.

Banners bearing the heroic images of Lenin and Stalin hang in a Moscow square in 1931. Stalin linked his image to Lenin's, even going as far as doctoring photographs and rewriting history books to make it look as if Lenin had chosen him to be his successor, which he had not.

Eugene Alexandrov, who was born in 1916, was a witness to the horror in the Ukrainian countryside.

During the famine, when I was a student at the Soviet School of Mines, the government decided to send out some students to help the collective farmers with the harvest—those who remained alive, that is. So in 1933 I was sent with a group of other students out to the Ukraine. By this time the famine had spread all over the territory. As we traveled into the area we noticed that there were no people left anywhere—they had all been deported or starved to death, all because of collectivization. Sometimes we would arrive at a place that our maps told us was supposed to be a village and there would be nothing there—just bricks and weeds.

When we arrived at Uman, the village where we would be working, we went to the family home in which we were supposed to stay and found only one girl there, of about thirteen years of age. Her wall was covered with photographs of nice-looking, healthy people. They were her grandparents, her parents, and her sisters; there were maybe twelve or fifteen of them altogether. We asked her, "Who are these people? Where are they?" She said, "They all died of starvation. I am the only one who's still alive, but I will die soon because I have already gone through the stage of being swollen." This meant that she was now in the dehydration stage and beyond medical help.

Living among the villagers, I learned what was going on with collective farming. The peasants had to give all of their grain to the government, but the government thought they were holding out and hiding the grain. Some of them did try to hide it under a roof or a floor, or they would dig a hole three meters deep and bury canvas bags full of grain. But then the Communists would come with long steel probes and wherever the ground was loose they would start digging. And when they took that grain away, the family was left without anything. If a

Peasants stand trial for hoarding grain in one of the Soviet Union's Central Asian republics in 1931. Party activists used false accusations, class hatred, and intimidation in an attempt to destroy the kulak class, a class of wealthier, landowning peasants.

family had a cow or pigs, they would slaughter them, too. In the villages you would never see a dog, or a cat, or a goose, or a chicken. Everything was consumed.

In Uman there was a small pond for fishing. And one day a group of men who were still strong enough were fishing there, and when they pulled in their nets they found a bundle of something. It was a human head, the head of a woman they knew, in fact, who had disappeared. When the authorities came to investigate, they traced it back to the woman's neighbor. He had killed her and was living on her flesh. He was shot, of course. I also saw two people arrested in a railway station near Kiev. They were a man and wife, peasants from some northern wooded area. When we asked the chief what was going on, he said, "They are cannibals. They are doomed to be executed by shooting." In fact, they were half insane, because when starvation starts, a person goes through various stages. The first one is a tremendous desire to eat something. Then the person gets almost insane. Then weakness appears. These people who were arrested were already in the stage of weakness. They were trembling, and not at all steady on their feet. Soon they would get swollen and desiccated, so they were doomed either way.

Workers dispose of the bodies of famine victims in the Ukraine, 1932.

Through it all, Stalin insisted that everything in the countryside was fine. Newspapers and the radio never mentioned the mass death in the fields. According to the government, the harvests were doing very well. Of course, many people knew otherwise. But it was too dangerous to talk. In fact, the world would not learn the truth about what happened in the Ukraine until decades later.

Whatever idealism Soviet Communism had started with was trampled to dust. The Soviet Union was now an iron dictatorship. Like Hitler's Germany, it began to revolve around the dominating personality of one man. Europe was in the grip of tyrants, and these men were setting the stage for a confrontation that would pull the whole world into war once again.

5 Over the Edge
1936–1941

A nail-biting sense of dread dominated life in the late 1930s. Everywhere people looked, there was proof that things were going very wrong. The American economy was still limping along, with little to show for FDR's New Deal programs. Yet even as people in the United States struggled to put food on the table and keep a roof over their heads, there were rumblings of war from around the globe. In 1936 Italy's dictator, Benito Mussolini, seized Ethiopia. In Spain another dictator, Francisco Franco, began a brutal civil war that would eventually bring him to power. In 1937 the Japanese began attacks on China. And Germany's Adolf Hitler was threatening to take over neighboring Czechoslovakia.

These world events felt closer to home than ever before because of the way news was delivered. Instead of reading about incidents in newspapers days after they happened, Americans turned on their radios for daily news flashes. Live broadcasts from Spain brought the sounds of exploding bombs into American living rooms. Whole families sat by their radios listening to the frightening sounds coming from Europe.

Bob Trout, who was born in 1908, was one of the early news broadcasters who brought world events home to America.

In the middle of the 1930s neither of the two big radio networks—NBC and CBS—had a news department. All we did was air a couple of five-minute news broadcasts a day, which were supplied by the Press Radio Bureau. But toward the end of the decade the country began to count on getting its news from us.

It was a standard evening ritual in houses: People would gather round these rather large radio sets when the news came on, and nobody would talk very much until it was over. They listened to H. V. Kaltenborn bringing them coverage of the Spanish Civil War with the crackle of the rifles in the distance, and certainly nobody had ever heard real gunfire on the air before. Radio was bringing things right into people's homes, and it was beginning to affect the way people felt about what was going on in the world. So when something important happened in Europe, the country was prepared to listen. Americans had always been somewhat interested in Europe's affairs, but they just didn't feel that they were intimately affected by them. Now they were fascinated.

As part of their coverage of the London blitz of 1940, American, British, and Canadian radio commentators broadcast a joint program called *Round London After Dark*.

When Hitler annexed Austria, we did a full half hour of reports from Europe, with correspondents in Paris, Berlin, Washington, and London, and me in New York, acting as what would now be called an anchorman. Then in 1939 came the Czech crisis, which was a major radio event, and the country was enthralled by it all. They listened as much as they possibly could. It's no exaggeration to say that radio brought the whole country together, all at the same instant, everyone listening to the same things. And the country liked being tied together that way. In the morning people would say, "Did you hear that last night? Did you hear Hitler speaking again? What was he talking about? Did you hear them all cheering, '*Sieg heil*'? What did you think?" It was on the tip of everybody's tongue. People didn't quite see just yet exactly how all these things overseas were ever going to intimately affect their daily lives. But it was the greatest show they'd ever been offered.

Still, few Americans were interested in seeing their country get involved in another war in Europe. Times were tough enough at home. The country's attention was focused inward, not outward. Just as new technology such as radio brought Americans closer to events in Europe, it also brought them closer to each other. A new sense of "we" encouraged Americans to celebrate their own country. And a new sense of "we" also energized workers. The 1930s were a period of resentment between the working class and the industrialists. Because of the Depression, jobs were hard to find, and working men and women were afraid to make demands. But in 1935 Congress passed the National Labor Relations Act, a law that gave unions bargaining power and encouraged workers to organize and demand better wages and working conditions.

Victor Reuther, born in 1912, was one of the first union organizers to fight for the rights of working men and women.

For me, the most exciting aspect of the mid-1930s was the growth of industrial unionism and the birth of the CIO [Congress of Industrial Organizations]. By "industrial unionism" I mean a concept of unionism that embraced the skilled, the semiskilled, and the unskilled as members of the same union. This was in great contrast to the old tradition of the AF of L [American Federation of Labor], which sought to unionize only the skilled elite. The way the AF of L saw it, unskilled factory workers didn't earn enough to pay dues, so why bother? By contrast, industrial unionists were committed to the well-being of the lowest paid, and also to the idea of bridging the racial gap. Black people worked beside whites in the coal fields, the steel mills, and auto and rubber factories.

The rise of the CIO was one of the most dramatic chapters in the history of labor—not only in the United States but in the world. But what came as the real surprise was how quickly the workers in mining,

After staging several successful strikes against small automotive parts makers, the upstart United Auto Workers was ready to turn its sights against one of the "Big Three" automakers: Ford, General Motors, and Chrysler. Here UAW members stage a sit-down at a General Motors plant in Flint, Michigan, in 1937.

steel, rubber, and auto responded to the idea of organizing. I know this came as a surprise to me and my brother, Walter Reuther, at the level we were organizing in Detroit.

I think I can best describe this rapid growth by telling the story of the factory in which I was working in the fall of 1936. There were five thousand workers in these two plants on the west side of Detroit. And we had all of seventy-eight members signed up in the union. I was working in a department that had a higher percentage of union membership than any others—though still not great. And there was a Polish woman working at the punch press next to me who had two small children at home, and I knew she worried about them. But the speed of the line and the pressure on all of the workers in there was so horrible in those days that it caused her to faint one day. And visibly, she dramatized a problem that was common to every worker among the five thousand: the incredible pressure under which they were working. There was a look of awe and bewilderment on the face of every worker in that department as they looked at this woman. And they were angry. And I came home and I reported to my brother what had happened that day. And he said, I want to meet with this woman.

Victor Reuther (seated at far left) at a strike meeting led by his brother Walter Reuther (standing).

We went to see her at home, and Walter said to her, "It is time we do something dramatic to overcome the workers' fear of organizing. Do you think you can faint again, but this time on schedule?" She looked at him with bewilderment. "Not Monday, but Tuesday. Give us a day to work on this." She promised to do it. Tuesday came, and sure enough she went into a dead faint. I walked over and pulled the main switch, and gradually all these huge presses ground to a frightening silence. It was an awesome silence, because the workers had never been in the factory when it was quiet before. And suddenly, they realized the incredible power they had in their own hands. They could shut the place down, and they did. And the strike began.

We had a ten-day strike. But as a result of that first stoppage that grew out of the woman fainting, we could not sign up workers fast enough. Fear was eliminated, wiped out in one dramatic move. Soon we had over three thousand workers signed up. Ours was a short and quick strike, but we won, and we raised our wages in one simple move from twenty-two and thirty-three cents an hour to a minimum of seventy-five cents an hour for everyone—blacks, women, it didn't matter. We were on our way.

Even as Americans focused on improving their own lives, it was get-ting harder for them to ignore the bloody deeds of the dictators across the Atlantic. On April 26, 1937, a squadron of German planes flew over the tiny Spanish town of Guernica. It was market day, and the town was filled with people from surrounding villages. The German planes were there to support Franco in the civil war, and that afternoon they ruthlessly bombed the town for three hours. Women carrying babies, shop owners, peasants—more than sixteen hundred people were killed. Guernica was not an important military target; the reason for the bombing was to terrorize the Spanish people. It succeeded in terrifying people around the world. Was this how battles would now be fought, with bombs raining down on children?

It was becoming more and more obvious that Hitler's policies were aimed at threatening people as much as governments or armies. In the spring of 1938 the Germans marched into Austria in an invasion that met almost no challenge from the Austrian people. Hitler called it the Anschluss, or "union." Within days, Austria was completely transformed into an extension of the Nazi Reich. Shops owned by Jews were looted, and synagogues were occupied by soldiers. As crowds taunted them with insults, Jews were made to scrawl anti-Semitic slogans across their own storefronts, or to get down on their knees to scrub anti-Nazi graffiti from the sidewalks. Policemen even forced them to clean toilets using their precious prayer bands, or *tefillin*, in place of rags.

The Spanish artist Pablo Picasso painted *Guernica* in 1937. It may be modern art's most powerful statement on the brutality of war.

Vienna had long been a center for anti-Semitism, but after the Anschluss life quickly worsened for the city's Jews. Here a group of Jews is publicly humiliated in what the Nazis sarcastically called a "scrubbing party."

Karla Stept, who was born in 1918, saw her world end when the Nazis marched into Vienna.

Stept in Austria one year before the Anschluss.

The winter before the Anschluss was a great time. We were happy, we danced the nights away, we made plans for the future. It never occurred to us that, as Jews, something bad could happen to us. Austria had always been an anti-Semitic country, but in a way it had never really touched us in Vienna. We thought that this was the place where we were born, that this was our country. Every time we heard about what was going on with Hitler in Germany, we said, "Oh, that can't stay that way. They'll get rid of that lunatic." And we believed it. That was our tragedy.

A few weeks before the Anschluss, the chancellor of Austria had gone to see Hitler, and when he came back, he spoke on the radio and told us that there would be no changes, that Austria would always be Austria. We believed it, and we were lulled into thinking that everything was going to be just fine. So when we heard on the radio that German troops had crossed the border into Austria and were met by throngs of people welcoming them with flowers, we were very much surprised. There were Nazi signs everywhere. There were large groups of men in brown uniforms and the SS in their black uniforms, wearing their Nazi armbands. They unfurled enormous swastika banners on all of the official buildings.

We found out later that everything was prepared down to the very last detail. Many Austrians, it seems, had wanted to be part of Germany, especially those who had Nazi inclinations. They knew exactly what would happen, but they thought they would be much better off. The Germans came to Austria and trained people who wanted to be Nazis, though the Nazi Party was illegal at that time. All the preparation had to go on without anybody knowing, and I'm sure today that they trained tens of thousands of people.

So Austria converted to Nazism within an hour. It was unbelievable. Then the telephones began to hum. People who lived in sections of the city where they could see what was going on would call and say, "Don't go out. Stay in. You don't know what will happen to you." We were all on the phones to each other. "Is everything all right? What are you doing? What's going on? Look out the window. What's going on on the streets?" Because we weren't sure what was going on.

On Saturday morning, twenty-four hours after the German troops had crossed the border, the brown shirts and the black shirts got to work against the Jewish population of Vienna. They forced Jewish men and women to get down on their knees and scrub the sidewalks free of graffiti, all the while being kicked by the people standing around them. They put detergents and other things into the water, which would eat away at the skin, so these people had to scrub with bleeding hands. And seeing the faces of the bystanders, it was terrible. They were enjoying it. They really enjoyed what was happening to those poor people.

In November 1938 the violence spread. Distraught over the suffering of his family at the hands of the Nazis, a young Jew named Herschel Grynszpan walked into the German embassy in Paris and shot a diplomat, Ernst vom Rath. When word of the murder reached Germany, it enraged the Nazi leadership. The minister of propaganda ordered troops into the streets for a night of violent attacks against the Jews. In Berlin, Stuttgart, Vienna, and other cities, crowds smashed the windows of stores owned by Jews and broke into Jewish homes, looting, burning, and attacking. One hundred and eleven Jews were killed and 177 synagogues were destroyed in what came to be known as Kristallnacht, the "Night of Broken Glass."

In Hamburg, Ralph Giordano, born in 1923, witnessed the terror of Kristallnacht.

Kristallnacht is a term that minimizes the event. It would be better to call it the "night of the imperial pogrom." That night was a clear turning point, a great divide, the beginning of a new era, and not only for the Jews. My family was not bothered on that night. But the next morning, on the way to school, there was a very strange, totally altered atmosphere. One could tell that the people were stirred up, that something had happened that was entirely new. And then I found out at school what had happened. There were some Nazis in my class, and they were happy, rubbing their hands together, saying, "Now the Jews will be dealt with, finally the time has come." And then after school, I went into the center of Hamburg, and I saw what damage had been done. It was so monstrous that you didn't want to believe it. It was like a terrible dream. Windows were shattered, goods were scattered in the street. There was smoke and fire. Merchandise was thrown out onto the street. There were people who walked in the midst of it without any self-consciousness at all, who showed themselves to be completely indifferent. There were also other people who you could tell were troubled. They kept their heads down and were probably extremely disturbed by what they saw. And from that point in time, everything was clear. It was plain that the Nazi regime was capable of doing anything. Suddenly there was the feeling that we could meet with a violent death at any moment, not because we did anything against the system, against the regime, but because we existed in the world as Jews, because of our biological existence. This feeling was very tangible, very palpable from that moment on.

A synagogue in ruins after Kristallnacht, Eberswalde, Germany.

A synagogue burns in Graz, Austria, after Kristallnacht in November 1938. While violence against Jews was not new under Hitler's regime, this was the first massacre organized and carried out by his government. In a crowning insult, German Jews were collectively fined one billion marks after the event for "their abominable crimes, et cetera," as Nazi aide Hermann Göring put it.

After Kristallnacht, there was outrage in the United States. Americans called for harsh sanctions against Germany. In Congress there was an effort to widen immigration quotas to let in more German Jews fleeing the Nazis. Robert Wagner, a senator from New York, introduced a bill that would have admitted ten thousand German Jewish children. But the bill failed, and in the end, the country did very little to support the Jews. Many people saw the acceptance of more European immigrants as a mistake. America was still suffering from the Great Depression, and refugees from Europe might take precious jobs away from Americans.

Many Americans tried their best to ignore what was happening overseas. They looked for an escape from their worries through entertainment. One of the biggest and flashiest distractions was the World's Fair, held in New York City in 1939–40. The pavilions of thirty-three states, fifty-eight foreign countries (minus Nazi Germany), and thirteen hundred businesses dazzled visitors with such marvels as television, nylon stockings, robots, and man-made lightning. "I have seen the future" was one motto at the fair, and people flocked to New York to get a peek.

Even the architecture of the 1939 World's Fair—with its towers, arches, fins, domes, and serpentine roofs—spoke of the hope for an exciting future aided by advances in science and technology. Shown here is the Perisphere, at the fair's Theme Center.

Gilda Snow, born in 1929, visited the fair at the end of the summer of 1939.

Snow's father, William (bottom row, fourth from right), with his coworkers in front of the yet-to-be-completed Perisphere.

New York World's Fair

Snow with her mother, Lillian, in a World's Fair souvenir photo.

My father was an electrician, and when I was about eight or nine he wanted to show me the kind of stuff he did. So he brought me to the place where he was working, and it turned out to be the New York World's Fair! My father took me around to all the buildings and exhibits that were starting to go up, and he said, "This is what I do, kid. This is it! And someday this place is all going to be lit up."

When the fair opened officially, it was quite an event, with lots of people there, of course. The crowds really gathered there because I think American people were ready for a pick-me-up. Everyone had been down in the dumps for so long from the Depression, and this World's Fair was helping everybody come alive again. Being at the fair was like having a bird's-eye view of the future, and people loved it.

There were all kinds of exhibits—Wonder bread, where they gave you a little loaf of bread; Heinz, where they gave you a little green pickle pin to wear. But the fair was called the "World of Tomorrow," and the most interesting exhibits were the ones that showed you what the future would be like. I remember sitting in a dark room and watching a rotating stage that would display first the old and then the new. We would see all the old washing machines, refrigerators, cars, and so on, and then little by little the stage would move, and we would be in the future. There were televisions, electric washers, electric dryers—everything was electrified. It was almost like a fairy tale, like a whole different way of living. It was so easy. Take the refrigerator, for example. It made its own ice. You didn't have to do anything with it except open and close it! And there was a light inside of it! There was a television demonstration where this man would film you. And to see your picture on the screen, well, that was just unbelievable. How it worked, we did not know. I didn't even ask! I was just in awe of the whole thing. It was hard to believe that we would ever see any of these things, because, let's face it, at that time we were just pulling ourselves out of a depression.

But then I remember going to the Polish pavilion. We were going up this huge, beautiful walkway, with flowers all around us. But as soon as we got up to the building, the lights went out. My father, he figured they had an electrical short, because the rest of the fair was all lit up. And then we heard over a loudspeaker that Germany had just invaded Poland and that they were closing down that pavilion. And that, of course, was the beginning of the war. I remember thinking, "War? Where?" I didn't even know where Poland was at that time. But there wasn't anything to see and we couldn't go into the pavilion, so we just walked away from it.

In late August, startling news came over the radio. Hitler and Stalin had signed an agreement that split Poland into two spheres of influence, with Germany poised on its western side and the Soviet Union looming over it from the east. Then at dawn on September 1, 1939, Hitler faked a Polish invasion of Germany to give himself an excuse for fighting back. A million and a half German soldiers were waiting on the German-Polish border for the order to attack.

When the signal came, German tanks rolled across the Polish country-side. The Polish army, still fighting on horseback, was almost powerless to resist. The frontier fell in a few days. Thousands of German soldiers, who had left Berlin in railroad cars painted with the slogan We're Off to Poland to Thrash the Jews!, now descended in tanks and troop carriers on Poland's capital, Warsaw. Wave upon wave of Stuka dive-bombers blasted road junctions and railroad lines. The Stukas, which emitted a piercing shriek that spread terror wherever they went, were backed up by heavy bombers, which pounded the city to rubble. Together, the tanks and bombers carried out the German blitzkrieg, or "lightning war." They hit both military and civilian targets. Within weeks, the Russians invaded Poland from the east to take their share of the spoils. Poland was finished.

Peter Pechel, born in 1920, was part of the invading German army.

Pechel in his Wehrmacht uniform, 1944.

Just before the invasion of Poland, Hitler sent the 3rd Armored Division through Berlin, and he was very disappointed by people's reactions. He thought they would be jubilant, as apparently the Germans had been in 1914 when World War I started. But the Berliners lined the streets and let the tanks go by, remaining totally silent. There was no movement, no reaction, nothing. I think this illustrates the general feeling among the people at that time, especially the young men in uniform, like myself, who would have to use their weapons sooner or later.

Not long after that, my company marched into Czechoslovakia and camped out on the Polish border. We were very scared because we didn't know what war was. We had only been told by our fathers that war was a horrible thing. And so we hoped and prayed that we would be spared. Then the order came to move into battle position. We were to march across the border at 4:45 A.M. on the first of September, 1939. For a young man, war means hearing the first shots, and suddenly having strange smells in your nose: burning houses, burning cows, burning dogs, burning corpses. It means seeing the first people killed; in Poland it was civilians. And then seeing young men like yourself in foreign uniforms being killed or wounded.

I was in an armored tank division, and of course we rode on and on and just kept on rolling. We were the spearhead of the German army. The Poles were very tough to fight. They fought bitterly and desperately. But it was easy for a modern army like the German army to beat them, because here we were in tanks being attacked by the Polish cavalry. Can you imagine? Soldiers on horses with lances moved against tanks.

German tanks head toward Warsaw after defeating a Polish battalion at the Brahe River. Once the front was broken, the Poles' only hope was for the British and French to attack Germany from the west. By the time the Allied forces were mobilized, however, Poland had already fallen.

Julian Kulski, born in 1929, described the effects of the blitzkrieg on the Polish countryside.

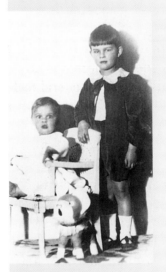

Kulski, standing, with his sister Wanda, 1934.

In the summer of 1939 my father, who was the mayor of Warsaw, rented a house out in the Polish countryside because he knew the war was coming soon. One day I was playing in the woods with my friend, and we heard this tremendous sound of motors, and watched the trees start bending. Huge planes with sinister-looking black crosses on them were flying over us, pretty much at the level of the treetops. They were headed north, toward Warsaw, and they must have been one of the first squadrons of the Luftwaffe. This was when I realized that war had begun, and it was a terrifying experience.

The little medieval town near us was bombed a few days later. And since it was not defended, the Wehrmacht took it over immediately. I was near the market when I first saw them coming, and while I expected something like cavalry on horses, they came on motorcycles and trucks. They wore greatcoats covered with dust, goggles, and very scary gray helmets. Somehow I expected that the invader would come in looking very well dressed, but they looked pretty beaten up and bedraggled. The Polish army had given them a hard resistance on the border, so they had been fighting every day. They put up a field gun in the middle of the square near the cathedral. They brought in a large military band and started playing *"Deutschland über Alles"* and other German marching songs.

At the same time, they started a fire in the synagogue and tied up the rabbi, letting the elders run into the temple to try to save him. My first impression was this was complete unreality. And absolute horror. I didn't stay in that town very long, but before we left, I remember that a nine-year-old peasant boy came over and touched the handle of a German motorcycle. And a soldier, who was inside the café, came out and shot him dead, right in front of my eyes. After that I stayed away from Germans, period.

Hitler's elite SS troops began the immediate persecution of Poland's Jews. Here, after the shooting of a German police officer in the city of Olkusz, Jewish men between the ages of fourteen and fifty-five were systematically rounded up, forced to lie facedown with their hands tied behind their backs, and mercilessly beaten for hours.

In spite of the terror being unleashed in Europe, American isolationists, those who wanted the United States to keep to itself, were still a loud voice. Nevertheless, Americans followed the progress of the war with great interest. While Hitler took Denmark and then Norway, maps sold out across the United States. People mounted them on their walls and, listening to the news flashes on their radios, marked the troop movements. But that didn't mean they wanted America to get involved.

Bob Stuart, born in 1916, was a student at Yale University who believed that Europe's troubles were not our concern.

A capacity crowd packs Madison Square Garden in New York for an "America First" rally, 1941.

Growing up in the thirties, I was educated by people who were seriously disillusioned about why we'd fought in World War I. So the general feeling of my generation was that we shouldn't do that again, especially during a time when we were just pulling ourselves out of a terribly tough depression. When I was in college in 1937 I traveled all through Europe and saw everything that was going on there, and I came back from that trip sort of wondering if all of their problems were really our problems. I was young, and hardly thinking profoundly about anything, but my overall reaction to it all was just, "God, it's great to be an American."

The following year the war clouds were gathering in Europe. As I talked about it among my friends, we began to think about what we could do to keep America from getting trapped in another European war. They were in a mess over there—France seemed disorganized, and the British didn't seem to have too much military capability either, but we felt that fundamentally it was not our concern as Americans. We were just convinced, after the experience of "trying to make the world safe for democracy" in World War I, that we'd better take care of our hemisphere first and avoid entanglements.

In retrospect, it's clear that some of the events going on in Europe, such as Kristallnacht, really didn't get the coverage they deserved. So our awareness level wasn't very high. Dorothy Thompson would write a column from time to time on the refugee situation, but I don't think we were aware of how serious that was. I think we all would have been horrified if we'd really known and understood it.

In the spring of 1940 my friends and I started to worry about President Roosevelt, because it was clear to all of us that he was anxious to help Britain and France. Everything he was doing seemed to lead toward more support and more involvement. We felt very strongly that there was still a lot to rebuild and do in the United States.

President Roosevelt was troubled that America's old allies, Britain and France, faced the growing threat from Germany alone. Yet American support for involvement in Europe wasn't strong enough to let him act. By the spring of 1940 Hitler was moving westward, toward France. His army plowed through Holland, unleashing a wave of civilian terror that forced thousands upon thousands to flee ahead of the tanks and troops. Belgium was next, and the Allied soldiers rose in force to meet the Germans there. Unfortunately, they fell into a deadly trap.

Most of the French army was in the trenches of the Maginot Line, which had been built in the 1930s to defend France from the west. (They had expected, mistakenly, that the next war would be fought much like the last one.) With most of the British army in Belgium, Hitler sent his troops into France from the north, in between the two Allied armies. The Allied forces in Belgium found themselves nearly surrounded, and the only strategy left to them was to retreat. Britain's prime minister, Winston Churchill, ordered his troops to flee to Dunkirk, the French port that was now their only way out. He sent 165 ships of the Royal Navy to meet them there, but the waters were too shallow for the navy vessels. London put out an emergency call for any boat that could cross the English Channel and rescue the soldiers. Some 850 yachts, fishing boats, ferries, and firefighting boats responded, while the Luftwaffe descended on the town, pounding the beaches with machine-gun fire and bombs.

Paule Rogalin, born in 1930, was a little girl in Dunkirk who saw the Luftwaffe's attack.

Rogalin in 1943.

Just before the war began I was living in Dunkirk with my mother. My father had been drafted and was stationed nearby. Since so many of the French ships were coming through Dunkirk we saw soldiers all of the time, and we just knew something bad was going to happen soon. It was like living on dynamite. All of us children went to school each day with a gas mask on our back, a school bag, and a blanket, because there was no heat in the classrooms due to shortages.

One night my mother and I went to see some friends in the port of Dunkirk. We started to hear these loud explosions, but the air raid signal had not sounded, so we didn't know what it was. And suddenly we were surrounded by fire. The big ships in the harbor were on fire, and men were jumping off them—some of the men were on fire as well. We were so shocked, we ran and jumped into a ditch shelter nearby. The bombs kept falling, and soon the shelter started collapsing. I was almost up to my nose in dirt. I was getting buried alive. And these three young men got my hands, and they pulled me out of the dirt.

We ran toward the town of Dunkirk, but bombs were just falling all over. It was terrible. It's something I cannot forget. Houses were collapsing, and we could hear people down in the basement who were screaming because they were drowning in the water from pipes that had burst. And we just kept on running. It seemed like we ran almost all night.

In the morning the bombing stopped for a while, so we started walking back to our house. It was still standing up, but as we got nearer, we could see the drapes flying out of the windows, and we could see that a bomb had exploded inside the house. We stayed there for a few days, because there was nowhere else to go; the whole city of Dunkirk was just gone, all gone. We kept hearing that the German soldiers were marching toward our town.

Though I can't remember the first German I saw, I do remember the sound of their boots and their voices. That's what scared me the most. They came into our house, which was half gone, and they kept saying to my mother, "Where is the man of the house?" They thought we were hiding something. And she kept telling them he was in the French army. I guess they wanted to take him prisoner. I'm not a hateful person, but I felt hatred toward the Germans. I hated them with a passion. And I felt like we were not French anymore. We were invaded by these people, who had done so much damage and so much killing, and I'm sure a lot of them got killed, too, but at that point I didn't care.

British and French troops on the beach at Dunkirk.

After a few days we left the house, bringing with us a few things that we carried on our backs. When we got onto the main road we saw that many others were doing the same thing. We looked for our friends but we couldn't find them. As we walked along we saw a lot of dead people; I remember seeing one man who had burned up inside his truck, and he was still at the wheel. Then the enemy started shooting at us from their airplanes, and even though we were mostly just women, children, and old people, they would swoop down low and shoot at us. We had to scramble down the hill into the canal in order to avoid getting hit.

We saw French soldiers in trenches who had no idea what to do. They were lost just like we were, running in all directions with no general to tell them what to do. When my father managed to find us, he was just like those men. He had left the army because they had no guns, nothing to fight with. He was almost crying when he found us, saying, "We can't fight. We don't have anything."

Many people in France saw the retreat from Dunkirk as a betrayal. But the makeshift fleet saved 200,000 British soldiers and 140,000 French soldiers. It also gave the Allies time to regroup in England. France fell in a few days, and utter chaos reigned on the European continent. From Paris alone, more than two million people had fled in cars and on bicycles and on foot, pushing baby carriages and wagons. They wandered the countryside, searching for someplace to hide from the Germans.

Now that Hitler was in command of Europe, Italy's Mussolini joined him. Japan was impressed by Hitler, too. Soon Italy, Germany, and Japan signed an agreement forming the Axis alliance. Only penniless Britain was left to stand against them. But Britain, short on money and weapons, had found in Winston Churchill a man who could inspire the nation. His

Left: In what would become known as the *"exode,"* or exodus, panicked civilians from northern and eastern France fled from the advancing German army. Entire towns and villages emptied as refugees headed south across the Loire River and into cities such as Bordeaux, where the population tripled in a matter of weeks.

dramatic speeches gave English men and women new hope. "Victory," he promised them. "Victory at all costs. Victory in spite of all terror. Victory, however hard and long the road may be, for without victory there is no survival."

In July 1940 the island safety of Britain was destroyed by bombers launched from France. The Luftwaffe, the German air force, was preparing the way for a full-scale invasion. To the Germans' great surprise, the Royal Air Force fought back bravely. Over the cliffs of Dover, British Spitfires engaged in fierce air combat with German Messerschmitts. But then the bombers began striking at the heart of Britain: London itself.

From September to November nearly 250 bombers attacked London each night, sending people running into air raid shelters and subway stations for safety. Entire blocks of houses were demolished. Factories were gutted. Every morning there were mounds of smoking rubble, deep bomb craters, dead bodies, and workers busy cleaning up the debris so that life could go on.

Sheila Black, who was born in 1920, remembers the London blitz.

Left: Black in 1939. Below: Londoners stroll the streets the morning after an air raid.

Most of us learned that the war had begun when we heard it on the radio. There was kind of silence before it and after it, or at least that's how it seems in my memory. It was a very short announcement: "We are now at war with Germany." But, of course, what was a war? Was it going to be the war of World War I, when soldiers got shipped over and walked through trenches and tried to shoot the enemy, or what? We had no idea, and we certainly didn't know then how much of the war would be in the air, right over our heads.

First the men were called to join the military. Then there was the building of the air raid shelters. In our gardens we got Anderson shelters, which were tin huts buried under the earth. And in our homes we

got what were called Morrison shelters, which were wrought-iron tables. We were to hide under these tables if there was a bomb. We also had to line all of our curtains with black fabric, to make sure our homes were absolutely light-tight. There was a group of men called the Home Guard who kept watch for bombs or other signs of invasion, and we were rather led to believe that at any moment a German might parachute himself into our midst. So there was a national feeling that we had to be ready.

We were all issued gas masks, which were horrid things with eyepieces, which you looked through, and long snouts, which you breathed through. They were bad enough as it was, but what was worse was the contraption they gave you for your baby. It was an enormous cabinet into which you fastened your child. And you had to pump fresh air into this for the baby to breathe. Ugh! They were horrible things, and I think they made me feel more like we were in a war than almost anything else. The toddlers got what was called a Mickey Mouse gas mask, which was the same as the adult model, but painted like Mickey Mouse.

I was married when the war actually started, and pregnant when the dogfights over Kent and London began. Then came the bombing. On the night of September 14, 1940, London was ablaze and the docks were alight. That was the night I went into labor. Our flat was at the end of a car park where antiaircraft guns were positioned. So the noise was absolutely deafening when the battle started. My midwife rode over on her bicycle at around midnight, and she stayed through the night because it wasn't safe for her to leave. My daughter was born at three o'clock that morning, and the midwife opened the curtains because we got more bright light from London burning than we got from the electric light in the middle of the room. That was the Battle of Britain, and that, for us, was truly the beginning of the war.

What else is there to say about the blitz? Yes, there was bombing, yes, we lived with it, yes, we woke up and some areas were devastated, but we got used to it. You lived for the day. And then at night you would get under your Morrison shelter, into which you put your mattress. And you got into bed with the children. And others packed up their mattresses and blankets and went down into the tube stations. And when you came up in the morning, you saw dead people. You would think we would have all been terribly squeamish about it, but we got used to it. Human beings are extraordinarily resilient. They get used to anything. Or almost anything.

London's subways continued to operate throughout most of the blitz, even though many of the stations were used as bomb shelters. At midnight, when the trains stopped, Londoners, seeking safety, bedded down on the tracks.

Across the Atlantic, many Americans, with FDR's guidance, were beginning to change their minds about this war. While London burned, isolationists and interventionists debated America's responsibilities to the Allies. And while they argued, Hitler's relentless aggression continued. In the spring of 1941 he broke his agreement with Stalin and marched his troops into the Soviet Union. In less than a month the Germans advanced more than three hundred miles into Soviet territory.

Perhaps it was because most Americans were of European ancestry, or perhaps it was because Hitler riveted the country's attention. But more Americans were focusing their attention on Europe than on Japan in 1941. That all changed on Sunday, December 7.

The Japanese attack on Pearl Harbor in December 1941 left much of America's Pacific fleet in smoldering ruins. Four days later Hitler, too, declared war on the United States.

In the early hours of that day, 189 Japanese bombers lifted off from ships in the Pacific Ocean. They were headed for the American naval base at Pearl Harbor in Hawaii. When they neared their target, the squadron leader spotted Battleship Row. He signaled for the bombers to begin their surprise attack. Within minutes Pearl Harbor was an inferno, as battleships, destroyers, supply ships, and cruisers went up in flames. When the assault was finished, the United States was left with 2,433 dead, 1,178 wounded, 18 warships sunk, and 188 planes destroyed. It was the worst day in American naval history.

Now there was no doubt as to America's point of view. Armed with grim resolve, the country would go to war, in Europe and in Asia. Army recruiting stations were jammed within hours of the catastrophe in Hawaii. As President Roosevelt said, December 7 was a date that would "live in infamy." The United States treated the attack as an invasion: It was a blow that must be swiftly returned.

6 Global Nightmare

1941–1945

As Allied troops advanced deep into Germany, they encountered cities destroyed by endless air and artillery bombardments. Here American infantrymen search the rubble that was once Waldenburg, Germany, April 1945.

From 1941 to 1945 the world experienced the most terrible period of modern times. The war that had raged in Europe for more than two years now spiraled out of control, becoming a truly global conflict. Americans were fighting against the Japanese in the Pacific and joining the Allies to face off against the Germans in the Atlantic, in North Africa, and in Europe itself.

The stakes had been raised. No longer did it seem that the war was being fought only to stop the advance of Germany. Now it was a fight to prevent the destruction of the world as people knew it, and the combat had no limits. Civilians had become targets, and millions of innocent people perished. Amazingly, millions also fought back. Struggling to survive, they enjoyed the one satisfaction that was left for them: the sense of companionship and purpose that came with fighting a war against evil—and fighting it together.

The entire populations of the warring countries were involved. Women worked in munitions factories, men flew lonely combat missions, and children collected materials for scrap drives. Yet the sense that this was "total war" developed not just because whole societies were involved. "Total war" captured the feeling of global madness that the war produced. Even after it was over and the Allies had triumphed, people wondered if the evil forces that Hitler represented had somehow won, too—because now there was a sense that the world had gone somewhere it could never return from. People had seen things they would never be able to forget.

After Pearl Harbor, there was no question left for Americans: The country must join the war. By February 1942 more than five million volunteers had joined community war efforts. Industry moved into high gear, churning out so many tanks, planes, guns, and ships that the economy was pushed out of the Depression.

The attack on Pearl Harbor was a unique moment in modern American history. An enemy had slipped across our borders, and it affected people the way a burglary at home does: They never felt totally safe again. Everyone was afraid. Weather reports were stopped for fear that enemy fliers might use them to plan attacks. Man-on-the-street interviews were ended for fear that someone might blurt out a national secret. Thousands

Posters like this one urged men to enlist, but the command to "remember December 7th" was hardly necessary: The shock of Pearl Harbor had been etched firmly into people's minds.

of Japanese Americans were forced to leave their homes and move into detention camps, for fear that they might try to help the enemy.

In the months after the Japanese attack on Pearl Harbor, the American forces in the Pacific were defeated again and again. Wake Island, Guam, Borneo, Singapore, and the Philippines all fell. Nearly half of the Pacific air force was destroyed. Even though these islands were far away, Americans at home were convinced that their own lives were in danger. And although they were afraid, they also wanted revenge.

This time, though, there were no cheerful tunes urging men to go into battle. The experiences of World War I had taught these soldiers and their families what war really meant. People were ready to fight, but they knew it would be an ugly job.

President Roosevelt defined America's war goals in terms everyone could understand. He called them the Four Freedoms: freedom from want, freedom from fear, freedom of belief, and freedom of expression. These were goals people were willing to work hard to achieve.

By the time American factories were running at peak production, cargo ships that used to take a year to build were being constructed in seventeen days. Bombers came off the line fifteen times faster than usual. A typewriter factory switched over to producing machine guns, and a corset company made grenade belts. With so many men at war, the workforce was flooded with women who took off their aprons and put on overalls. Everyone was pulling part of the load.

America's armed forces were already getting ready for combat. In 1940 Congress had begun the country's first peacetime draft. By the war's end, nearly sixteen million Americans had served.

Neil Shine, born in 1930, was a boy when America entered the war. His family, like millions of others, pitched in.

Shine (back row, center) at age twelve with his brothers and a neighborhood friend.

"I'm Making Believe"

"I'll Get By"

"I'll Be Home for Christmas"

"Don't Sit Under the Apple Tree with Anyone Else but Me"

"I'll Walk Alone"

"I'll Be Seeing You"

"Good-bye, Mama, I'm Off to Yokohama"

"Ma, I Miss Your Apple Pie"

—Wartime songs, appealing to Americans' overwhelming sense of separation

In 1941 I was living in Detroit with my parents and my two younger brothers. I came home one Sunday afternoon from the Plaza Theater to a household that was somber and quiet. The radio was on, and I was told that the Japanese had bombed Pearl Harbor. I spent the whole next day talking with other kids about this war and what it would mean, and the excitement level was high. I mean, I was eleven years old, and I just didn't understand that people died in wars and that war was a horrible thing. To us it was simply excitement.

My parents understood what war was. My father was a veteran of the First World War. My brothers and I were constantly asking him questions, but he didn't talk about it much. Once I asked my father, "Did we kill more Germans or did they kill more Americans?" And he didn't answer me for quite a while, but then he said something like, "It's hard to say because dead soldiers are all on the same side." I didn't know what he meant at the time.

To us kids, combat was a sort of lifestyle, with the good guys and the bad guys. And suddenly here was this exciting thing happening, with the good guys versus the bad guys, and we were the good guys and we were going to win! We played war constantly. We constantly roamed the empty fields near our house, attacking the abandoned buildings and hurling clumps of mortar at them. But nobody would be the Japanese, and nobody would be the Germans. We were all the good guys.

We watched the newsreels, the Hollywood version of World War II, with scenes from the battlefields, where we were always winning. We would come out of the movies so fired up. In fact, we even got fired up in the movies. Once during a movie called *Bataan*, we were losing badly to the Japanese, and Lefty Brosnan, one of the kids in the neighborhood, stood up and threw a golf ball at the screen to try to stem the Japanese onslaught. All he did was mess up the screen so that for the rest of the war it had a big patch in it that you could always see there. Eventually the newsreels became so popular that Detroit opened a newsreel theater downtown. It was all flamethrowers and bombs and shells, and we indulged ourselves in this chaos.

We were always on the lookout for spies, so to us, people with foreign accents were automatically suspect. Now, in an immigrant neighborhood, this is pretty ridiculous, right? I mean, my own father had a foreign accent. But we'd pick out people we thought were likely spies because they wore long overcoats and slouch hats.

We all felt Detroit was at risk, as much as anyplace else, that is. The word ENEMY was everywhere, in capital letters. We had to protect our shores from this "enemy." We learned the silhouettes of all the airplanes, and we spent countless hours lying on our backs at the playground, looking skyward, watching for Messerschmitts and Stukas and Mitsubishis and Zeros. But all we ever saw were the planes from the local air base. If they had ever tried to slip one airplane over Detroit airspace, without a doubt some kid in my neighborhood would have sounded the alarm.

With a theme song entitled "Slap the Jap with the Scrap," the Office of Civilian Defense organized nationwide recycling drives to provide materials for the war effort and to boost morale on the home front.

My father was an air raid warden, but he could have been Eisenhower's aide-de-camp and I wouldn't have been any prouder. He had a white helmet with a symbol on it, an armband, a flashlight, and a whistle. We were so absolutely proud of him as we watched him striding up and down the street making people close those drapes and shut off those lights during the air raid drills. We also had air raid drills at school, where we would get under these tables in the basement.

There was this thing called "the war effort" that took on a life of its own; you had to be doing something for it. One day my mother got herself a pair of slacks, a cap that held her hair in the back, and a lunch bucket and went to work in a factory. My mother was this nice lady who baked and cooked and cleaned house and kept her kids in line, and suddenly she was running a machine at an aircraft supply factory. Every day for three years she marched off to Continental Motors and ran a machine, and I think she enjoyed it.

I remember being jealous that I didn't have an older brother. Other kids came to school with patches on their jackets that their brothers had sent them, souvenirs from overseas. I felt deprived because I didn't have an older brother who would send me a German helmet. But then there was a sort of ritual at my Catholic school when someone was killed, where someone would come into the classroom and get the siblings of whoever was the casualty, and then announce the name over the public-address system, you know, that "Jack Callahan had been killed in action," and we would all get up, put our coats on, go next door to church and pray, and then go home. I found myself being thankful that I didn't have a brother who was at risk, so that I wouldn't have to sit with my mother while she wept in church, while they played taps and folded the flag and gave it to her. So the realization that this was not so fun anymore finally came to me when the kids from the neighborhood started dying.

With much of the male population at war, women, such as these at Douglas Aircraft's plant in Long Beach, California, became the backbone of the nation's war industry. At the peak of production, U.S. companies produced $6 billion worth of war materials each day. Even Russian premier Joseph Stalin later raised a toast "to American production, without which this war would have been lost."

Many of the young men who went into combat never returned. Perhaps the greatest difference in this war—as far as the soldier was concerned—was that it depended on machines more than any war before it. Far more than World War I, World War II made use of the tank and the airplane, and of modern rifles that were capable of firing rapidly at the enemy. But if these new guns could fire faster, they were also less accurate. More powerful weapons, and more of them, meant even greater destruction. The two world wars involved about the same number of fighting men and lasted about the same length of time. Yet more than twice as many people died in World War II.

The Pacific war was especially brutal. To the Japanese soldier, there was no higher duty than fighting for his emperor. Death was thought of as a sublime event, and surrender was an intolerable dishonor. It was considered unmanly, and a soldier who surrendered was less than human. The other side of this philosophy was that a surrendering enemy was also less than human: Captives were to be scorned and abused.

Like the Germans, the Japanese were in the grip of an ideology that regarded all other peoples as inferior. The combination of this racism and their contempt for captives resulted in behavior that shocked Americans. Its terrible effect was to encourage the opinion that the Japanese themselves were barbaric, less than human, and deserved barbaric treatment. In the end gruesome acts were committed by both sides.

At least some of this behavior was caused by the strange conditions of the war in the Pacific. Most of these battles happened far from signs of civilization, on tiny coral-reef islands that seemed almost like another planet.

On Corregidor Island in the Philippines, thirteen thousand American troops were forced to surrender after withstanding a monthlong artillery barrage; then, in a further humiliation, they were paraded before Japanese troops.

Earle Curtis, born in 1918, was a private in the Marine Corps. He suffered from shell shock during a battle in the Pacific, though he later received a citation for bravery.

Top: Earle Curtis at age twenty-five. Above: Marines advance after a destroyer bombardment on Tarawa, 1943.

I was sent with my regiment to Tarawa in the Gilbert Islands. A battle was going on there on one square mile of sand. We arrived on the third day of the battle. It was scorching hot, and corpses were piled everywhere. I was the telephone man, which meant I had to string telephone wire from the command post to where the company was.

We advanced about two hundred yards, and at nightfall we were attacked. Shells were exploding all around me. The first time you get shelled, it's a real rush. Especially when a piece of shrapnel bounces off your shoe or something like that. But the power of high explosives is very demoralizing, because it's this sudden force which has nothing to do with humanity; it's the force of an enormously powerful machine, and there's nothing in the world you can do to resist that. After a while you start to feel like someone who's been in an automobile wreck; you get into a state of shock, and you can't really comprehend everything that's happening around you. There really is no way in the world to prepare yourself for the reality of battle.

During my trips from the front to the rear of the battle, I was stopped every fifty feet or so by soldiers guarding their shell holes with rifles. I soon realized that all of these shell holes were full of marines who were either wounded or too afraid to go out into battle. The war stories never seem to mention all of these guys who are literally paralyzed with fear, unable or unwilling to fight.

One shell landed so close to me that I was thrown to the ground. When I sat up, I had to pick the pieces of coral gravel out of my face. This was really the climax of my battle experience, and it put me over the thin red line into shell shock. I went and told my captain that I needed a break, and I dug out a little area in a bomb crater and fell asleep. When I woke up a few hours later, a huge noise shook me, and I looked up to see an American fighter plane roaring straight toward me. I wasn't surprised or afraid at all—nothing happening around me seemed to have any bearing on my life. When the plane opened fire I felt the muzzle blast of the machine gun on my face, but I wasn't hit. I scrambled out of my crater and saw that the battlefield had gone quiet.

A shouting voice kind of jolted me into reality; it was a corpsman looking for casualties. He had found a body, and he wanted me to help fix the guy up. I looked down at the man's face and I realized I knew him. His eyes were open, rolling from side to side, the sightless eyes of a dying man. Then I noticed that his right leg was entirely missing. The absurdity of the whole situation suddenly hit me, and I broke into an uncontrolled laugh. All the fear and horror melted away, and I felt nothing but relief. Then suddenly I was sober again. I was watching a man die, and the reality of the violence was back with me. All I could think was, "This is insane, this is too much. Nobody will ever get me to do this again." To live through a battle like Tarawa shakes your faith in humanity forever.

With their reservoirs in ruins, Leningrad residents tapped frozen canals, the Neva River, and streets that had turned to glaciers for drinking water. While many people became ill, the intense winter cold prevented full-scale epidemics from sweeping the city.

While soldiers were fighting all over the world, ordinary citizens in central Europe and Russia fought for their lives every day in the streets of their cities. In Russia, Hitler had ordered a blockade of the city of Leningrad, hoping to starve its three million people. But even as the Germans bombed warehouses and supply routes to cut off food supplies, Leningrad's citizens showed they would not be easily conquered. People made "bread" with sawdust. They boiled weeds to make soup. Starving people died in the streets and at home, but the city held on.

In Stalingrad the fighting was on the ground, house to house, and in the air. In a single night six hundred German planes dropped bombs that ignited fires throughout the city. But the Russians—soldiers and civilians alike—fought back with everything they had. Housewives fired artillery, snipers crouched on rooftops. Grenades flew from above, behind, and below. The brutal fighting continued for months.

"What really boggled my mind was that the only sounds made were by the tools and the stones. The people didn't speak. Their eyes seemed extinguished, and the overall impression was that these were not men but, rather, beings from another, fearful world—the world of the dead."

—*German businessman Hans Deichmann, describing a visit to Auschwitz in 1942*

Ernest Michel was born in 1923. He was one of the few survivors of the Auschwitz camp.

Michel in 1939.

As Hitler's forces rampaged through Russia, SS divisions followed them. Their job was to round up Jews for mass execution. The victims were marched to the countryside, where they were forced to dig their own graves, then were shot. When that method of slaughter proved to undermine the morale of even the hardened Nazi soldiers, they began using mobile gas vans.

At last Hitler's maniacal hatred of the Jews led him to employ what was darkly referred to as the "final solution" to the Jewish "problem." With Germany gaining control all over eastern Europe, Jews from cities and towns were stripped of their belongings and sent to "resettlement camps." These were really death camps. After an initial examination, some were judged fit to work. The rest were ordered into "bathhouses" where what looked like showerheads actually dispensed Zyklon-B, a poison gas used to kill rats. After they had been gassed, their corpses were hauled off to ovens for burning.

The six most active camps were in Poland, out of sight of the German citizens. The camps took the industrialization of killing to a new level. Now there were not only weapons factories but actual killing factories, too. The staff of Auschwitz, the most notorious of the Polish camps, proudly claimed to be able to "process" twelve thousand inmates a day.

I was living in a work camp called Paderborn in northern Germany, cleaning the streets and sewers in the town. We were guarded by policemen, but at least we had something to eat and nobody got shot or killed. In February 1943 we were told to get ready because the entire camp was going to be evacuated toward the east. We walked at night, through the streets we had been cleaning, to the train station, where we were put on cattle cars. We spent five days and five nights in these cars with hardly any food or water, never knowing where we were going. There was no room to sleep or sit down. Several people couldn't take it and they died right in the car; we had to just put them in a corner. Then we came to a place, and somebody called out, "Oświęcim!" That's the Polish word for Auschwitz.

There was a peculiar, sweet smell in the air. I couldn't figure out what it was. We heard noises—dogs barking—and all of a sudden it became very light. The doors of the car were opened up and we heard, "Everybody out. Leave your luggage." Everywhere there was screaming and yelling: "My son, my father, where are you?" We saw for the first time that we were in a line of thirty or forty cars, full of old people, young people, children.

We were forced into two columns, women on one side, men on the other side. I held on to two of my friends. The screaming and yelling continued as mothers looked for their children, and mothers tried to hold on to their babies. I would never have believed that anything like this could happen to human beings, but this was just the beginning. An SS man asked us, "How old?" If you were between the ages of sixteen and thirty, the thumb went up, and you went to one side. Over thirty, the thumb went down, and you went to the other side. The screaming, the whips, the dogs—that picture will be with me as long as I live. "How old?" he asked me. I said, "Nineteen." The thumb went up.

They piled us into trucks, and then a guard said something to me that I didn't understand. He said, "You're the lucky ones. The others are already up the chimney." That's when we started to realize what this place was. All the girls were gassed that same day. But they needed labor, so when the thumb went up, I was given a chance to live. I wasn't hungry anymore. I was scared for my life. "The others are already up the chimney." So that was the smell.

In the morning we were shorn of hair. Then every one of us was tattooed. That's when I got my number, 104995. The normal food rations in Auschwitz were such that you had approximately half a year until your body gave out—they had figured it out very scientifically. And after that, up the chimney.

We didn't live, we existed. That's all it was. The camp was surrounded by two sets of electrically charged wire. The moment you touched it you were electrocuted. I saw inmates by the hundreds run into that barbed wire just to get it over with. But I never wanted to. My parents instilled in me a feeling of responsibility, even during very difficult times. So I told myself and the others around me, some of us have got to hang on in order to tell the story of what happened.

To survive under those circumstances took fortitude and a desire to hang on, but it also took plain old dumb luck. Without a lucky break, something extra that helped you survive, you would never make it. And eventually I got my lucky break. Now, I was getting very thin—probably eighty-five pounds or so—and my bones were starting to show. One day I got hit over the head, and I went to the prison hospital to get taken care of. By some fluke, a man came through the hospital and asked if anyone had good handwriting. Now, in 1939 my father had sent me to take calligraphy lessons. At the time I said, "What do I need this for?" And he said, "You never know when it could come in handy." That ended up saving my life. They sat me down with a logbook and told me what to write: "Weak of body." "Heart attack." The Germans kept immaculate records, and of course nobody was ever gassed. Everybody died of weak body or heart attack. So because I could write neatly I became an official recorder.

Michel's sister, Lotte (right), and their parents in 1939. Lotte left for France the day after this photograph was taken. She survived the war and lives in Israel. Michel's parents died in Auschwitz.

Jews weren't the only victims. Gypsies, Slavs, Catholics, homosexuals, and the mentally retarded were sent to their deaths, too. But the Jews were by far the largest group of victims—more than six million Jews died in the Holocaust. Still, when news of the camps began reaching the West in 1942 and 1943, many people found the stories too outrageous to believe. It had to be an exaggeration, they thought; even Hitler could not go that far.

By January 1943 the tide of the war began to turn against Germany. Hitler had not planned for a long war, and his factories began to run out of oil and gas. There were other problems, too. The Allies had begun bombing German cities. Now it was German refugees who were clogging the roads searching for shelter. As in London in 1940, people hurried into shelters at night, then rebuilt their homes during the day. All the while they waited for the Allies to launch their land invasion, which everyone knew would come soon.

On the night of June 5, 1944, President Roosevelt announced that the fascists had been defeated in Italy. But Roosevelt was preoccupied. For even as he told Americans this wonderful news, 175,000 Allied soldiers were getting ready on the coast of England for a secret invasion of France. Operation Overlord, as it was called, was an enormous challenge. Along with a massive fighting force, it involved moving fifty thousand motorcycles, tanks, and bulldozers across the sixty miles of the English Channel. It would take more than five thousand ships and eleven thousand airplanes. All told, the operation of D-Day was, one historian noted, like moving the Wisconsin cities of Green Bay, Racine, and Kenosha across Lake Michigan—every man, woman, child, car, and truck—and doing it all in one night. On the morning of June 6, no one was sure it was possible.

As he toured the bases, General Dwight D. Eisenhower, the supreme commander of the Allied troops, went to see off British troops boarding a landing craft. Then he said farewell to twenty-three thousand Allied paratroopers, knowing that experts had predicted that as many as 75 percent of them might be killed. He saluted the planes as they took off for France. Then the tough Kansan who would later become president turned away in tears.

For most Americans D-Day was the climax of the war. People cheered the news of the invasion, which they had eagerly awaited. Churches rang their bells, factories sounded their whistles. Then, just as suddenly, everyone huddled in fear for their young soldiers. Roosevelt went on the radio to do the only thing that he or any other American could do: pray.

"I've done all I can . . . ," proclaimed General Eisenhower to the 101st Airborne Division before the invasion of Normandy. "Now quit worrying, General," replied one soldier, "we'll take care of this thing for you."

In the English Channel, thousands of terrified men from twelve Allied nations floated toward the coast of France, toward beaches code-named Sword, Juno, Omaha, Gold, and Utah. Clair Galdonik, who was born in 1919, was there.

Just before they shipped my infantry unit over to Europe, we were given a ten-day furlough to visit our wives and children. I, being single, went back and spent those ten days with my mother and dad. For me it wasn't a joyful occasion. I didn't tell them that I knew we'd be going into combat; I tried to spare them as much as I could.

When we got to England we were stationed in a huge tent city. We got there in March of 1944 and trained a bit. By May we still hadn't heard what we were doing there. Then on June 1 all letter writing was stopped, and that was our first clue that something was ready to happen.

On the third of June all the troops were assembled, and it was just a mass of humanity—people loading the ships, loading trucks and tanks onto ships. It was a pretty gratifying feeling, looking at this and saying, "Holy smokes, look at all this stuff. How could we lose the war?" When we got on our ship we were told what our destination was, and there wasn't much we could do at that point but prepare ourselves. We were very well trained physically for what lay ahead. Mentally, though, each person is different. When you think you are going to face the enemy and you wonder, "How long have I got? Will I survive?" you want to be in the best shape spiritually to face your Creator.

Galdonik in Germany near the end of the war.

When we finally crossed the Channel on the morning of the sixth, we had to go from the ship onto those landing crafts that would take us to the shore. There were big scramble nets that led down into the landing crafts because they were probably about twenty-five or thirty feet below the level of the ship. Here we were with all of our gear—I don't know how we even got our legs over the side of the ship. We had a gas-resistant suit that was very cumbersome, we had our rifle belt, and we had to carry ninety-six rounds of ammunition, our canteens, our entrenching tool, our gas mask, our life jacket, our K-rations, and our rifles. I mean, we were weighed down. I had a strange, nightmarish feeling, sort of like, "Is this a dream or is this reality?" But then we lined up and they called my name and over the side I went. I don't know how we did it, but somehow we got down that net, even with the huge waves bobbing up.

Our battleships had already started firing on the beach by the time my unit got there, and it was glorious to see the big belches of orange flame coming out of our guns. Then we saw the 82nd and the 101st Airborne, and to see those darlings up there gave us a marvelous feeling. It was reassuring to think that we might have it relatively easy going in. But as we got closer to the beach we saw these big black plumes of smoke, and we knew that the German artillery had opened up and was zeroing in on the beaches where we were headed.

Then the ramp on the landing craft went down. A good buddy of mine started to cry and scream, "I can't go in, I can't." The poor guy just broke up. I said, "You gotta go, you gotta," and I grabbed him with one arm and inflated our life jackets, and threw him in the water. I jumped in and tried to help him by myself, but he was hysterical. Another one of my buddies came along and got on the other side of this guy, and I said, "We gotta go, we gotta go," because the longer we were out there the longer we were subjected to artillery fire, and we could get hit at any time.

American soldiers in a landing craft off Omaha Beach.

We held our rifles over our heads and submerged ourselves in the water to protect us as much as we could. I was exhausted, weighed down, but then I got mad. I started cursing, and I told myself, "Nothing is going to stop me until I get on that beach." Fortunately, I got there, and I took off as best I could up the beach to some kind of wall, where we took cover until we could regroup.

At a time like that you don't hold out too much hope that you're going to survive this whole war. Some of us did, and some of us didn't. God rest their souls that lie over there in foreign soil.

"My decision to attack at this time and place was based upon the best information available. If any blame or fault attaches to the attempt it is mine alone."

—Note carried in the wallet of Supreme Commander Dwight Eisenhower on the morning of D-Day, the invasion of Normandy

An American electrician's mate, who was in the first wave of American soldiers to land at Omaha Beach, later recalled, "We hit the sandbar, dropped the ramp, and then all hell poured loose on us."

The first units of the invasion, taking advantage of the element of surprise, made their way quickly into the farmland at Gold, Juno, and Sword Beaches. But the Americans pushing in at Omaha Beach were not so lucky. There, in the center of the front, soldiers walked into a wall of German gunfire. Attempting to scale a cliff well covered by German defenders, more than 2,000 GIs were killed or wounded. But by nightfall they had secured it and joined the 156,000 other Allied soldiers on their way to liberating France. The invasion of Normandy had been a success.

By August the Allies had freed Paris and turned east. But the Germans were not ready to give up. They mounted one last strike through Belgium in what became known as the Battle of the Bulge. Hitler was still fighting, but by early 1945 Germany was surrounded. From the east, the Russian army pushed through Poland and headed for the German capital, Berlin. Meanwhile the Allies were advancing from the west. Hitler retreated to his bunker in Berlin, hoping for a miracle. But his fate—and Germany's—was sealed. In April 1945, as Russian shells began pounding Berlin, Hitler swallowed a lethal dose of cyanide. Within days Germany surrendered.

On August 25, 1944, French army units rolled into Paris and liberated the capital after four years of German occupation. Despite Hitler's orders to reduce the city to a "blackened field of ruins," the German commander opted to surrender to avoid senseless destruction.

A crowd in Times Square, New York City, celebrates the end of the war in Europe, May 1945. Fighting in the Pacific remained vigorous, but there was a sense of an ending in the air. The most murderous conflict in history was racing to a conclusion.

Crowds in New York, London, Paris, and Moscow went wild with excitement. But the news from Berlin did not slow the pace of the war on the other side of the globe, in the Pacific.

When the marines landed on Saipan in 1944, within striking distance of Tokyo, they battled fiercely against Japanese soldiers, losing more than sixteen thousand men. Then they found themselves fighting wave upon wave of Japanese civilians. Fighting on Guam later that year, marines encountered desperate Japanese soldiers armed only with pitchforks, baseball bats, bottles, and rocks. On one coral-reef island after another, Americans waged war against an enemy whose will to fight never faltered. By the summer of 1945 the United States was bombing Tokyo, Osaka, Kobe, Kawasaki, and Yokohama, obliterating every military target and killing hundreds of thousands of civilians. Yet the Japanese people's devotion to Emperor Hirohito meant that Japan would fight on. Throughout the Pacific, American soldiers nervously waited for the invasion of Japan to begin, dreading another long, gruesome battle.

Named after a "divine wind" that saved Japan from a Mongol invasion in the Middle Ages, Japanese kamikaze corps were made up of young pilots whose devotion to the emperor was so total, they were willing to perform suicide runs on enemy targets. Here the men of one kamikaze unit pay their final respects before embarking on missions that will bring them certain death.

Even though Japan was on the brink of defeat, the nation still refused to surrender. Bracing for an expected Allied invasion, the country's leaders ordered the military training of civilians. Here an army officer instructs Japanese housewives on how best to resist the enemy with bamboo spears.

Only a few people knew that America was testing a secret weapon in the summer of 1945. And they never called it a bomb. The secretary of war called it "X." The scientists at the New Mexico test site called it "the gadget." But it was really the first atomic bomb, and its power to destroy was incredible.

Seventy-five crack fliers had been training for months, having volunteered for a mysterious secret assignment. All they knew was that they would be doing "something different." During practice flights, the men had been instructed to wear welder's goggles and never look back at their target. That was strange enough. But when they were told they would be dropping one bomb and only one bomb, they were really puzzled. Then they learned that this one bomb would carry the force of twenty thousand tons of dynamite.

Late on August 5, 1945, this special bomb was loaded onto Lieutenant Colonel Paul Tibbets's plane, a B-29 he had named *Enola Gay*, after his mother. At 2:45 A.M. the plane lumbered down the runway and lifted off into the darkness. Its mission was nothing less than a quick and sudden end to the Pacific war. Seven minutes after the flight began, Tibbets asked his crew if they knew what they were really carrying. "A chemist's nightmare?" asked the tail gunner. Tibbets told him to guess again. "A physicist's nightmare?" he asked. Then the truth dawned on him. "Colonel," he said, "are we splitting atoms today?"

The crew flew onward without talking much. Then, at 8:15 A.M. on August 6, the bombardier squeezed the release latch, dropping the bomb over the city of Hiroshima.

Junji Sarashina, born in 1929, was a student in Hiroshima who survived the destruction of the city.

In the summer of 1945 I was sixteen years old and a junior in high school. August 6 seemed like any other day. All my classmates and I were working in a munitions factory, as we had since we were freshmen. I had just stepped out of the factory and walked behind a two-story building when I saw this big ball of orange fire. The whole building— and the earth itself, it seemed—moved once to the left and once to the right, and then everything started to fall on top of me. I hit the ground immediately. After everything settled down, I found that I was covered with glass, boards, rocks, and sand. I walked to the nurse's office to find bandages and medications, as we had been trained to do. I broke the medicine chest open with a bat and carried some first-aid supplies to my friends.

A while later we went out into the street only to discover that the entire town of Hiroshima was ablaze. We could see the smoke of those famous mushroom clouds, and the skies were all dark. We started to walk toward the bridge, which was only about a quarter of a mile away, but we couldn't cross it because it was covered with people. They were all hurt, all burned. Some were dead. A lot of people were floating in the river; some were swimming, but some of them were dead, drifting with the current. Their skin was red and their clothes were nothing but strips of cloth hanging from them. Our teacher decided we should go back to the factory to spend the night. All night long we watched the town burn.

Early on August 7, some of us left the factory and started to go toward my high school. We walked through the town. Since the town was still burning, you had to be careful where you walked, tiptoeing to keep from stepping on people. When we got to my school, we found that about 285 out of the 300 students died. I tried to help some of the kids out of the swimming pool, but they just rolled right back in, their skin peeling right off from their arms. I walked back to the dormitory, where I stayed for about two days more. People began to fear typhoid, and they wanted to start cremating bodies. Someone had to do it, so I helped cremate some of my fellow students.

On the third day I went back to where my mom lived, in the countryside. The train was full of wounded people, dying people. When I finally made it to my house my mother couldn't believe I was still alive. I remember she hugged me so hard that I told her I couldn't breathe. The course I had taken, walking through town, trying to help people and cremating some of my friends, that was a really terrible thing. I actually took a step through hell and returned.

In one of only five known photographs taken in Hiroshima on the day the bomb was dropped, a bandaged policeman certifies victims for emergency aid.

The crew of the *Enola Gay* had seen the atomic bomb do its terrible work. The devastation was stunning. "My God," wrote the copilot, "what have we done?"

The bombing of Hiroshima left the city in ruins. Three days later an atomic bomb was dropped on the industrial city of Nagasaki. History's most destructive war was finally over.

7 An Uneasy Peace

1946–1952

The end of World War II was the beginning of prosperous times in the United States. The booming wartime economy had turned the Great Depression upside down, and now the future of the nation seemed limitless. Of all the warring countries, only America came out of World War II stronger than before. Europe had been bombed and shelled into rubble. Japan had been burned by two atomic bombs (a second bomb had been dropped on the city of Nagasaki). But America in the late 1940s was a bustling, busy nation of abundance.

No problem seemed too big for American know-how and energy. American medicine unveiled the first forms of penicillin and other antibiotics, suggesting that disease was just one more enemy that Americans could lick. American scientists also built the first electronic computer. It was a thirty-ton monster with the computing power of a 1980s pocket calculator, but for its time, it was incredible. It suggested that Americans could tackle any problem, no matter how complex.

After living through the gloom and poverty of the Great Depression and giving 100 percent for the war effort, Americans felt they deserved some rest and relaxation. It was great to be home, swinging in the hammock in the sunshine, watching the kids play. And it felt great to be an American, a savior to much of the world.

Left: In 1951, when the government began a series of atomic tests in the Nevada desert, mushroom clouds became a regular part of the Las Vegas skyline. Aware of the public's curiosity about the A-bomb, the government heavily publicized the tests, and one explosion was broadcast live on local television. Forty-six years later, the government would admit that fallout from these and later Nevada nuclear tests might have caused as many as seventy-five thousand cases of thyroid cancer.

Walter Girardin, born in 1919, was a GI from California who summed up the feeling of many veterans when they finally got home.

When I got discharged and sent home from Europe at the end of the war, they flew me down to Burbank, where my family was. My wife met me at the airport. She was beautiful, as usual. I just didn't want to let go of her. And that was the first time I'd seen our daughter since she was a little over a year old, and there she was, almost four. My wife told me that during the war, whenever my daughter saw a photo or a film of a man in uniform, she would say, "There's Daddy." Coming home, it's a joyous occasion. You're filled with tears, but you're so happy.

In southern California at that time, things were booming. Jobs were plentiful, and salaries were better than they were in other parts of the country. It seemed to me that everything was moving more rapidly than it had been before I left. Cities were growing, big highways were popping up everywhere—even the cars seemed faster. I felt excited by it

A veteran of the Pacific war is doted on by his mother and fiancée after returning home. This marine was one of the six soldiers featured in the famous flag-raising photograph shot at Iwo Jima.

all, and also determined to succeed and make something of myself. Suddenly I felt very confident about my future.

I got us a Veterans Administration loan and bought a bigger house down the street. Somebody had bought up an old strawberry field, divided it up into lots, and built forty-two houses. They looked a little different on the outside, but they were all pretty much the same floor plan on the inside. I had to work overtime to help pay for it, but oh, how wonderful it was. And there was a great camaraderie between all of the young families in the neighborhood. We used to have barbecues and parties, play golf together, and our kids ran around together. In fact, when my wife was pregnant with our second daughter, I think there were ten or twelve other women in the neighborhood who were pregnant at the same time.

In the early days after the war, we used to think we were struggling, but we were really having a wonderful time. We were just doing all those kind of things that young families do, trying to make up for those years that we didn't have together, and everyone was having fun. It was a very happy time.

Owning a home was the dream of nearly every veteran returning from the war. Affordable houses were in demand. Builders all over the country began constructing low-cost suburban homes. Before the war, the American suburb had mostly been the playground of the rich. Now Americans were moving out of the cities and into small houses springing up in former cow pastures and cornfields. And they were moving out by the millions.

The suburbs promised green grass, safe streets, and an escape from the worries of the dawning atomic age. Americans had had enough drama during the war years. Now they wanted to enjoy the good life, with cookouts and Little League teams and bake sales. But this American dream was still out of reach for many people. Many suburbs were built for whites only. Black Americans returned from the war to find that little had changed while they had been off fighting for the world's freedom.

New cookie-cutter suburban developments like this one addressed the housing demand in the United States after the war. The number of houses being built jumped from 114,000 in 1944 to 1.7 million in 1950.

Howard "Stretch" Johnson, who was born in 1915, received two Purple Hearts for injuries suffered in World War II. He decided to do something to help black veterans.

Throughout the war I was in the 92nd Division, along with ten or twelve thousand other black troops. In Europe, the men of the 92nd were regarded as heroes. We liberated a number of Italian towns, including Lucca and Pisa, and when the Italian people saw these brown troops coming into their community, they just hailed us as conquering heroes. So when we came back to the United States, we expected to be treated as if we had made a contribution; we didn't like coming back into a Jim Crow scene. Most of the enlisted men in the 92nd were from the South, and it was ironic for them to return to a country for which they risked their lives, and they still had to go to the back of the bus, could not sit downstairs in the movie theater, and could not leave the plantation except with a pass from the owner.

A number of us got together and decided that it would be a good thing for us to form a black veterans' organization. One of the first things we took on was the issue of terminal leave pay. Each veteran was entitled to anywhere from $100 to $300 for having served in the U.S. Army. In the South, plantation owners attempted to prevent many of the returning veterans who worked on their plantations from getting into town to apply for their terminal leave pay. You see, blacks could only leave the plantation with a pass, and the passes were usually given for Saturday noon until Sunday evening; you couldn't leave the plantation during the work week. The application blanks for terminal leave pay were at the post office, which shut down at noon on Saturday, so it was impossible for a black veteran to pick up the application blank. So our group went to the War Department and got them to agree to release terminal leave pay blanks to our organization so we could distribute them through the Baptist Church, NAACP, and the Negro Elks Clubs. A number of our GIs went onto the plantations, sometimes dressed in blue overalls and things like that. It was almost an underground operation. We helped veterans throughout the South to get their terminal leave pay.

We also organized early bus boycotts and marches of veterans to county courthouses, to get their ballots to vote, because they had been denied the right to vote prior to World War II. We organized picket lines against job discrimination. All of these activities laid the basis for the civil rights movement of the late fifties and sixties. It was a direct outcome and carryover of the goals of World War II. The war was still being fought, in a sense.

Battles for black equality in America were being fought on several fronts. In 1947 Jack Roosevelt "Jackie" Robinson won an important victory. When Robinson strode to the plate for the Brooklyn Dodgers baseball team, he broke the "color barrier." The world of professional sports was suddenly integrated. A year later, President Harry S. Truman signed an executive order that officially integrated the armed services.

Sharpe James, born in 1936, went on to become the mayor of Newark, New Jersey. He described how Jackie Robinson's achievement changed his life.

Sharpe James at age twelve.

Jackie Robinson as a Brooklyn Dodger, 1947.

I was born in the South, but in 1944 we moved to 43 Emmett Street in Newark, which was a predominantly Irish American neighborhood. Being the only black kid in my crowd, I used to hear my white buddies say things like, "Let's get them blacks, run them blacks out of the neighborhood." But then they would always add, "We don't mean you, Sharpe." To them, "good blacks" were those that lived in their neighborhood and participated with them. Bad blacks were those in other neighborhood. So I was a "good black."

When you're poor, you've got to have a vehicle that you believe in, some kind of dream. And for all of us playing on that street, baseball was it. We all dreamed that someday we would grow up and be major-league players. The key to getting out of the ghetto for us kids was not to be a movie star or a football player. Baseball was our game, because we could wake up, go out on the street, and get a game going, which is something you couldn't do with basketball or football.

Before 1947 major-league baseball was white only. So here you had thousands of black kids like me playing baseball, but the ones with superior talent could never hope to get the same recognition that the white players would get. So as a black kid I knew I didn't have the same opportunities that the whites did, and that was really a frustration.

Then one day we got the news about Jackie Robinson. I remember all the folks in the black neighborhoods sitting around playing their card games and saying, "Did you hear? [Brooklyn Dodgers general manager] Branch Rickey's going to bring Jackie up to the majors." Everywhere you went, people had their newspapers out and they were talking about it. It was the talk of the black community because it gave hope and spirit to the downtrodden. Once Jackie broke the color barrier, I guess the thinking was that if you could break it in baseball, anything else in the world was possible. People said, "Here is a man of color who's going to make it."

To everyone in my neighborhood, white or black, Jackie Robinson was a hero. He was our role model. When we played baseball, suddenly everybody was saying, "I'm fast as Jackie Robinson," "I can catch like Jackie Robinson"—even the white guys would say that. Jackie was a thrill to watch because he was such a great athlete; his skill and aggressiveness changed the game of baseball.

Jackie's success started to affect my self-esteem, because my friends started to see my skills a different way. These white guys realized that my playing could really take me somewhere. But I think when they realized that a man of color had made it into the major leagues, they suddenly became aware that they had this good baseball player living in their community, that someday maybe I would make it like Jackie did.

Social progress now seemed to be joining economic prosperity. But even as Americans enjoyed the good life, many people realized that the United States could not turn its back on the world. In fact, as the Allied nation that had suffered the least, America, many people now felt, had a new responsibility. It would be up to the United States to reconstruct the war-torn world and defend it from a new enemy: the growing menace of Soviet Communism.

During the war, America and the Soviet Union had put aside their differences to fight a common threat. Now, with Germany beaten, all traces of friendship quickly disappeared. To the Soviets, America was acting like a new imperial power, ready to deny Russia the spoils of a war that had cost it dearly. To Americans, the Soviet Union looked like a nation of godless fanatics bent on spreading Communism to the four corners of the world, crushing freedom and democracy as they went. Mutual suspicion ran deep. But neither side wanted another war, especially one that might involve the new atomic weapons. And so the "Cold War" began.

As Stalin tightened his grip on eastern Europe, one British diplomat declared, "Our relations with the Russians . . . are drifting into the same condition as that in which we had found ourselves . . . with Hitler." Here the Soviet Union flexes its military muscle during a traditional May Day celebration in Red Square, 1952.

Left: Despite emergency shipments from the United States, 125 million Europeans were still not getting enough to eat. Here Greek children sing while waiting for rations of powdered milk in 1948.

In the negotiations that hammered out the rules of the peace, Russia was allowed to exert its influence over the countries its armies already occupied, but that "influence" quickly evolved into a demand that eastern Europe serve the will of the Soviet Union. Stalin took control of Poland, Hungary, Bulgaria, Rumania, East Germany, and Czechoslovakia. In the words of Winston Churchill, an "Iron Curtain" now descended across Europe.

Americans feared that the rest of Europe was also in terrible danger. European cities were in chaos, their bridges broken, their roads torn. Many factories had been destroyed, and unemployment was rising. Poverty was spreading, with Europe's starving children crying for food. How long would it be before the Soviet Union tried to take control of these weak and desperate countries? Perhaps the most devastated country of all was Germany. Once the enemy, it was now Europe's most vulnerable nation.

American pilot Jack O. Bennett, born in 1914, had been a student in Berlin before the war. He was one of the first Americans to visit the German capital at the war's end.

Jack O. Bennett in the cockpit of one of the first planes to land in Berlin after the war.

When the war ended, because I was in the right place at the right time, I got to fly the first American airplane into Berlin. I took off from New York in a DC-4, a civilian airplane with big American flags on the side. As I circled around where I thought Berlin used to be, I couldn't find the city. There were no navigational aids. Even though I knew Berlin well, I nearly flew into the North Sea. And when I landed, I couldn't believe it. The city was nothing but a rubble pile.

The first thing we saw when we landed at Templehof Airport was a woman having a baby on top of a junk pile, right there amid the wrecked planes. Then all of a sudden the Russians started to lob rockets over our heads. I figured they had seen the American flag painted on the tail. A few of them came out onto the airstrip carrying these stubby machine guns. They tried to get me to take off and leave, but I wouldn't do it.

I tried to get a Jeep that afternoon. There were only two or three American officers in the whole town, and when I got in touch with them, they said, "Sure, we'll lend you a Jeep, but you're not going to be able to go downtown. There are no bridges anymore." I said, "Listen, I know Berlin well." So they gave me a Jeep, but I couldn't even get a thousand meters from the airport. I had no sense of orientation, no way to navigate. So I came back, and the officer laughed and said he would give me a German driver the next day.

The following day when my German driver picked me up, he said, "I've heard you were here, before the war." I said I was, and he said, "You're not going to like this." It turned out that every main thoroughfare was piled up five stories high with rubbish, wrecked tanks, and wrecked airplanes. We made our way to Pragerplatz and then walked a ways to find the street where I used to live. There was no apartment house there at all, and I sat down and had tears in my eyes. My driver had tears in his eyes as well. I said, "They'll never rebuild this city." He said, "No, they never will."

Once the center of Nazi power, Berlin was a wasteland after the war. Desperate Berliners rummaged through the refuse of the Allied occupation forces looking for scraps of food, cigarette butts, or anything they could trade.

In 1947 General George Marshall, the secretary of state, proposed a plan to rescue Europe with billions of dollars of U.S. aid. There would be direct aid in the form of food, fuel, medicine, and emergency housing to help Europeans get back on their feet. But the bulk of the Marshall Plan would be spent on reconstructing industries so that Europeans could again take care of themselves. First Marshall had to convince Congress and the American people that they should give more aid to Europe. He got help when seven Cub Scouts from Maryland came to him to propose their own "Junior Marshall Plan." They wanted to raise money themselves to send to suffering European children their own age. Marshall was very moved by these generous Scouts. He declared that a new generation understood America's new responsibilities in the world.

The Marshall Plan began in June 1948. In just months Western Europe began to recover. Cases of malnutrition decreased. Factories started up again. People had heat for their homes. At the height of the plan, 150 ships a day brought tires, tractors, drilling equipment, chemicals, oil, cotton, and more to European ports. The Marshall Plan would save Europe for democracy.

Berlin was the setting for the first Cold War showdown between the United States and the Soviet Union. Because it was the capital of Germany, it was being governed by all the victorious powers: the Americans, the British, the French, and the Soviets. But the entire city was deep within Soviet-controlled East Germany. In June 1948, as the Marshall Plan began, Stalin decided to challenge the United States by blocking the road into Berlin from the west.

Stalin had gambled that America would not want to risk war over Berlin, and he was right. But President Truman took a gamble of his own. He decided to simply ignore Stalin's blockade and supply Berlin by air. It was an enormous challenge. For Berlin to survive, the United States would have to land four thousand tons of supplies every day—one planeload every three and a half minutes.

At first, only a thousand tons a day were getting through. Then the people of Berlin, using twenty thousand volunteers, built a third airport. By December, forty-five hundred tons of supplies were being flown in every day; by the spring it became eight thousand tons, then thirteen thousand. American and British pilots flew on little sleep, their planes dangerously overloaded. But they still managed to do something extra, dropping bags of candy from their planes as German children ran to greet them. By the middle of May, Stalin realized he was beaten. The blockade was over.

George Marshall, 1880–1959.

To keep deliveries moving as fast as possible, Berlin airlift flight crews were ordered to remain in their planes between landing and takeoff. Food was brought out to them, and the planes were refueled and serviced as they were being unloaded.

"Stalin cutlets"

*—Berliners' name for
warmed-over toast*

Children in Berlin called
American airlift planes
"chocolate bombers" because
pilots dropped candy tied to
miniature parachutes as they
flew into the city.

Three young survivors of the Buchenwald concentration camp head for the British colony of Palestine, June 1945.

One of the most far-reaching consequences of the Second World War was the end it brought to the old colonial powers. All over the world new nations were emerging. At the same time that the Marshall Plan's ships were carrying their valuable cargo to Europe, Jewish refugees were making their way to the former British colony of Palestine. There the recently formed United Nations had established a new country, Israel. And in China the Communists, led by Mao Zedong, finally won their long battle for power.

The Communist victory in China stunned Americans. And when China and Russia signed a friendship treaty, it confirmed Americans' worst fears of a Communist world revolution. There was still more bad news. In September 1949 Americans discovered that the Soviet Union had exploded its first atomic bomb. Cold War tensions were growing.

In this environment of suspicion, people began to worry that Communists were infiltrating the United States. A rabid anti-Communism gripped many people across the country. Senator Joseph McCarthy of Wisconsin became the most influential anti-Communist of the time by playing on people's fears. In a speech one day in 1950 he announced that he had a list of 205 known Communists working in the State Department. In fact, there was no such list. (In later speeches he changed the number to 57, to 81, and then to 4.) But the uproar that greeted his statement was enormous. So McCarthy continued with his wild accusations. He went on to lead his supporters in a witch-hunt that would last for years and ruin thousands of lives. *McCarthyism* has since entered the language as a word that describes the making of unfounded accusations against innocent people.

Senator Joseph R. McCarthy signs autographs for a group of adoring students, 1950. At the height of the McCarthy hysteria, six detention camps were readied to handle the anticipated arrest of Communist agents. But McCarthy was unable to produce enough legal evidence to support a single charge.

Liberal Hollywood came under heavy attack by McCarthy's forces. The entertainment industry created a blacklist— a list of "suspicious" people who were not allowed to work on television or in movies. Actress Lee Grant, who was born in 1927, found her name on that list.

In 1951 the first play I was ever in, *Detective Story*, was made into a film, and I got my first Academy Award nomination. Around that time, I was asked to speak at the memorial service for an actor I had been working with, who had been questioned by the House Un-American Activities Committee as a suspected Communist. I got up there and said that I felt he was hounded to death—that his constant appearances in front of the committee had contributed to his death. The next day, at an Actor's Equity meeting, somebody turned around to me and said, "Congratulations. You made it into *Red Channels*." This was a weekly periodical that listed the names of the people who were to be blacklisted. I felt the floor rush out from under me and my heart drop, and I said to myself, "That's it."

Of course there really weren't very many Communists in Hollywood. But once the anti-Communists had taken care of the real Communists, they started picking on people who had given money to certain organizations, people who had shown up at the "wrong" party, or people who voted for the "wrong" person—people who weren't even political at all, like me. And the entertainment industry buckled under the pressure.

Red Channels became the bible of the television industry. It was easy to make it in there—all you had to do was stand up at a union meeting and ask, "What are you trying to do about blacklisting?" Then somebody from the union board would write your name down, and the next day you'd be on the list. The Screen Actors Guild, run by Ronald Reagan, did the same thing. And once you were blacklisted, you were out of work unless you got up in front of the

Grant in *Detective Story*, 1951.

union and said, "I'm sorry that I gave money to that," or "I'm sorry I showed up at that party. I am a good American. I never meant to do it." You had to humiliate yourself in front of your peers, or maybe give some money to *Red Channels* as a way of showing that you supported their patriotic effort.

When I got the subpoena from the House Un-American Activities Committee asking me to testify against other actors, it was very frightening. They asked me lots of personal questions, things that could have put other people in jeopardy, because I knew all the other people in the union who were fighting blacklisting. And I could have hurt them if I talked. Being an informer meant placing your fellow actor, fellow friend, or fellow director in jeopardy. It meant that a person didn't work anymore. So taking that step was about the worst thing that you could do to anybody.

When I made a choice not to give names, I never really knew if the whole thing would ever end. It seemed like it might go on forever. Fighting the blacklist became my career.

IS THIS TOMORROW

AMERICA UNDER COMMUNISM!

A Minnesota-based religious group printed and distributed four million copies of this Red scare publication.

Senator McCarthy was not the only anti-Communist who ruined careers and smeared reputations. There was a hysteria sweeping through the United States that sometimes became ridiculous. Schools banned the Robin Hood story for its "Communist" themes. The Cincinnati Reds baseball team even changed its name to the Red Legs so no one would get the wrong idea.

But there were also real Communist spies in America. Klaus Fuchs, one of the physicists who worked on the atomic bomb, had given information about the bomb to Soviet agents. He belonged to a spy ring that included nine other people, among them Julius and Ethel Rosenberg. The Rosenbergs were convicted of espionage and sentenced to death in 1951.

In the midst of this Communist scare, in 1950, President Truman decided to go to war in Korea, which had been divided at the end of World War II. The success of the Communists in China had people fearing a "domino effect": that one country after another would fall under Communist control. The Korean War began when Communist North Korea, with Stalin's blessing, invaded South Korea. The U.S. government, joining with other countries in the United Nations, believed that it had to support South Korea, especially when Chinese Communists joined the North Koreans. American forces entered the fight, and three years passed before the war ended. Korea was left ravaged. But it was still divided politically, much as it had been when the war started. Nobody really won. Nobody really lost—except the fifty-four thousand Americans and other Allied soldiers and more than two million Koreans and Chinese who died in the fighting.

Len Maffioli, who was born in 1925, fought in the Korean War and was taken prisoner by the Chinese. He described the Chinese attempts to convert American prisoners to their cause.

On the twenty-eighth of November, 1950, I was in a convoy in the Chosin Reservoir that was completely surrounded by Chinese troops. We fought them off for twelve hours, but we had an awful lot of dead and dying in the ditches, so we eventually had to surrender. We had heard about the North Koreans, that they were just as apt to execute a prisoner as they were to imprison him. But the Chinese fighting with them were different. They had the idea that they were going to put us through a political indoctrination course—what some people called a low-power brainwashing course—and actually convert us to their cause.

On December 24 they threw us a Christmas party. They had actually gone and cut down a pine tree and decorated it with pieces of colored paper. They handed each of us a few pieces of candy, five or six salted peanuts, and a tailor-made cigarette—these were our Christmas presents. And then they started this bit where they wanted us to get up and make confessions. This was a big deal in Communist brainwashing, to confess your sins.

After about a week or two, they started giving us English editions of Chinese newspapers, with certain articles circled in red. We had to read these articles and make sure we understood them, because later the Chinese would test us on them. And they were so ridiculous—stuff about Chinese soldiers who jumped on the back of an American tank, ripped open the hatch with bayonets, and threw grenades down there and killed the crew, and you were supposed to believe it. There were also stories about the terrible situation that we had in the United States. I remember one about how people were dying of starvation on the streets of Bakersfield, California. Of course, we knew all this was rot, but when we told them so, we had to listen to long-winded lectures in a barn, which meant three or four hours of freezing to death. So eventually we got the idea. They never interrogated us much on military matters; what they were more interested in was our family life, our social life. They couldn't believe that a lot of the people captured, me included, owned our own automobiles. I remember one of them saying one morning that in China he could have an egg every morning for breakfast if he wanted. And somebody laughed and said, "God, we could have a dozen if we wanted, every morning." Well, he refused to believe that food was so plentiful.

Maffioli, the day after his escape, holding cigarettes, candy, and toiletries given to him by the Red Cross.

One day they called out the names of nineteen of us. They drove us in a truck and we had no idea where we were, but we could hear the sound of Allied artillery. Our Chinese guards took off in fear, and, surprisingly, some Korean civilians helped us hide out in a house. We couldn't figure out why these Koreans were helping us. Then we asked where we were and found out that we were in South Korea. That's why the Koreans were so friendly.

We were just overjoyed to be back with the Allies. We were the only group ever to escape from the enemy in Korea. And we were the first Allied troops to come home as graduates of the political indoctrination course.

General MacArthur was given a hero's welcome when he returned to the United States. Here his motorcade makes its way through downtown San Francisco.

The conflict in Korea left many people in the United States confused. If it was a war worth fighting in the first place, why wasn't it worth fighting to a real victory? General Douglas MacArthur, the commander of the American forces in Korea, agreed. He had driven the Communists out of South Korea, and he'd wanted to go further, to push his troops through North Korea and into mainland China. But President Truman had ordered MacArthur to turn back. He was afraid that any move directly against the Chinese could trigger a nuclear war.

The Korean War was America's first limited war. Though it frustrated many Americans not to fight on to a real victory, the terrifying specter of nuclear weapons demanded caution. No one wanted to risk starting World War III—because now that both the United States and the Communists had nuclear weapons, fighting an all-out war could mean the end of the world.

8 Mass Markets

1953–1961

America was transformed in the 1950s. Home life changed as people left farms and cities for the suburbs. Work life changed, with more people now employed at desk jobs and in stores than on farms and in factories. Shopping changed, making room for new chain stores and the first suburban malls. Supermarkets began to replace grocery stores, McDonald's started to push out the old-fashioned roadside diners, and Holiday Inns were forcing downtown hotels to shut their doors. The American economy was booming, and more people than ever before shared in the good life.

Many Americans were enjoying the fruits of success for the first time: health insurance, vacations, savings accounts, their own homes. They flocked to the suburbs to find a new way of life. But leaving hometowns behind often meant losing connections to ethnic traditions and family support systems. In an attempt to create new ties, these people tried hard to blend in, to be just like their neighbors. They wanted to create a place where they felt comfortable, part of a community. The promise of suburbia was safety and newness. If the price was, for some, a loss of individuality, well, was that really so important? Wasn't it better to be a team player, to put up a united front—especially to show the Soviets that the American way of life was a superior one? It felt almost like a patriotic duty to show your team spirit.

Left: "Never has a whole people spent so much money on so many expensive things in such an easy way as Americans are doing today," wrote *Fortune* magazine in October 1956. Here a shopper samples perfume at a department store in Washington, D.C., 1953.

Commuters return from downtown Chicago to Park Forest, Illinois, in 1953. As in other suburbs across the country, the population of Park Forest more than tripled between 1950 and 1960. Most of its inhabitants were young white families with a husband in a promising corporate job and a wife who stayed home to raise their children.

Harriet Osborn was born in 1928. Her experience of moving to a brand-new suburb was typical for many families.

Top: The Osborn family—John, Harriet, and their son, Francis, Christmas 1955. Above: John Osborn checking the camping equipment in the back of the family station wagon, summer 1956.

Moving into the suburbs was an adventure. We traveled twelve hours from Boston with a truckload of furniture. I sat in the front with the goldfish, the plants, and my son on my lap. We lived too far away to prepare our new home before our arrival. In fact, we hadn't even seen the house. We arrived and took our first steps through the back door and into our new home. I remember it took me five hours to get from my back door to the bedrooms because of the parade of salesmen waiting to greet us on our arrival. They were selling landscaping, storm windows, and milk and bread and diapers. It was really something. One day after we were all moved in, the property was landscaped.

One of the most important things about suburban life was forming a bond with your neighbors. Our town was a veritable melting pot, with people coming from all over upstate Pennsylvania, New Jersey, and Philadelphia. I think we confided in each other to alleviate the loneliness of coming from different sections of the country. Mothers and dads and grandparents weren't there. Sisters and brothers weren't there. We shared the same problems of trying to build a home, raise children, and find work. Everybody was the same age, and everybody wore the same clothes.

The woman's role was to keep the home fires burning. We were expected to keep a clean home, to look after and discipline our children, and to take care of our husbands. It was very easy, really, yet we were all a bit lonesome. There were many, many get-togethers. Around ten o'clock in the morning we'd sit out and have coffee klatches, and there'd be kids running all around and you'd be watching this child and that child.

The suburbs were the perfect place to raise children, and children were our primary focus. The statistics said that every home had at least two and a half children. When we first moved to our town there were only three obstetricians. As the birthrate rose, the obstetricians extended their office hours to 2:00 A.M. Many times in the newspaper we'd see at least three columns of names listed in the birth announcements for the week. There was much emphasis placed on babies and bringing them up during their first year of life. Once in a while we'd hear a seminar on how to raise children. Everything in the stores was geared toward children. It was always, "What do children want and what will parents buy for their children?"

The television also served as a baby-sitter. You could just put your children in front of the TV, and while they watched *Davy Crockett* and *Ding Dong School,* you could make supper. TV was our information box and our link to the outside world, and, of course, it entertained us. My family always loved the dramas and the variety and comedy shows. We saw Elvis on *The Ed Sullivan Show.* We loved the programs that focused on family, like *Ozzie and Harriet* and *Leave It to Beaver.* We identified with these pictures on the television screen, and they became an integral part of our lives.

Television had arrived shortly after World War II. Many people regarded it as a miracle, a miniature theater right in their own homes. Americans had bought more than forty-five million television sets by the end of the 1950s, and they were spending a third of their waking hours watching television.

More often than not, TV programs conformed to the same family values that people looked for in the suburbs. Old radio shows that had ethnic or working-class characters didn't make the transition to television. New shows such as *Father Knows Best* and *Ozzie and Harriet* showed Americans what they wanted to see in themselves: a complete family with a working father, an aproned mother, and cheerful, friendly children living in a comfortable home. Comedy changed, too. Because television was visual, it was perfect for sight gags and goofy slapstick. Variety shows with a mix of comic sketches and pop music were the rage.

Sid Caesar, born in 1922, was the star of *Your Show of Shows*, one of the most popular programs of the 1950s.

Left to right: Carl Reiner, Sid Caesar, and Howard Morris in *Your Show of Shows.*

Your Show of Shows boasted one of the finest teams of writers and producers in television. Left to right: Mel Brooks, writer; Mel Tolkin, head writer; Hal Janis, NBC representative; Sid Caesar; Pat Weaver, president of NBC TV; Mark Harris, Caesar's dresser.

In the 1950s I think people liked television so much because it was about them. They would see things on television that would remind them of events in their own life. That was the key to the success of *Your Show of Shows*: We always wrote sketches about things that happened to normal people. Quite often it was drawn directly from things that happened to us. When we would write a sketch, the most important thing was how does this affect the people—the people that have to wait in line, that have to park the car. Writing for television, you had the feeling that you were communicating with the people.

Most of the time we had little choice but to write from our own experiences. We had an hour-and-a-half-long show to write every week. So we needed new ideas, as well as things we could always go back to. If we did a certain kind of sketch—like a husband-and-wife sketch—and it went well, then we'd do another husband-and-wife sketch. If we did a satire of a movie, we'd say, "Hey, we can do more movie satires." One time, the writers and I went into a delicatessen for lunch and it was so crowded you couldn't move. They seated us at this table by a swinging door that led to the kitchen. So I'm sitting there eating my sandwich and bang—the door keeps flying open and hitting me on the back. The next week we wrote a sketch about that very same thing. There's this guy who gets seated next to a kitchen door, and every time the waiter tries to serve him, the door comes flying open and he gets smashed all around. So, in taking our sketches from things that happened to us firsthand, we hoped we were giving the audience something they could see themselves in and laugh at.

In the fifties ideal, women dedicated their lives to becoming good home-makers, mothers, and wives. Often isolated inside their suburban communities, housewives such as these relied on each other and the ubiquitous television for social interaction and companionship.

Swanson's first TV Dinner, above, featured turkey, corn bread dressing, gravy, peas, and whipped sweet potatoes in a package designed to look like a television set. By 1955 the company had added three other entrees and was selling twenty-five million TV Dinners a year.

One of the things that separated television from radio was that people had to sit still to watch it. Before television, people could do chores or housework or eat meals while the radio played in the background. But television required people to change their behavior to fit the program schedule. Studies showed an increase in toilet flushing when the most popular shows broke for commercials. The Swanson food company realized that television was interrupting the family meal. In 1954 Swanson created the first TV Dinner, a frozen meal packaged in a little foil tray that could be rushed from the oven to the living room and eaten in front of the television set.

The advertisements on television helped reinforce a uniform American culture. For the first time products could actually be seen, not just described, to millions of customers all over the country. Television commercials began to create the desire for products that Americans hadn't even known about.

By the end of its first year on the air, more than thirty million viewers tuned to CBS to watch *I Love Lucy* every Monday night, making Lucille Ball, left, one of the most popular stars on television.

As automobiles became larger, fancier, and more expensive, commercials for them became louder and livelier and used more visual tricks. Ads such as the one for Ford being filmed below, for instance, were less about cars than the dream of an auto-centered suburban life.

Maxwell Dane, born in 1906, founded an advertising firm that quickly recognized the power of television for selling new consumer products.

Left to right: Dane, Bill Bernbach, and Ned Doyle, 1950.

When we first started the company, we relied primarily on print advertising with some radio sprinkled in. Then as the fifties wore on, television came into its own and really changed things. Suddenly you had this visual medium where you could reach millions of people—coast to coast—all at one time. And you could control exactly what the people would see and what they would hear. It was a very powerful medium. No advertising agency could ignore television. One of our earliest and most successful major television campaigns was for the Polaroid Land camera, which took pictures that developed instantly. Of course, live television was the perfect medium to show off the virtues of an instant camera. The viewers actually got to see the picture develop before their eyes. Since it was live television, we had no control when things went wrong. Once one of our spokesmen, I think it was Steve Allen, took a picture that didn't develop properly. Being the professional that he was, he just simply took another photograph and said, "See? You know instantly whether or not you've got the shot."

In addition to handling American companies overseas, we also acquired a few foreign clients—Volkswagen being our most famous. When we first landed the Volkswagen account in the early fifties, they were selling very few cars in America. This was the era of the big American car. The Volkswagen was unique in its smaller size, lower cost, and low fuel consumption. It was a simple, reliable, and very unusual car, so [my partner] Bill Bernbach developed an advertising campaign that reflected that. His ads stressed the quality and reliability of the car and were aimed at people looking for an affordable second car, as well as the growing youth market looking to buy its first car.

In 1958 the Wham-O Manufacturing Company started one of the biggest fads of the decade when it introduced the Hula Hoop. In less than six months, Wham-O and dozens of imitators had sold nearly thirty million hoops, both in America and abroad.

The growing youth market began to drive cultural change in America. After World War II the baby boom brought an enormous number of children into the world. These children, together with teenagers, created a huge youth population. Even the term *teenager* was only first used widely in the 1940s. In the years before World War I, children usually finished school by the age of fifteen and went to work. The expansion of secondary education in the 1920s and, now, the prosperity of the 1950s allowed childhood to last longer. Children enjoyed their parents' higher standard of living as well. With bigger allowances and more leisure time, they became consumers, too.

Television eagerly grabbed hold of this huge audience. *American Bandstand* was a wildly popular television dance show, introducing new music, dance styles, and fashions to children who watched at home. The younger crowd wanted to shake things up, and music was one way they were going to do it. At the same time, shows such as *American Bandstand* helped make popular culture even more uniform, with teens around the country dressing alike and dancing alike to the same tunes.

Bunny Gibson, who was born in 1946, was one of the teenage dancers on *American Bandstand*.

Above: Bunny with Don Travarelli, whom she eventually married.

Right: Dick Clark (with microphone) and dancers on the *Bandstand* set.

A*merican Bandstand* was kind of like the first televised revolution of teenagers in this country. We could watch the show and see our peers dance, and then we could go out and buy records of the music that we heard. That show brought all the teenagers together. It's the first time that we could identify with other teenagers that were on TV. When I was growing up in Darby, Pennsylvania, I would run home from Catholic school every day to watch *American Bandstand*. I couldn't wait to turn on the TV. When I watched the show, I felt liberated. It made me forget about my problems at Catholic school and the difficult life I had at home. I would watch the kids on the show dance, and I would dance along. I would spin around and do all the steps using the banister or the refrigerator door as a partner. I got pretty good with that old banister. I figured if I could dance that well alone, imagine how I would be with a real partner. So I decided to go down and try and get on that show.

One day I stole fifty cents from my mother's purse, played hooky from school, and hopped on a bus downtown. I tried to look older by putting on lots of makeup. You see, I was only thirteen, and the minimum age for *Bandstand* was fourteen. I was so nervous while waiting in line to get in. I was sure somebody was going to tap me on the shoulder and say that I was too young. But the minute I walked through those green doors, I knew I was at home. And that little studio became my home for the next several years. It was really the first place where I felt like I belonged.

Even on *Bandstand* we had to conform. We had a strict dress code. The guys all had crew cuts and wore ties and jackets. All of the girls' dresses had to come up high on the neck and could not reveal too much. I think that really helped change the image of rock and roll. How could rock and roll be the devil's music when all of the kids on *Bandstand* looked so nice and clean? I think the show really helped to smooth over the image of rock and roll and to bring it into the mainstream.

In the fifties we were supposed to listen to our parents and not really have a lot of thoughts of our own. We were supposed to do what we were told, which didn't really allow for much freedom. But like me, a lot of teenagers wanted to be able to find things out for ourselves: who we were inside, what we liked, what we wanted to do. Rock and roll was music from the heart and the soul that gave us a feeling of freedom. And once we got that freedom, it was like the parents really lost their control over us.

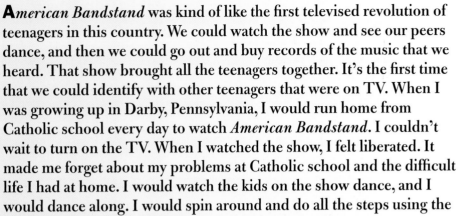

The "theme park" was an invention of the 1950s. Disneyland, the most celebrated of all of them, featured attractions based on cartoon characters, such as Dumbo.

To bring his Disneyland dream to reality, Walt Disney put together an "Imagineering" team to design a park that would seem larger than life. In Sleeping Beauty Castle larger stones were used at the building's base, followed by smaller ones toward the top to make the seventy-five-foot spires appear even taller.

Rock and roll was the music of a new generation. To many parents, it seemed like a revolution. The most famous rock-and-roll revolutionary was Elvis Presley. Elvis's songs seemed innocent enough, with silly lyrics about "hound dogs" and "blue suede shoes." But his music and his performance style were something else entirely. The roots of Elvis's rock and roll were in the rhythm-and-blues music of America's black community. But Elvis added a country-and-western beat. Onstage, he curled his lip and swung his hips, and teenage girls swooned. Boys copied his "duck-tail" hairdo. America's white teenagers found their role model in Elvis and made rock and roll their music.

Sam Phillips, born in 1923, founded Sun Records, where Elvis first recorded.

Phillips, far right, at the Memphis Recording Service, 1954, with, from left to right, Elvis Presley and his band, Bill Black (bass) and Scotty Moore (guitar).

In the early 1950s rhythm and blues was considered the music of black people. It was even called "race music," which meant that it was black music played by and for black folks. At Sun Records, I recorded primarily black rhythm-and-blues artists. And in talking to friends at radio stations across the country, it was evident that a lot of white kids were listening to black rhythm and blues. A lot of the adults I talked to were worried about that. I would always just look them straight in the eye and tell them, "Your kids aren't falling in love with black or white or green or yeller. They're falling in love with the vitality of the music."

From very early on, the biggest thing that I hoped to achieve was to find a white person who could help broaden the base of rhythm-and-blues music and to help us get over this black and white thing. To me, Elvis Presley was the perfect person to take black rhythm and blues and combine it with white country blues into something interesting. Now, I was criticized plenty by people saying, "Hey, man, you have been recording our black artists, and now you're going to steal it and give it to some white kid." But I never set out to steal anything. I just wanted this exciting music to be heard by the widest audience possible.

When I sent a copy of Elvis's first record to the editor of *Billboard* magazine, he said that I had to either be a fool or a genius to have Elvis sing a blues song on one side ("That's All Right, Mama") and a country bluegrass anthem ("Blue Moon of Kentucky") on the back side. Nobody had ever combined a black rhythm-and-blues song with a white country hit; you just didn't mix things up like that. Also, Elvis's versions of these songs were unlike anything ever done before; they were fast, exciting, and powerful.

When "That's All Right, Mama" and "Blue Moon of Kentucky" turned the corner and became hits, that was the defining moment when people began to feel the music and not think about whether it's black or white. Once word got around about what was happening with Elvis, it opened the doors for a lot of other singers, and it ultimately helped change the way people felt about music and about race.

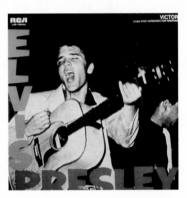

Released March 13, 1956, Elvis Presley's first album became the first in history to sell a million copies.

"I'm not kidding myself," a candid Presley once told an interviewer. "My voice alone is just an ordinary voice. What people come to see is how I use it. If I stand still while I'm singin', I'm dead, man. I might as well go back to drivin' a truck." Here he performs at the Municipal Auditorium in New Orleans, August 12, 1956.

On December 1, 1955, after a long day at work, a forty-two-year-old seamstress named Rosa Parks boarded a bus in Montgomery, Alabama, for her ride home. Montgomery, like most southern cities, operated a segregated bus system—the front rows of seats were for white riders, the back rows for black riders. Being a "Negro," Parks took her place at the front of the black section. But when the bus reached the next stop, enough whites got on to fill the seats at the front, leaving one white man standing. The bus driver told Parks and three other black riders to give up their seats. The three others moved, but Parks remained where she was. The driver warned that he would have her arrested, but Rosa Parks stayed calm and stayed put.

Rosa Parks's arrest set off a chain of events that could not be stopped. Within hours a well-organized network of civil rights leaders in Montgomery had decided to organize a boycott of the bus system. It was the perfect opportunity to challenge the constitutionality of the city's segregation laws. To lead the effort, the black community chose a young minister named Martin Luther King Jr.

King's strategy was one of passive resistance. He called it "Christianity in action." He told his followers to commit no violence, no matter how strongly they were provoked. "Blood may flow . . . before we receive our freedom," he said, "but it must be our blood." To keep the boycott going, more than twenty thousand black citizens formed car pools, rode bicycles, hired taxis, or walked to work. By saying no, Rosa Parks had triggered one of the most dramatic demonstrations of nonviolent protest in American history.

During the Montgomery bus boycott, Montgomery's black citizens relied on an efficient car pool system that ferried people among more than forty pickup stations like this one. Support for the protest came from within the black community—workers donated one-fifth of their weekly salaries—as well as from outside groups such as the NAACP, the United Auto Workers, Montgomery's Jewish community, and sympathetic white southerners.

The Montgomery bus boycott lasted more than a year, and Inez Jessie Baskin, born in 1916, was part of it.

I took the bus to work every day. Our bus system was segregated, just like practically everything else. There was no specific line of demarcation separating seats reserved for white and black passengers. It was usually at the bus driver's discretion, and it varied depending on the time of day and the driver, but you were just supposed to know. One thing was for certain: When a white person occupied a seat, even if it was one man to an entire long seat, blacks had to walk right on past. About six o'clock one evening I received a phone call from a friend's mother telling me to go to the Dexter Avenue Church. That's where I heard about Rosa Parks's arrest. I had first met Rosa Parks during the time that I was a member of the NAACP. She had always impressed me. She was just an angel walking. When I arrived, a small group of people were gathered in the church basement, and they were already talking about boycotting the local bus system and spreading some leaflets around about it.

News of the boycott spread pretty quickly. The telephones were ringing off the wall all over town. I was wondering how many people were going to get on the bus in the morning, because some of us had to travel five or six miles to get to work. But when Monday morning came,

Baskin riding a bus after the end of the boycott, with the Reverend Ralph Abernathy (to her right), Martin Luther King Jr. (second row, left), and the Reverend Glenn Smiley, a white minister from New York.

there were empty buses wherever you looked. That night a mass meeting was held at the Holt Street Baptist Church. It was not a large church, but it was packed to the rafters with people from all walks of life. We were all waiting for Dr. King, who had just been chosen as our spokesperson. There were people singing the Negro spirituals. You just don't need an organ and a cathedral the size of St. Peter's when a thousand black voices are singing with all their feelings and pathos. Everything was coming out in these songs. Dr. King finally arrived and came in through the side door while everyone was singing. There was first a hush, and then the whole place exploded. Martin Luther King spoke in a very soft, rich voice, and as he was going along, you'd get the feeling that this was not just something on paper, but rather that here was a person who really cared.

I remember one particular day during the boycott when everyone was asked to walk to wherever you had to go. From where I lived to my office was approximately eight miles, and it was drizzling and it was cold. As we walked we just kept conversing and singing, but by the time I was halfway to work, the singing and conversation weren't helping me very much because I was damp and cold. But then I heard that an older woman had said, "My feets is tired, but my soul is resting." There were plenty of elderly persons walking with us, and when you saw them walking, singing, and smiling, you knew you just had to go on. I thought, "If they can do it, so can I."

The night the boycott ended, I was thinking about getting a little sleep when the telephone rang. It was a friend saying, "Get up. I'm picking you up. The buses are running." Well, that opened my eyes. We went right over to the bus stop in front of Dr. King's house on Jackson Street, just as the bus pulled up. I got out of the car and waltzed up to the bus. I stepped onto the bus, and the bus driver held out his hand for the bus fare. I didn't have a dime in my pocket. Fortunately, one of the ministers gave me bus fare, and so I got on the bus with Dr. King and Dr. Abernathy, right up in front.

I had been living in Montgomery most of my life, and up until then, you couldn't even get three people to stay together for two hours. And here we had all come together as one for 381 days. It made me feel that there was more to this cohesiveness. There was more than Dr. Martin Luther King and Rosa Parks involved in this. It was Providence. I still believe that.

The bus boycott and other civil rights protests throughout the South were covered on national television. On television, the issue of civil rights was made plain and simple through the power of images. While the nation watched, peaceful demonstrators asking for the most basic equality and respect were blasted with water from fire hoses and attacked with police dogs.

Some of the most frightening civil rights clashes were over integrating American schools. In 1954 the Supreme Court had ruled that whites-only schools were illegal. Three years later nine black students were chosen to integrate Central High School in Little Rock, Arkansas. The governor of Arkansas, Orval Faubus, opposed integration. He sent the Arkansas National Guard to turn away the black students when they came to school. The mayor of Little Rock, fearing violence, asked Washington for help. President Eisenhower sent troops to Little Rock to restore the peace and make sure the black students were allowed to go to school.

Before leading the Montgomery boycott, Martin Luther King Jr. (seated) had been reluctant to take a leader's role outside his own congregation. Even after spearheading the civil rights movement of the 1950s and 1960s, King modestly referred to himself as merely a "drum major for justice."

Starting with a list of eighty volunteers, Little Rock school officials carefully interviewed both parents and children before selecting three boys and six girls to become the first black students at Central High School.

Even though plans for integrating Central High School had been going smoothly, Arkansas governor Orval Faubus falsely announced that the city was on the brink of a riot and that the city's stores were selling out of guns and knives (sold "mostly to Negro youths," he said). He then encouraged one of his closest friends—a local athlete and professional strikebreaker—to stir up trouble outside the school. According to an assistant police chief, "Half the troublemakers were from out of town."

Anne Thompson, born in 1942, was a student at Central High when integration first came to the schools.

Thompson at age sixteen.

Thompson (left, carrying books) and schoolmate Hazel Bryant (center background, with mouth open) shout epithets at Elizabeth Eckford. In 1956 a white citizen paid to have this photograph published in the Little Rock newspaper along with the line, "If you live in Arkansas, study this picture and know shame. When hate is unleashed and bigotry finds a voice, God help us all."

I was a fifteen-year-old tenth grader when they made the announcement that they were going to integrate Little Rock Central High. At first many of the parents refused to believe that it was actually going to happen. Some parents formed groups and committees to try and stop it.

The day the black students arrived, there was a circuslike atmosphere around the school. There was fear and there was anger, but there was a lot of excitement, too. It was almost as if something fun was about to happen. There were all of the cameras and reporters, and all of the parents were there, urging us on and telling us to go out there and not let them in. The parents gathered in this vacant lot directly across the street from the school. There was so much electricity and tension coming from that vacant lot that something big was bound to happen. Every now and then fights would break out among the parents. There were things said and done over there that frightened me much more than these black students did.

At one point an elderly black man in a blue and white Chevrolet drove up Fourteenth Street alongside Central High School. Suddenly all of these white parents surrounded the car and started yelling. I was so afraid they were going to turn that car over with the elderly black man in it. I honestly believe that had the parents stayed away, there wouldn't have been a problem. The whole thing was at their insistence. We were all thinking, "Well, we're just doing what our parents want us to do." We almost felt like we didn't have a choice; we had to get out there and protest.

Many white Americans were sympathetic to the black struggle. For years now, they had been displaying the American democratic dream before the world, especially the Soviet Union. But here in their own country many Americans were being treated as second-class citizens, simply because they were black. Americans were beginning to examine their national values with a critical eye.

By the end of the decade, the United States had formed the National Aeronautics and Space Administration (NASA) and named the first seven American astronauts, shifting the focus of space exploration well past the simple orbiting of unmanned satellites, as pointed out by this August 1959 issue of *Popular Mechanics*.

A new challenge to American complacency became visible in the sky on October 5, 1957. The first satellite ever launched was orbiting the earth. The trouble was that this satellite had been launched not by America but by the Soviet Union. The Russians had beaten the Americans into space.

This news was hard for Americans to accept. They had always believed that democracy's free exchange of ideas would keep American science ahead of Soviet science. For Russians, the launch of *Sputnik* (Russian for "fellow traveler") was a major achievement, signaling their importance on the world stage.

Semyon Reznik, born in 1938, was a Russian student in Moscow when *Sputnik* was launched. He shared his country's excitement.

Reznik (left) with two friends at the Moscow Civil Engineering University, 1958.

One of the reasons that scientific progress took on such importance during those years was our belief that through technological progress, the Soviet Union would be victorious over the United States. I myself loved science and believed in scientific progress, because it would move history forward faster, just as the Marxists claimed it would. Science and technology would make our production more efficient, making life easier for us, the workers. I thought science would make our society better in a moral sense and a social sense. So I was very excited about the fact that the Soviet space program was advancing so rapidly.

The day our satellite *Sputnik* was launched, a special voice came over the radio to announce it to us. Traditionally in the Soviet Union a few of the radio announcers were hired to read only the most urgent news on the radio. We always knew when something extra special was coming over the airwaves, as we would hear a special signal, *ta ta toe, ta toe, ta toe*, and then one of those readers with a deep voice would begin speaking. And if your radio wasn't on at home, a neighbor would let you know immediately.

On an October morning in 1957 we heard one of those voices announce, "Attention. All radio stations of the Soviet Union are broadcasting. . . . Our satellite *Sputnik* is in space." I felt so proud. Who did it? We did it! The Soviet Union is first in space!

There was a growing uneasiness in America in the late 1950s. Perhaps it came from the moral challenge of the civil rights movement. Perhaps it came from the technological challenge of the space race. People felt that a new, more difficult era was coming, and they looked for a new leader to inspire them. In 1960 television brought the presidential candidates before an audience of millions, and the handsome young Senator John Fitzgerald Kennedy of Massachusetts shone. He was confident, energetic, and ambitious, and he had lofty goals. His message was just what the youthful American culture wanted to hear: Let's all work together to make this nation worthy of its high ideals. Kennedy electrified America's youth.

Journalist Jeff Greenfield, born in 1943, was inspired by presidential candidate John Kennedy.

If you were a teenager in the 1950s, the president, Dwight Eisenhower, looked a lot like your grandfather. In fact, he was old enough to be your grandfather—the oldest man ever to have served as president at that time. By the late fifties he'd been through a heart attack and a stroke, and he was never particularly good with the English language. To my parents' generation, he was the guy who won World War II. But to my generation, he just looked like a somewhat befuddled elderly gentleman.

So along comes this 1960 campaign and John Kennedy. The idea that this guy, who looked like your cool older brother, might be president of the United States was a really exciting proposition. Kennedy came to my college, the University of Wisconsin, and I had a seat several miles high up in the bleachers. There was this impossibly tanned, impossibly energetic young guy giving a rousing speech about our generation and what it meant. And it connected, because we were not cynics then. It was possible to listen to somebody running for president of the United States talk about our responsibilities as the next generation, and believe it.

John Kennedy and his wife, Jackie, would bring youthful energy and a glamorous style to the White House.

I watched all the debates in the common rooms on campus, and they were absolutely packed. I think we all felt a sense of identification, and it wasn't just that he was young. Kennedy seemed to suggest that there was some role for us in the world.

The idea of a White House run and staffed by younger people suggested that government and politics were not simply the province of people impossibly older than we were. There was the feeling that, well, if they're running the political system, surely we can be somehow involved in it. It gave us a sense that we were entitled to be part of the political process, even as naysayers and protesters. Because, after all, look who was running the country.

On November 8, 1960, John Fitzgerald Kennedy was elected the thirty-fifth president of the United States. With Martin Luthur King, he shared the flame of idealism. President Kennedy, or JFK, as he was known, gave one of the most persuasive inaugural addresses in history. It was short, poetic, and inspiring. The torch had been passed to a new generation, he declared. Then he called on all Americans to live up to their ideals. "Ask not what your country can do for you," he said, "ask what you can do for your country." JFK challenged Americans to look deep into their consciences and create a better nation.

Not only was Kennedy young, he inspired the nation's young, too, such as this crowd that greeted him on the campaign trail in rural Wisconsin and thousands of others who now jumped at the chance to work for the government.

9 Into the Streets
1961–1969

The 1960s were a turning point in America's history. Ideas that had been introduced in the 1950s now began to gain momentum. The civil rights movement, begun as a series of peaceful protests, grew more violent as some of its followers became impatient with the slow pace of change. U.S. involvement in the war in Southeast Asia, intended to hold back the tide of Communism, grew rapidly. And the new political awareness of youth bloomed almost overnight into a rejection of many of the values of an older generation. Both exciting and confusing, full of hope and despair, the 1960s witnessed a cascade of events that changed the way Americans looked at themselves, at each other, and at the rest of the world.

At first America's youth eagerly answered the call to service by President John F. Kennedy. As a result of the baby boom, there were now more young people in college than there were farmers in the United States. The youthful president was the natural leader of this army of students, and one of the first missions he created for them was the Peace Corps.

The Peace Corps was a generous way of extending American influence into parts of the world where poverty and ignorance could make the promises of Communism appealing. Young, enthusiastic volunteers were sent to underdeveloped countries to build schools, teach modern agricultural practices, and develop community services. When Kennedy began the Peace Corps just three months into his presidency, hundreds, then thousands of college students jumped at the chance to serve.

Left: Thousands of protesters demonstrated against the Vietnam War at an army induction center in Oakland, California, in October 1967. In a prelude to the more violent protests of 1968, they pulled parked cars into the street to block traffic, overturned trash cans, and fought with the police.

Marnie Mueller, who was born in 1942, was one of the willing volunteers in the early years of the Peace Corps.

When Kennedy was elected there was definitely a feeling that he was going to somehow lead the country in a different way. He was young and handsome, and he talked a language that I could understand. When he said, "Ask not what your country can do for you, ask what you can do for your country," it struck a very profound chord in me. I was a junior in college when he announced the formation of the Peace Corps, and I immediately thought, "I'm going to get an application, and I'm going to join this Peace Corps." I was going to go and help the poor people of the world do something better with their lives. The idea was to go there and help people to help themselves.

I was assigned to an extremely poor barrio on the northern side of Guayaqil [a city in Ecuador], on a very picturesque hill, full of cane shacks. The running water only went up to a certain place on the hill. Beyond that, water had to be carried in buckets up to people's houses. Many of the houses had dirt floors, and none of them had windows. There were holes in the roofs. There was garbage and sewage overflowing down the hill. It was a pretty big shock to me. My job was to organize activities for a new community center, which was built by previous volunteers. You have to understand, I was a twenty-one-year-old girl. I not only had to live in a very rough-and-tumble community, but I then had to try and work some miracle within the community. I was alternately thrilled, moved, excited, terrified, and filled with the desire to go home.

We had a library in the community center. We had mechanics classes in there. We organized football teams for the boys to play. Whatever the community wanted, we developed. Out of that grew more serious projects such as a preschool. Out of the sewing classes grew an economic development project where the women made mosquito nets and sold them to CARE to make money. On the one hand, I was very accepted in the community. On the other hand, whenever you're a First World person working in the Third World, there is always a certain anger and resentment toward you.

Mueller, above, at home in Hempstead, New York, 1960, and, right, three years later during her second day of Peace Corps training in Puerto Rico.

Out of the activities at the center grew a notion that the community could begin to demand bigger, more fundamental changes. And when we began to deal with the true needs of the community, we got into some trouble. One of the first indications that something was wrong occurred at a party I threw at my house. The president of the Small Business Organization pulled me aside and pointed to somebody in the room and said, "What is he doing here? He's a Communist." And then sometime after that, when the people in the community marched on the *municipio,* the city government, to demand a new sewage system, the money for the center disappeared. Then the U.S. ambassador called me in and warned me not to enter into the politics of the country.

Many of us suspected that there was something else going on, that there was another purpose for our being there that we weren't told about. There was something wrong with young, inexperienced kids coming like gangbusters into these Third World communities as though we knew everything about the world—as though we knew how to help these poor people. There was a certain arrogance about our being there, and it was very disturbing for us to find that out.

America's attempts to topple Cuba's Communist leader, Fidel Castro, only helped to strengthen Cuban feelings against the United States and increase the fiery dictator's popularity. Here an enthusiastic supporter pulls playfully at Castro's beard, 1964.

More and more, the developing world became the battleground for the Cold War between democracy and Communism. The United States and the Soviet Union both tried to extend their influence over smaller, poorer countries around the world. Cuba, an island nation just south of Florida, became Communist when Fidel Castro took power in 1959. Tensions ran high between Cuba and the United States, especially after President Kennedy mounted a secret invasion of the island in 1961. The invasion at the Bay of Pigs was a total failure.

The leader of the Soviet Union, Nikita Khrushchev, sensed from the Bay of Pigs disaster that Kennedy might be weak. He decided to challenge the young president by arming Cuba with nuclear missiles aimed at the United States. The idea of an enemy missile base so close to home terrified Americans. Still, photographs taken from American reconnaissance planes did not show any missiles ready to launch—yet. In an attempt to keep the Soviet missiles from reaching their launch site, President Kennedy ordered a blockade of all Russian ships headed to Cuba. Then he waited to see what the Russians would do.

Sixteen navy destroyers and three cruisers blocked access to Cuba while twenty-five Soviet merchant ships stayed on course for the island. Around the country—around the world—people watched nervously. In a California high school, a student reportedly broke down, sobbing, "I don't want to die." Pope John XXIII pleaded with Kennedy and Khrushchev to consider their moral duty to the world. At last, after thirteen nail-biting days, Khrushchev turned his ships back in exchange for a promise that America would never invade Cuba. The Cuban missile crisis was over, but the feeling endured that the end of the world might be only a heartbeat away.

Although terrified at the prospect of nuclear war, most Americans supported Kennedy's handling of the Cuban missile crisis. Others, such as these demonstrators in New York City, took to the streets to protest what they viewed as senseless saber rattling between the two superpowers.

Crisis followed crisis as the country continued to struggle with the issue of civil rights. The nonviolent campaign of the fifties, led by black churches, had made progress, but for many people it was not enough. More and more African Americans felt bitter toward a white power structure that still denied them basic equality. And many now grew impatient with Martin Luther King Jr. and other moderate leaders. They also began to doubt the support of the federal government. The Supreme Court had ruled again and again that segregation was unconstitutional. Yet so long as local authorities refused to change anything, these legal victories were hollow. Only the federal government could ensure that the local authorities obeyed the law.

In 1961 the Supreme Court ruled that segregated interstate bus terminals were unconstitutional. A group of activists calling themselves Freedom Riders rode buses into southern cities, hoping to be arrested. They wanted to force the federal government to stand up for them and uphold the Constitution. But it seemed that the Freedom Riders were on their own. In one Alabama town a mob set a bus on fire. In Birmingham, Alabama, the Ku Klux Klan attacked a bus with the full support of the police commissioner. In Montgomery, Alabama, home of Rosa Parks, a white mob went after the Freedom Riders with metal pipes and baseball bats, while the city's police chief declared that his department had "no intention of standing guard for a bunch of troublemakers coming into our city." When Martin Luther King showed up in Montgomery the next day to lead a church rally, the church was firebombed. Finally, U.S. marshals arrived to drive the white mob back. Attorney General Robert Kennedy, the president's brother, asked King to observe a cooling-off period. Organizer James Farmer replied to reporters with righteous anger, "Please tell the attorney general that we have been cooling off for three hundred and fifty years."

After Freedom Riders were beaten and their bus set on fire outside Anniston, Alabama, right, segregationist governor John Patterson called the riders "a bunch of rabble-rousers" and warned them "to get out of Alabama as quickly as possible. ... The state ... can't guarantee the safety of fools."

Diane Nash, born in 1938, was one of the student Freedom Riders who joined the struggle against segregation.

Nash (far right) at an integrated lunch counter.

I grew up on the South Side of Chicago, and while there was segregation there, I didn't really notice it that much. I always knew things were much worse in the South. While I ran into some discrimination growing up, it wasn't until I went to school in Nashville, Tennessee, that I experienced real segregation. When I arrived at Fisk University, I visited a few of the places near campus that were available to blacks, but everything else was segregated. I resented not being able to go downtown to the Woolworth's and have lunch with a friend. Also, when I was downtown, I saw lots of blacks sitting out on the curb or on the ground eating their lunches because they weren't allowed to sit in the restaurants and eat. It was so demeaning. The first time I had to use a women's rest room marked Colored was pretty humiliating, too.

Pretty soon I started looking for an organization—someone, somewhere—that was trying to do something to change segregation. I heard about a series of workshops conducted by Reverend James Lawson, who was extremely well versed in nonviolence. So I went to these workshops, and I listened very carefully. After a few weeks I decided this nonviolence couldn't possibly have any impact. But because they were the only group in Nashville that was trying to make a change, I kept going.

In the fall of 1959 we started going to restaurants downtown and trying to get served. When we were refused service, we would ask to see the manager, ask him why we were being refused service, and then tell him we thought it was morally wrong. We called that testing. In February of 1960 we heard on the radio that sit-ins had begun in other southern cities, and then we decided to have our sit-ins at the same chains that the students were targeting in other cities.

By 1962 I had left Fisk University to devote all my time to the civil rights moments. In May I was in Mississippi, where the bus system was still legally segregated, encouraging black young people to sit at the front of the bus and conducting workshops on nonviolence to prepare students for the things they needed to know in order to join the Freedom Riders. I was twenty-three at the time, and since I was encouraging these minors to do something illegal, a warrant was issued for my arrest, charging me with contributing to the delinquency of minors. I faced a two-and-a-half-year jail term, and I was about six months pregnant with my first child. My husband drove me down to Jackson and I surrendered to the sheriff, and the following Monday I surrendered to the court. I sat in the first bench in the first row and refused to move to the rear when the bailiff ordered me to do so, so I was put in jail for ten days for contempt of court.

Those days were really hard. The jail had so many cockroaches that I soon learned to sleep during the day so that I could sit up at night and dodge them as they dropped off the ceiling onto my cot. One night there was an insect that was so large I could actually hear it walking across the floor. I had taken a toothbrush, comb, and my vitamin pills (since I was expecting), a change of underwear, and an extra skirt and blouse, because I knew I was going to jail. But the prison officials would not let me have anything, not a toothbrush, not toothpaste, nothing. I remember combing my hair with my fingers and working out a way to brush my teeth. I emerged from the experience even stronger because I learned that I could get along with nothing if I had to—except food and water, perhaps.

When you are faced with a situation of injustice or oppression, if you change yourself and become somebody who cannot be oppressed, then the world has to set up against a new you. We students became people who could not be segregated. They could have killed us, but they could not segregate us any longer. Once that happened, the whole country was faced with a new set of decisions. I think most of the students that were participating were confident that we could change the world. I still think we can.

Police chief Bull Connor ordered the use of high-pressure fire hoses on black protesters as they attempted to march on Birmingham's city hall in 1963. While many of the marchers were forced to retreat, one small group braced themselves against the onslaught and repeatedly chanted the word *freedom*, inspiring the remaining marchers to continue.

Martin Luther King Jr., 1929-1968.

The choice of the Lincoln Memorial as the rally site for the March on Washington was a profoundly symbolic one, particularly since 1963 was the centennial of Lincoln's Emancipation Proclamation. The D.C. police liked the site as well, but for a more cynical reason: With the monument grounds surrounded by water on three sides, any violence among the demonstrators could be easily contained.

Martin Luther King had not given up hope of a better America. On August 28, 1963, he addressed nearly a quarter of a million demonstrators at the March on Washington, the first massive display of sixties "people power." The people in the audience—many of them the great-grand-children of slaves—had come together in one of the crowning moments of the civil rights movement. King stood at the Lincoln Memorial, beneath the statue of Abraham Lincoln, and gave one of the most stirring speeches in American history. "I have a dream," he said, describing his vision of America as it could be and as it should be. "When we let freedom ring, when we let it ring from every village and hamlet, from every state and every city, we will be able to speed up that day when all of God's children, black men and white men, Jews and Gentiles, Protestants and Catholics, will all be able to join hands and sing in the words of the old Negro spiritual, 'Free at last! Free at last! Thank God almighty, we are free at last!'"

King's words were electrifying. For the first time, many white Americans understood that the civil rights workers were patriots, challenging the nation to live up to its best traditions. The March on Washington was a grand, hopeful spectacle. But only two weeks later a bomb exploded in the Sixteenth Street Baptist Church in Birmingham, Alabama, killing four young black girls as they were putting on their choir robes.

On Friday, November 22, 1963, President Kennedy was in Dallas, Texas, trying to smooth his relationship with members of the Democratic Party there. Many white southern Democrats had felt he was too supportive of the civil rights movement, and with an election coming up, JFK wanted to repair his image in the South.

The president and the First Lady, Jackie Kennedy, were in the backseat of an open convertible, waving to the crowds lining the parade route in downtown Dallas. The president smiled and waved, raising his right hand to push back his hair, when he suddenly slumped forward, clutching his throat. Almost immediately his head was thrown back by a second impact. President John Fitzgerald Kennedy had been shot. Secret Service agents flung themselves toward the dying president and his wife, who was unhurt but covered with her husband's blood. John Connally, the governor of Texas, had also been shot, though not fatally.

News of the shooting in Dallas spread quickly throughout the world via television, radio, news wires, and word of mouth. Here stunned New Yorkers in Times Square anxiously wait for word on the president's fate.

Reporter Richard Stolley, born in 1928, covered the assassination of the president for _Life_ magazine.

On November 22, 1963, one of my colleagues, who was watching the AP [Associated Press] ticker, suddenly shouted to me that Kennedy had been shot in Dallas. I got on the phone to the New York office, and they told me to get to Dallas as fast as I could.

I set up a bureau office in a downtown hotel. At about six o'clock I got a phone call from a _Life_ [reporter]. She had heard from a cop that a Dallas businessman [Abraham Zapruder] had been in Dealey Plaza with a movie camera and had photographed the assassination from beginning to end. If that film actually existed, I just knew I had to get it, but I wasn't sure where to look. So I picked up the Dallas phone book

Stolley in 1963 with a copy of *Life*'s special issue on the assassination.

The opening spread of the *Life* story.

and just ran my fingers down the *Z*'s, and God, there it was: Zapruder, comma, Abraham. I called the number every fifteen minutes for about five hours, but no one picked up. Finally, late that evening, around eleven, this weary voice answered, and I said, "Is this Abraham Zapruder?" He said, "Yes." "Is it true that you photographed the assassination?" "Yes." "Have you seen the film?" "Yes." And then I said, "Can I come out and see it now?" And he said, "No. I'm too upset. I'm too tired. Come to my office at nine."

I got there at 8:00 A.M. Saturday. Zapruder was slightly annoyed that I was an hour early, but he let me come in anyway. Inside the room were four very grim-faced Secret Service agents who had also come down to see the film. Zapruder got out this creaky old projector, with, of course, no sound, and he beamed the film up on a plain white wall. Within just a few seconds I knew that I was experiencing the most dramatic moment in my entire career. I was sitting there with these Secret Service agents as they watched a film of their failure at their number one job, which was to protect the president. We watched the motorcade snake around onto Elm Street around Dealey Plaza. It went behind a sign and Kennedy was briefly out of the scene. The next time we saw the president, his hands were up around his throat, and Connally's mouth was open and he was howling in pain—they had both already been shot. Jackie turned her head and looked quizzically at her husband. Less than two or three seconds later, without warning, the whole right side of President Kennedy's head just exploded in pink froth. Everyone watching the film in the room, including the Secret Service agents, just went, "Ugh!" It was like we had been gut-punched. Zapruder, who had already seen the film, turned his head away just before the image of Kennedy getting shot appeared on the screen. It was an absolutely astounding moment. There was Jackie crawling up onto the trunk, and Secret Service agent Clint Hill leaping up onto the car, pushing Jackie back in, and holding on for dear life as the limo sped away to the hospital. The camera ran out of film just as the limo disappeared under the underpass.

The assassination of President Kennedy stunned the nation. A rush of events followed: On Friday Vice President Lyndon Johnson was sworn in as president on the plane carrying Kennedy's body back to Washington. That same afternoon the assassin, Lee Harvey Oswald, was arrested in a Dallas movie theater. On Saturday, while it poured rain in Washington, the body of the president lay in state in the East Room of the White House. On Sunday, in front of live television news cameras, Oswald was shot dead in the police station by a nightclub owner named Jack Ruby.

On Monday came the funeral itself, with the heart-wrenching image of JFK's small children mourning their dead father.

America's young were in shock. The president had formed a special bond with them, a bond that had helped them to feel that these times were particularly theirs. With his leadership gone, young people experienced a feeling of both freedom and responsibility. The decade now appeared to pass even more completely to them. A youth-oriented subculture emerged around the arrival of more sophisticated rock groups such as the Beatles, and a growing political awareness was centered around protest over American participation in the Vietnam War.

No novelist's imagination could have created an assassin better suited to early-sixties fears than Lee Harvey Oswald, shown here at Dallas police headquarters. Oswald had connections to the Soviet Union (his wife was Russian and he had once lived in Moscow), Cuba (the pro-Castro Fair Play for Cuba Committee), and the mob (he had tenuous links to a New Orleans Mafia figure).

Never before had a single event instantly summoned so many Americans together in mourning. Hastily organized memorial services for President Kennedy were conducted nationwide, allowing many, such as these students outside a ceremony at Harvard University, to share their grief.

Not since Elvis Presley had a musical performer or group caused such a frenzy as the Beatles did when they arrived in New York City on February 12, 1964. Thousands of screaming fans greeted them at the airport and then shadowed their every move throughout the city. Here a group of "Beatlemaniacs" waits across the street from New York's Plaza Hotel hoping to catch a glimpse of the Fab Four.

In June 1963 a Buddhist monk burned himself to death in downtown Saigon to protest the cruelties of South Vietnamese president Ngo Dinh Diem, leading many Americans to begin to question U.S. support of the repressive leader.

Vietnam, once the French colony of Indochina, had won its own war for independence in 1954. It ended with the country's being split into two halves: Communist North Vietnam and South Vietnam, which America would come to support. The war had also ended with an agreement that both North Vietnam and South Vietnam would hold elections on reunification. But when it became clear that the Communists would win the election, South Vietnam put off the referendum. Over the next few years, Vietnamese Communist guerrillas gradually infiltrated South Vietnam, eventually renewing the war.

Like Cuba, Vietnam was of little actual importance to the United States. But as with Cuba, Vietnam's embrace of Communism would be a serious blow to American prestige. And it was argued that if Vietnam became Communist, other nations in Asia might also fall under Soviet influence, like a tumbling row of dominoes. At first Americans gave their wholehearted support to South Vietnam in its struggle against the Communist North Vietnamese.

But in June 1963 several Buddhist monks burned themselves to death in protest against the brutally oppressive government of South Vietnam. Suddenly Americans began to wonder what they had gotten into. Perhaps the conflict in Vietnam was more complicated than it had seemed. Exactly what sort of government was the United States supporting in South Vietnam? As President Johnson intensified America's military presence with troops and arms, the antiwar movement intensified as well. For many of the young soldiers who went to Vietnam, the experience was baffling: They went into battle without really knowing what they were fighting for.

The way this war was fought was different, too. American GIs in Vietnam were not prepared to fight against smiling villagers who hid grenades behind their backs, or an army of snipers who fired on the Americans and then quickly dissolved into the jungle greenery. The GIs were supposed to be soldiers of democracy. But it wasn't at all clear that the government of South Vietnam had much support from its own people. What the people of Vietnam seemed to want most was a future free from domination by any foreign power, even the United States, which said it was trying to help them. For lack of any other cause, many American GIs fought for their fellow soldiers.

"We are not about to send American boys nine or ten thousand miles away from home," Lyndon Johnson declared in the 1964 presidential campaign, "to do what Asian boys ought to be doing for themselves." But by the time Johnson left office in 1969, he had delivered half a million GIs to do just that.

Larry Gwin, who was born in 1941, received a Silver Star for extraordinary heroism. He described the soldier's experience in Vietnam.

I arrived in Vietnam in July of '65. I landed with a group of soldiers on an airstrip just outside Saigon. Walking out of the airplane, the heat hit everyone in my entourage simultaneously, and everybody started to sweat. The roads into Saigon were dirt, and en route we passed homes which were nothing but tar paper and aluminum shacks with pigs and chickens in every yard. I thought, "This is the Third World." After an hour and a half, the school bus crossed a bridge into the teeming capital of Saigon. There were two traffic lights, and only one was functioning, so it was absolute bedlam between the jeeps, the trucks, the taxis, the buffalo carts, and the people on bicycles. Just before we pulled into headquarters, someone smashed a bottle against the bus. This person obviously didn't care about Americans and really didn't want us there. It was my first indication that maybe our presence wasn't quite as welcome as we had been led to believe.

I was sent to a base at An Khe to prepare for the arrival of fifteen thousand troops in mid-September. The troops arrived, and by early October had constructed a defensible perimeter around the base, and then we began our operations. On the afternoon of the fourteenth of November, we heard that the first battalion was engaged in heavy contact at a landing zone code-named X-ray in the Ia Drang Valley. My company was quickly sent in, in three waves of six helicopters each. We lifted up over the tall trees of our landing zone and we could see the clouds of smoke drifting from Chu Pong Mountain, where we were headed. I thought, "Oh, my God, we're not going to fly into that mess, are we?"

The helicopter set me down in the midst of chaos. There were air strikes against the mountain, and the *pop-pop-pop* of rounds in the air sounded like firecrackers. I saw three or four Americans huddled around a tree saying, "Get down, get down, man, they're all around us." I had been on the ground for all of ten seconds when a fellow jumped up next to me and said, "I'm hit, sir." Carrying our wounded guy, we dodged and weaved forward for about a hundred yards until we got to where we could see the battalion commander's post. In between there was nothing but burnt grass, where napalm had killed some people, stacks of empty ammo crates, and bent and broken weapons scattered around. There was a row of American dead covered with ponchos, but we had to spring past it and get ready to fight.

On the morning of November 17 we received orders to move to another landing zone about three miles due north. We knew there were

Gwin (left) with a fellow marine in Vietnam, 1965.

American soldiers rush their wounded
to safety during a firefight in a northern
province of South Vietnam, 1966.
Despite vast superiority in logistics and
firepower, the U.S. forces were unable
to make substantial gains against the
guerrilla tactics adopted by the North
Vietnamese.

North Vietnamese in the area. The temperature was maybe a hundred, and everybody was exhausted because we'd been awake for two days and were weighed down with our equipment. We set up in a clump of trees, waiting for the other platoons to go around and secure the area. All of a sudden we heard some shooting from the vicinity of our first platoon. After two or three single shots, the whole jungle opened up in one massive crescendo of fire. It seemed that everybody I knew and everybody behind us was firing every weapon they had. We had run into the North Vietnamese, and they had attacked us immediately.

I remember jumping up to go to a tree for some cover when the firing got bad, and as I was looking at the tree, right in front of my eyes, this chunk of wood came out at me, and I realized it was a bullet and that it had almost taken my nose off. I crunched down in the grass and ran back to where my company commander and radios were. The guys I was with were all down in the grass, hugging the dirt. Since I was lieutenant and had to know what was going on, I stuck my head up and saw about forty North Vietnamese soldiers coming across the grass at us. All I did was say, "Here they come," and start shooting at them. Everybody got the message and we cranked out a lot of fire, killing all the North Vietnamese. I remember those were the first men I ever killed, and I remember each one of them very distinctly. But if we hadn't killed them, they would have killed us. The Vietnamese came back that night and killed a lot of our wounded lying in the grass. Most everybody I knew was dead, and the stench of the battlefield was just unbelievable. It took us two days to clean up our dead and wounded and get us out of there.

We lost 70 percent of our men in the battle. General Westmoreland came down for Thanksgiving a week later to congratulate us on what he called our "distinguished victory," and as he did every one of us looked around and counted our losses. We thought, "Is *that* a victory, General?"

The Battle of Thanh Son 2 in May 1966 was a turning point for me. On the morning of May 6 we attacked a village complex surrounded by trees. We didn't really know what was behind the trees, because we followed a walking artillery barrage. It wasn't until we got to the site that we realized we had devastated a village, killing many civilians. We saw children and little kids with their legs blown off and old couples under smoking wreckage. It broke my heart, and it broke the hearts of the guys I served with. I know after we left that village, none of us could talk and none of us could look back.

There was no point during my year in Vietnam when I realized that the U.S. had made a mistake and that we shouldn't have been there. But I also know in my heart that any American soldier who went to Vietnam didn't have to stay there long before he knew that there was something wrong with our presence there, either by the look in the Vietnamese eyes or in the way that we were treating them or what we were doing in the countryside.

Malcolm X (right), 1925–1965.

Detroit erupted in violence after police raided a black nightclub for a liquor violation. For six days rioters ransacked stores, overturned cars, smashed windows, and set fires. Frightened Michigan National Guard troops frantically tried to quell the violence while snipers shot at them from above.

In 1964 Martin Luther King was awarded the Nobel peace prize. His efforts had helped convince Congress to pass the Civil Rights Act and the Voting Rights Act, and his moving speeches had brought many white Americans to his cause. But within the black community, impatience with the white establishment was growing, as well as impatience with King's turn-the-other-cheek leadership. Now, in the mid-sixties, other voices rose up, not from the South but from the northern ghettos, asking: Why should we strive so hard to join a white community that doesn't welcome us? Why shouldn't we embrace our own heritage? The writings and teachings of Malcolm X offered a powerful alternative to King's message.

Malcolm X, born Malcolm Little (the *X* was his way of refusing the name given to his ancestors by white slaveholders), turned to the teachings of the black Muslim movement for guidance. He began to describe America in a deliberately provocative way, saying that southern whites were morally superior to northerners because at least they were honest about their racism. He mocked the image of the North as free. Preaching separation of the races, he urged African Americans to use the term *black* to describe themselves instead of the then common term *Negro*. Malcolm X's speeches set off alarm bells throughout white America.

"Black power" was the motto for activists who wanted to see more dramatic change in American society. To many, "black power" could only mean a black revolution intended to destroy the white establishment. With riots erupting in Los Angeles, Chicago, San Diego, Philadelphia, and other cities across the country, it looked as though the violent racial confrontation Americans had long feared might finally come. When Malcolm X was assassinated in 1965, his followers picked up his banner and carried it onward.

Kwame Turé, whose original name was Stokely Carmichael, was born in 1941. His experience demonstrated why Malcolm X found so many willing listeners.

Turé (known then as Stokely Carmichael) instructing a group of marchers in Montgomery, Alabama.

I was with the first group to take trains from New Orleans as part of the Freedom Rides in 1961. It was a rough ride, because we were confronted by segregationists breaking train windows at every single stop until we got to Jackson, Mississippi, where the police arrested us for refusing to leave the white waiting room. We were sent to Hinds County Jail, and then, just to increase the pressure on us, a group of us were transferred to the Parchman Penitentiary on death row. The police were beating us and torturing us every night. I respected Martin Luther King for sticking to the nonviolence under all conditions, and I believed in it as long as it was effective, but if it wasn't working, then I decided that I would be throwing blows. By the time I walked out of Parchman Penitentiary, I was prepared to carry a gun in my work.

When I was growing up in Harlem, Malcolm X was there all the time, so I knew all about him and the Nation of Islam. Malcolm X presented a clearer, more direct political analysis, stripped of sentimentality, that saw the reality of the enemy we were fighting. Since Malcolm X aimed his message directly at African Americans, he could touch us more deeply, while Martin Luther King's message also had to speak to white society. King would say, "What we need is morality," while Malcolm would say, "What we need is power." To Malcolm, nonviolence just meant that you're giving your cheek left and right to a man who has no conscience. He thought we needed an eye for an eye.

Malcolm X's assassination had a profound effect on us. After his assassination in 1965, those of us who really understood him made a conscious decision to pick up Malcolm's points and to build on them. We wanted to keep his philosophy alive. We decided to go into Lowndes County, Alabama, to use the vote as a means to organize the people. There was not one single black registered to vote there in 1965, yet 80 percent of the population in the county was black.

For three months before the arrival of election day, white terrorists sent out word that if any Africans went to vote, they'd be left there for dead. In order to encourage Africans to get out and vote, we let them know that young brothers and sisters were coming, armed, from the big cities to help out. I remember the Justice Department sent somebody to see me who said, "You know, your people are bringing in guns. What are you gonna do?" I said, "We're gonna vote." He said, "The whites are very upset about this." We had already decided that we would not fire the first shot, so I said, "You tell them they've got the first shot, but we're voting." When election day came, the people turned out to vote and not one shot was fired. For the first time, black citizens of Lowndes County felt they had exercised their political rights. They began to understand the power of politics.

Like much of America, Robert Kennedy, the former attorney general and now a U.S. senator, was changing his views on many different issues: the ongoing war in Vietnam, civil rights, the growing unrest among the country's young people. More and more people looked to him to challenge President Johnson to become the Democratic candidate in the 1968 presidential election. Many people were dissatisfied with the way Johnson had led the country since JFK's death. Eugene McCarthy, a senator from Minnesota who was against the war, was running for the Democratic Party's nomination, and in March of 1968 Bobby Kennedy also entered the race. Johnson, with so much of his own party against him, decided not to run again. Excitement was high; many Americans thought their troubles might be over if they could get another Kennedy into the White House.

But in 1968 it sometimes seemed as if every hope was destined to end in tragedy. In April Martin Luther King Jr. appeared in Memphis, Tennessee, in support of striking sanitation workers. There, on April 4, America's greatest prophet of nonviolence was shot and killed. When the news broke, violence erupted all over the country, with riots, arson, and gunfire. Though the deep anguish at King's death was heartfelt, the violence that followed was a sad tribute to a man who had dedicated his life to peaceful change.

The riots that followed the assassination of Martin Luther King Jr. charred America's cities, including Washington, D.C.

Robert Kennedy was boarding a plane for a campaign stop in Indianapolis when he heard that King had been shot. He was scheduled to speak at a rally in Indianapolis's black ghetto, but when he arrived the chief of police told Kennedy the city could not guarantee his safety. Kennedy ignored the warning and went anyway. The crowd waiting for him did not know King had been killed. They gasped when Kennedy told them. Then he appealed to their best instincts. "You can be filled with bitterness, with hatred and a desire for revenge," he said. "We can move in that direction as a country. . . . Or we can make an effort, as Martin Luther King did . . . to replace that violence, that stain of bloodshed . . . with an effort to understand, with compassion and love." While the rest of the country burned, there were no riots in Indianapolis. There people took their grief home quietly. Two months later Bobby Kennedy, too, became the victim of an assassin's bullet.

College and university campuses were in an uproar, and not only in the United States. Students took to the streets in Paris and London. Czechoslovakia, a Communist country, had begun some modest but daring democratic reforms, nicknamed the "Prague Spring." But on August 20, 1968, some 650,000 Soviet troops marched into Czechoslovakia to force the country back into the Soviet camp. Mobs of Czech youths climbed onto Russian tanks and chanted, "USSR go home." But the Prague Spring was over.

Approximately five hundred student radicals seized five buildings in the 1968 Columbia University protests, even occupying the president's office, above.

The most notable American uprising came at the Democratic National Convention in Chicago. Ten thousand demonstrators traveled there to make their voices heard. Twenty-three thousand police officers and National Guard forces were waiting for them. An army of students faced off against an army of police in riot gear outside the convention center. Inside, party leaders nominated Johnson's vice president, Hubert Humphrey, as the Democratic candidate for president. The demonstrators outside claimed that the party leaders had ignored them and betrayed their hopes. It felt as if a civil war between America and its own young people had begun.

Jane Adams, born in 1943, was a member of Students for a Democratic Society who was in Chicago for the convention.

I had been active in the student Left throughout the sixties, but by 1968 I was so alienated from the political system that I was not following the processes of the Democratic candidates very closely. I remember many people saw Bobby Kennedy and Eugene McCarthy as hopeful forces for change, but after Martin Luther King's assassination, I began to feel that there was a rottenness at the core of the political system of this country.

I was a marshal out in the streets during the Democratic National Convention in Chicago. My most vivid memory of the convention was at the demonstration down at the McCarthy campaign headquarters. A crowd of thousands of people gathered outside, and the police were pushing us closer and closer together. Those of us who had experience protesting kept saying, "Stand up, stand up, stand up," because we knew the police were gonna charge and were gonna go in and slaughter them. After the police charged in, I saw this young man in a suit and tie and a woman who looked like she was a sorority girl, very well dressed, and she had blood pouring out of her hair. This young man had picked her up and was trying to push her in the door, and he was hysterical. I was so furious, because these kids were doing nothing.

When Humphrey was nominated, I was in the YMCA watching it on TV. I ran out in the streets, and armored personnel carriers with barbed wire on the front of them moved into position. The young people chanted, "The whole world is watching," which really meant that the whole world is watching this massive injustice that's going on here, the ripping off of our democracy from us.

Chicago police beat back protesters attempting to reach the convention headquarters.

When Soviet tanks rolled into Prague, the capital of Czecho- slovakia, on August 20, 1968, they clashed head-on with a population determined to hold on to their nation's recent modest democratic reforms. The fiercest fighting erupted when the Soviets tried to storm the national radio station, which had vowed to continually play Czech composer Bedřich Smetana's "My Country" as long as the station remained free. Early in the morning of August 21 the station went silent, signaling the end of the "Prague Spring."

On the night of July 20, 1969, Americans put away their anger. Along with billions of television viewers around the world, they watched as American astronaut Neil Armstrong stepped out of the lunar module and became the first man to walk on the moon.

The American space program had also been caught up in the Cold War struggle between democracy and Communism. After the Soviets had launched the *Sputnik* satellite in 1957, beating America into space, the United States had thrown its support behind NASA, the national space agency. JFK had pledged to put a man on the moon before the 1960s were over. Now, in 1969, that promise had been fulfilled.

Among those at the crowded Apollo XI launch site was the 1920s pilot Charles Lindbergh. It had been only forty-two years since his heroic flight across the Atlantic, but the world had changed a great deal. His had been an individual achievement; he had navigated his own plane through near disaster. The Apollo program was the work of billions of dollars of taxpayers' money and more than four hundred thousand people in assembly plants and control rooms.

Still, like Lindbergh's flight in the twenties, the mission of the three Apollo XI astronauts gave their wounded country something to be proud of, something to share. And when the nation's weary citizens saw pictures of their planet taken from space, they were moved: It was not the troubled world they knew, but a beautiful, peaceful globe, ordered and still.

When astronaut Neil Armstrong radioed Earth, "The *Eagle* has landed," a relieved mission control in Houston replied, "You've got a bunch of guys [who were] about to turn blue.... We're breathing again." Below, the mission control staff celebrates the successful completion of the lunar landing mission.

The lunar module, *Eagle*, returns to the mother ship, *Columbia*, after the first lunar landing. With Apollo XI, the American space program made good on President Kennedy's promise to put men on the moon by the end of the decade, and it did so with six months to spare.

10 Years of Doubt
1969–1981

In the 1970s the booming postwar economy finally went bust. There was no single event that announced this decline, nothing like the 1929 stock market crash, which announced the arrival of the Great Depression. Instead, high unemployment and rising prices crept up on Americans. The unpopular war in Vietnam and the crisis in the economy combined to spread a feeling of mistrust of the government and its leaders. There was a new awareness that the growth of industry had helped to damage the environment. People worried about pollution, overpopulation, inflation, and recession. The earth itself, and the United States along with it, now seemed fragile and the future uncertain.

Prices were going up and up, and the most painful price increase was the one at the gas pump. Oil was—and still is—the lifeblood of America. Every plane, tank, and car needs it. Every skyscraper and industrial plant runs on it. Oil is part of the fertilizer that helps farmers produce crops for the world; when used in drugs, it helps fight disease. Like no other raw material, oil created the American way of life. And it fueled the American dream machine, the automobile.

Since the 1920s the car had become a symbol of American prosperity. GM made big cars after World War II, and people bought them according to their status: the more successful you were, the bigger your car. For years America had been buying cheap oil from the petroleum-producing countries of the Middle East: Saudi Arabia, Iran, the United Arab Emirates, and others. But when America supported Israel in the 1973 Arab-Israeli War, the oil-producing countries punished the United States. They organized an oil embargo, cutting off America's pipeline.

Suddenly the price of gasoline and heating oil went up. Everything in the American economy that had depended on cheap energy got more expensive. People had to turn down their thermostats, cut back on driving, make do with less. A new thrift was force-fed to the country.

Long lines formed at gas stations, whose owners were asked to sell a maximum of ten gallons per customer. Now the large cars that Americans had been driving for so long were a handicap. Still, the powerful American automakers kept right on rolling big cars down the assembly lines. People began buying smaller, more fuel-efficient foreign cars instead. The era of the gas guzzler was over.

As the price of crude oil climbed, the combined earnings of the OPEC nations rose from $23 billion in 1972 to $140 billion in 1974. The Saudis used the new profits to modernize their desert country. Here King Khalid, center, examines a model of the $8.5-billion King Khalid Military City, a town for seventy thousand troops being built near the Iraqi border.

In Detroit the big automakers started laying off their workers. LaNita Gaines, born in 1950, was a Chrysler employee who watched as the oil crisis began hurting people's lives.

When I first started working at the plant, Chrysler was manufacturing these giant-sized cars. They had gigantic gas tanks and got little mileage, but they were big and comfortable. It seemed as if people were changing cars every two years, and they weren't really going for the quality of the car; they just wanted to keep up with the latest model. I swear at one point they were moving down the assembly line so fast that we'd sometimes miss a screw.

In 1973 we began to see a downturn in the industry as a whole. We workers would read about the oil crisis in the papers, and we didn't quite know what to make of it. All we knew is that people were waiting on seemingly endless lines to get a tank of gas, and Chrysler just kept building those huge cars. The public started paying closer attention to gas mileage and began turning to smaller, more fuel-efficient cars from abroad like the Germans' Volkswagen Beetle and Japanese cars. We had a Chrysler Imperial at that time, and it was a real gas-guzzler. We were getting eight miles to the gallon on it, and it seemed as if you could barely get from one gas station to the other before you had to fill up again. Eventually I had to say good-bye to it because I couldn't afford to keep gas in it.

LaNita Gaines speaking at a UAW convention in 1975.

The American companies were refusing to change to what was now going to be the new road for the auto industry. We workers just kind of looked at that and said, "Well, why don't they change? When are they gonna get the message that we're not in love with those big cars anymore?" We'd try to tell them that we were the ones that were buying those little cars, but the company didn't want to listen. We were looking for companies that made smaller cars, of course, that were American-made, but if America was not making those cars, then you had to buy what you could find. We had to get to work, we had to get our families around, and with gas prices climbing much faster than our wages, we had to do something. We had to buy what was economically feasible for our families.

I worked at Chrysler until around 1974. I had bought my first home and started a family. That November they came around and told us that we were permanently laid off. I was terrified. I thought, "What does this mean? I've had a job for all these years, and now I'm being put in the street." All of a sudden there was not enough money for the mortgage note and the car note. We could barely keep food on the table. I thought I could rely on unemployment for a while, but the industry had recently changed some of its policies in the cutbacks, so the sub fund, which was to help laid-off workers, was depleting quickly, and I realized there was just one step between me and the welfare line. There was a sentiment of despair everywhere. These were very shaky times, and we just didn't know what to do.

During the 1973 OPEC oil embargo, many gas stations, such as this one outside Boston, simply ran out of gas. Even after the embargo ended, gas prices remained high. The OPEC nations had raised the price of crude oil to $11.65 per barrel, an increase of 387 percent.

The faltering economy led many people to feel that their leaders were failing them. This disappointment in the government had really begun with Vietnam, a war Richard Nixon inherited from Democrat Lyndon Johnson when he became president in 1969. At first many Americans were pleased when Nixon set up a policy of "Vietnamization," which placed more of the burden of their own defense on the South Vietnamese, and started bringing American GIs home. But this good feeling did not last. In 1970 it was revealed that U.S. soldiers had massacred Vietnamese civilians at My Lai, and that same year the United States illegally invaded Cambodia. Protests against the war continued to divide the nation. In May four college students were killed by National Guard troops during an antiwar rally at Kent State University in Ohio. Rage and resentment seemed to be the only emotions Americans had in common.

A young woman grieves over the body of a twenty-year-old man, one of four shot and killed by National Guard troops during an antiwar protest at Kent State University in Ohio, May 1970. This photograph became famous as a symbol of the violence caused by the American divide over the Vietnam War.

The 1972 presidential campaign was under way when a seemingly minor crime took place. One night in June seven men broke into the offices of the Democratic National Committee in the Watergate office complex in Washington, D.C. The burglars were arrested. But when it was discovered that they were on the payroll of the Committee to Re-Elect the President, a chain of events was set in motion that would eventually create a constitutional crisis known as Watergate. Americans watched with fascination and disgust as a complicated story of intrigue and obstruction of justice reached higher and higher in the government, eventually touching the president himself.

Hugh Sloan, born in 1940, was a White House aide who became caught up in the Watergate scandal.

Hugh Sloan and his wife, Deborah, who worked for President Nixon's wife, stand with the president in the Oval Office.

I started working at the White House as an assistant to the president's appointment secretary during Nixon's first term in office. I was very young and driven, and it was exciting to see the inner workings of government. When election time neared I was put on a team to help organize the Committee to Re-elect the President. Working on the campaign was even more exciting than working at the White House. We were all working for a cause and by and large we were all believers, so there was a lot of enthusiasm around the office.

One morning I was in the office and I saw G. Gordon Liddy, who was in charge of campaign security, hurrying down the hall in a state of panic. As he ran by, I heard him say something like, "My boys got caught last night. I told him I'd never use anybody from here. I made a big mistake." I didn't know exactly what he was talking about at first, but it got me thinking. Then I read in the papers about the Watergate break-in, and I saw that James McCord was one of the people arrested. I knew McCord; he was directly involved in the Committee to Re-elect the President. The pieces fell together pretty quickly in my mind. It was obvious by the way everyone was acting around the office that the campaign was somehow involved in the break-in. The men who were arrested had a fair amount of cash on them, most of it new hundred-dollar bills. I suspected that cash might have come from money that I had given Liddy, purportedly for campaign security. All of a sudden I started wondering whether the investigators would be able to pick my fingerprints off of those bills.

As the Watergate situation ballooned, the atmosphere around the office became very bizarre. I couldn't get straight answers about anything. I told some people at the White House that there were real problems over here at the committee and that they needed to do something. But their reaction was to just turn their backs on it.

Next I talked to the two attorneys who had been hired by the campaign committee. They said that if what I was telling them [about the money] was accurate, then they'd been lied to by other people in the campaign. They were worried that I would be subpoenaed before they had time to deal with this, and they asked if I had any legitimate reason for being out of town. When I got home that night, Fred LaRue [the director of the reelection committee] called me and said that I should fly to California to help raise money for the campaign. He wanted to know if I could be on the morning plane from Dulles Airport [in Washington, D.C.]. And then he said, "Oh, by the way, could you spend the night at a motel near the airport so you won't be subpoenaed in the meantime?" So I did.

The next day on the flight I had a long time to think. Everything started to seem so crazy to me. Here I was, fleeing from the authorities. It was like I was a character in a movie. The lawyers for the campaign were there to protect the more senior people, and they weren't concerned about what happened to someone like me. Obviously I was in the chain of command that paid all of these people to do something that was illegal. The question was, would anybody know that I was not part of the conspiracy in the first place?

It was during that flight to California that I decided I could no longer work every day with people that were clearly trying to abort the investigation and, in essence, cover it up. I knew I would have to testify, and I felt an immense pressure to be as accurate as possible because I knew my testimony was going to have an impact on people's lives. I think the tragedy in all of this was that I saw a lot of young, enthusiastic people make terrible mistakes and get chewed up in the gears. Particularly people who had no direct involvement, but who perjured themselves to protect more senior people. So many people went to jail because they lied about the cover-up.

It is unlikely that President Nixon knew about the break-in itself. The attempt to cover it up afterward was the mistake that finally forced him to resign. And what Watergate revealed about the Nixon White House turned the public against him. Nixon had gathered around him a loyal group of advisers who followed orders without question. In the interest of serving the president they faked information, attempted to slander his opponents, tried to steal documents, and were involved in other "dirty tricks" that had become a way of life at the White House.

As the Watergate scandal slowly enveloped the Oval Office, Richard Nixon looked for a break from his troubles when he greeted several hundred former POWs at the State Department auditorium and then treated them to a lavish party on the South Lawn of the White House in May 1973. "[Richard Nixon] has a deeper concern for his place in history than for the people he governs," observed Congresswoman Shirley Chisholm. "And history will not fail to note that fact."

Richard Nixon bids farewell to the White House staff and members of his cabinet in the East Room of the White House.

On August 8, 1974, Richard Nixon became the first president ever to resign his office. His vice president, Gerald Ford, was sworn in as the thirty-eighth president of the United States. Just four weeks later Ford issued a "full, free, and absolute" pardon to Richard Nixon, guaranteeing, to the disappointment of many, that the man who had brought such shame to America would never be asked to explain his part in the Watergate scandal.

Just six months after Nixon's resignation, South Vietnam fell to the Communists. Americans watched the humiliating spectacle of marine helicopters taking off from the roof of the U.S. embassy in Saigon, leaving desperate South Vietnamese friends behind. It was yet another blow to American pride. Now, with the defeat of South Vietnam, America had undeniably lost a war. Fifty thousand American soldiers had died for nothing.

With the North Vietnamese army descending on Saigon, the U.S. Armed Forces Radio station played "White Christmas" to signal the beginning of a massive helicopter airlift of one thousand Americans and five thousand South Vietnamese from the U.S. Embassy. Thousands of other desperate South Vietnamese frantically tried to storm the compound in the hopes of gaining a place on a helicopter.

In 1970, fifty years after the Nineteenth Amendment to the Constitution gave women the right to vote, feminists across the country held rallies and marches, such as this one in New York City. The protesters demanded reproductive rights, equal opportunity, child care, an end to violence against women, and approval of the Equal Rights Amendment (which was first submitted to Congress in 1923).

The collapse of faith in American leadership and the defeat in Viet-nam further undermined Americans' self-confidence. People responded by turning inward and becoming more focused on themselves. Instead of identifying themselves as Americans, many people began to think of themselves as members of groups with particular interests and rights. Many people now saw themselves first as women, or Latinos, or senior citizens, or environmentalists. The population seemed to be separating into special-interest groups, each fighting for its own cause.

Women were by far the largest and most successful of these groups. Feminist claims to equal rights had begun in the days of the suffragist movement. By the 1960s, the light cast by the civil rights movement made it increasingly obvious that African Americans weren't the only ones being denied equal opportunity.

In 1962 Betty Friedan had published a landmark book called *The Feminine Mystique.* In it she gave voice to the powerful but hard-to-explain feeling that so many women shared: that there was something missing from their lives, that motherhood and housework alone did not nourish the spirit or bring fulfillment. In 1966 Friedan established the National Organization for Women (NOW), which quickly focused on two main goals: the Equal Rights Amendment (ERA) and the right to safe, legal abortion.

In 1972 Congress passed the Equal Rights Amendment. And in 1973 the Supreme Court ruled in favor of abortion rights in a landmark case called *Roe v. Wade.* While both of these victories would come under severe attack (the ERA was never ratified by the states), they signaled an important shift in the way American society viewed women. Many people began to take another look at the traditional roles of men and women. Why were girls always sent to home economics classes while boys were assigned to shop classes? Shouldn't boys learn to cook? Shouldn't girls know how to use tools? Why was it always the husband who worked and the wife who raised the children? Couldn't women be the family breadwinners? Couldn't fathers stay home to take care of the kids?

But these questions also awoke a backlash against some aspects of feminism. By using the same argument that had been used against suffragists—the idea that rights for women would destroy the family—conservatives encouraged an antifeminist campaign. The issue that brought the emotions of both sides to a fever pitch was abortion. To many feminists, abortion was the most fundamental of rights, the right of a woman to control her own body and her own health. By contrast, their conservative and religious opponents saw abortion as an act of human arrogance, an attempt to replace the will of God with the will of the individual.

For many women, the goals of the women's movement—equal pay for equal work, affordable child care for working mothers, the ability to control their reproductive lives—were very close to home. Marie Wilson, born in 1940, was typical of the women who began to demand change.

I was quite certain that after college I'd marry, have children, stay at home, and have this great life that I saw in the Betty Crocker ads. But I was living in a very interesting time, sort of on the cusp between two eras. Half of me wanted to do something different, but half of me felt loyal to this vision of life as a wife and mother. So when my boyfriend proposed to me in 1962, I decided to drop out of college and marry him, but then I immediately changed my mind and canceled the wedding, deciding to go to graduate school instead. Just as suddenly I changed my mind again and had the wedding after all. Within nine months I was pregnant with my first child.

I felt like things had gone badly for my mother because she had to work outside the home, but it would be different for me, I thought, because I would stay home and be a happy, loving, perfect mother. Of course, things didn't happen that way. My husband and I moved around a lot and I didn't have a very good support system, so I was home alone with the baby quite a lot. I started to feel like you would feel on an airplane when they tell you the mask is going to drop and that you should just breathe normally. You can't breathe normally with a child in an apartment, without a lot of money, without friends and family. Children aren't meant to be raised in a home with just one adult who never leaves the house. I didn't like it. And I was also disappointed with myself for not absolutely loving this motherhood experience.

I got pregnant again—my fourth time in four and a half years. I had been sick a lot during those years—my body was just worn out—and I remember sitting in the bathtub and crying. I asked myself, "What am I gonna do? I really can't deal with having that many children, and the only alternative is abortion. Can I risk getting an illegal abortion?" There was a good chance then that I could die from it, and I didn't want to leave my children motherless. It suddenly hit me that something was wrong with this picture. For the first time, I realized I had been working for African American rights, for peace in Vietnam, but that I still had no choices, nor any peace, in my personal life.

The push for women's rights in this country really was a kitchen-table movement, started by women like me who needed changes in their lives. I found a number of women out there who felt the same way I did, and we started working together in our homes. Everything we wanted in life—whether it was to choose how many children to have, to go back to school, to get involved in the workforce—we were determined to go out and create in the world. So we gathered around kitchen tables and pieced together legislation, wrote petitions, and planned events while our children ran around the room. We figured out who to write to in the legislature in order to pass the Mondale child-care bill in the early seventies. I remember working on the Mondale bill, talking to a labor economist in my kitchen; I had a child in one hand, and I was stirring spaghetti sauce with the other.

Meanwhile, the media was creating a movement that was unrecognizable to me—people who burned bras, who hated men and all of that. I had no idea who these people were, what they did, what they looked like. That branch of the movement was never something I could identify with. My feminism came straight out of my own circumstances. I needed to space my children, so I worked on [reproductive] choice. I needed child care in order to work, so I worked on child care. I needed a better job, so I worked on creating good work for women. It wasn't about a national movement. It was simply something that was happening to me, to my friends, to my community. That was feminism.

The Supreme Court's 1973 decision in *Roe v. Wade*, which established abortion as a "fundamental right," galvanized the antiabortion movement and intensified an emotional debate that would continue for decades to come. On January 22, 1979, sixty thousand antiabortion protesters held a rally in Washington, D.C., on the sixth anniversary of *Roe*.

Arguments over the future of the environment, like the battles over feminism, occupied Americans more and more in the 1970s. Once it had seemed as though there was no limit to America's material progress. Factories had produced an endless stream of products. The land had produced enough food to feed the country and export the surplus around the world. But the image of the earth seen from the Apollo XI moon landing had given Americans a new perspective, one of a vulnerable planet that had been contaminated by people and industry.

Many Americans began to question their way of life: Was mass consumption morally right? They also began to question science: Had technology been exploiting natural resources without considering the consequences? Americans looked around and noticed what they had done to their own country: pollution, toxic-waste dumps, poisoned rivers, and endangered species.

In March 1979 the nation's attention was riveted on a nuclear power plant in Pennsylvania: Three Mile Island. A nuclear accident had brought the plant dangerously close to a meltdown. The sense of science gone awry filled people's minds with frightening images of birth defects and cancers. There was a growing belief that American prosperity was risking the health of the earth itself.

"Remain in your homes and stay off the street . . . this is a stage-one emergency," announced emergency workers after a nuclear accident at Three Mile Island spread a radioactive stream throughout a twenty-mile area of rural central Pennsylvania. Pregnant women and small children were evacuated from the area, and an estimated fifty thousand to sixty thousand people decided to leave on their own.

Lois Gibbs, who was born in 1951, personally suffered the consequences of the industrial machine. She and her family lived in Love Canal, a small town in upstate New York where people mysteriously began to get sick.

When I moved to Love Canal, in 1972, I felt I had achieved the American dream: I had a husband with a good job, a healthy one-year-old child, a station wagon, and my very first house, which even had a picket fence. I was living in a thriving community directly across from the mighty Niagara River. Everything in Love Canal seemed to be meant for families. We felt it was just the perfect neighborhood.

Above: Lois Gibbs in the office of the Love Canal Homeowners Association. Below: One of hundreds of abandoned homes at Love Canal.

Then my son, Michael, got very sick. When we moved into our house, he was one year old and perfectly healthy. Then he developed skin problems, asthma, epilepsy, a liver problem, an immune system problem, and a urinary tract disorder. When I asked the pediatrician what was going on, he told me, "You just must be an unlucky mother with a sickly child." My second child, Melissa, who was conceived and born at Love Canal, at first seemed to be perfectly healthy. Then one Friday I noticed bruises on her body. On Saturday the bruises were larger. And by Sunday the bruises on my little girl's body were the size of saucers. She looked like a child abuse victim! I took her to the pediatrician, but he didn't know what was wrong. He just took a blood test and sent us home. Later that afternoon he called and said, "Mrs. Gibbs, I believe your daughter has leukemia." We had no family history of any of these types of illnesses. It just didn't make any sense to me why my kids were so sick.

Around that time articles started appearing in the *Niagara Falls Gazette* that talked about hazardous waste in dump sites all across the city of Niagara Falls. Then I read one article that talked about a dump next to the Ninety-ninth Street Elementary School, where my son attended kindergarten. In this article they listed the chemicals that were buried there and what could result from exposure to these chemicals. I literally checked off every single one of my children's diseases and said to myself, "Oh, my God. It's not that I am an unlucky mother. My children are being poisoned." I couldn't believe that somebody would build a school next to a dump site.

I found out that other people were going through the same thing I was. One person had a thirteen-year-old daughter who had to have a hysterectomy due to cancer. There were eight other epileptics living in houses that practically encircled ours. And it wasn't just children who were sick; adults were getting sick as well. People would walk me down to their basement and show me orange goo coming up from their sump pumps. In some homes the chemical smell was so strong that it was like walking into a gas station.

In the spring of 1978 the state department of health came in and did some tests around Love Canal. And then they denied, denied, denied, and denied from that point on. They told the people living closest to the canal, "Don't go in your basement. Don't eat out of your garden. Don't do this, don't do that, but it's perfectly safe to live at Love Canal." We did our own house survey. And we found that 56 percent of the children at Love Canal were born with birth defects. And that included three ears, double rows of teeth, extra fingers, extra toes, or mentally retarded.

Before Love Canal, I believed that if you had a problem, you could just go to your elected officials and they would fix it. I now know that that's not true. The state didn't do anything until we forced it to. Eventually nine hundred families were evacuated from Love Canal. But what outraged me the most was that a state health department knew people were sick, knew people were dying, and decided to do nothing about it.

There were many things that worried Americans in the 1970s: rising oil prices, high unemployment, toxic waste, untrustworthy government, a crumbling international reputation, and the breakdown of traditional gender roles. But in 1979 one unfolding drama in a Middle East nation closed out the decade with a new and ferocious attack on American pride.

Once again, Cold War fears had led America to become involved in the affairs of a Third World country. Iran, which was a southern neighbor of the Soviet Union, was considered strategically important because it was so rich in the oil that America needed. For years the United States had supported the shah of Iran as a way of maintaining its influence there. But, as in South Vietnam, a government that was opposed to Communism proved to be anything but democratic.

Within Iran, anger at America's interference had been growing steadily. As Muslims, its people resented the pressure to give up their traditions and embrace American materialism. They had been listening to the words of an exiled Muslim cleric, Ayatollah Khomeini. Khomeini taught the lessons of the Shari'a, the seventh-century Islamic law, and

Millions of ecstatic Shiite Muslims took to the streets to celebrate the Ayatollah Khomeini's return from exile in February 1979. The seventy-six-year-old religious leader promised to create the nation's first "government of God."

denounced the modernization forced on Iran by the shah. In early 1979 the shah was overthrown in an Islamic revolution that brought Khomeini to power.

The revolution in Iran was a rejection of much that the United States stood for. The Ayatollah Khomeini and the religious leaders now in power in Iran saw American culture as lacking moral fiber, a civilization that had grown fat and weak. And with Iran's oil fields in the grip of a hostile power, prices rapidly rose, impressing upon people just how dependent the United States was on foreign oil. But it wasn't until later in the year that the Iranian revolution became a personal issue for most Americans.

On November 4, Iranian students loyal to Khomeini cut the chains on the gates of the American embassy in the capital city of Teheran. They stormed past marine guards and took sixty-six members of the embassy staff hostage. They demanded the return to Iran of the shah, who was in New York City undergoing cancer treatment.

With mounting horror, Americans watched the evening news to see what would happen. American hostages were paraded blindfolded in front of television cameras by students who burned American flags and shouted "Death to America!" Calling the United States "the Great Satan," they declared that Americans were their mortal enemies.

President Jimmy Carter seemed helpless to end the crisis. Khomeini considered himself a messenger from God and refused to negotiate. Military threats wouldn't work, for the militant Islamic revolutionaries were willing to die for their cause. "Why should we be afraid?" asked a defiant Khomeini. "We consider martyrdom a great honor." For 444 days Americans waited, tying yellow ribbons on trees across the nation as a symbol that the hostages were not forgotten.

"All Western governments are just thieves. Nothing but evil comes from them."

—*Ayatollah Khomeini*

Barry Rosen, born in 1944, was one of the hostages who endured the long ordeal.

In the months before the shah left Iran you could see a tremendous deterioration of the government's power. The Iranian people were up in arms. Every night I would hear shouting on the rooftops, "*Allah hu akbar! Marg bar shah!* God is great, down with the shah!" I would walk around and then report what was going on back to the United States embassy. Sometimes, of course, I'd get rifle butts stuck in my back and people would tell me to move on. But I could feel it, sense it, smell it— the regime was falling. The day the shah finally left was one of the most potent and vivid days imaginable. It's difficult to fully understand just how much the Iranian people hated him. And then when Khomeini returned, ecstatic crowds carried him through the streets of Teheran. It was as if the Messiah had landed.

To me, November 4, 1979, seemed like just an ordinary gray, rainy Sunday in Teheran. I was at work at ten o'clock that morning. All of a sudden I heard marching sounds coming from the main avenue in Teheran. I looked out my window and saw Iranian students climbing the gates and jumping over the walls of the embassy. They had photographs of Khomeini on their chest and they were yelling, "*Marg bar*

Amrika! Death to America!" The students banged on my door, and then came storming in with clubs and some small arms.

We were taken to a library in the embassy, where the hostage takers interrogated me and my Iranian coworkers. They eventually let all the Iranians go. I had become good friends with the Iranians in my office, and I cried because I was happy that they were being let go. They cried because they were sure that I was going to be executed. I was tied up and blindfolded and then led out of the library into the courtyard, raindrops hitting me on the head. That's when I started to think about my family, and I began to wonder, "Will I live through the rest of the night?"

My captors dragged me into the cook's quarters, where they took off my shoes and started searching them, trying to tear the heels apart. They thought that I had some secret message machine in the heels of my shoes. They were convinced that we were all CIA agents and would do anything to escape. That's why they tied us up day in and day out.

One of the most wrenching moments in my captivity was when the students tried to get me to sign a letter indicating my crimes against Iran. This young man held an automatic weapon to my head and started to count down from ten to one. It was then that I realized that I would do anything to survive. I wanted to be a good American, and I didn't want to sign something that would state that I was not, but I knew that the best thing to do to survive was to sign whatever needed to be signed, so I did.

Above: Barry Rosen being examined before his release from captivity in Iran. Below: Rosen (with beard, waving) and the other former hostages, with their families, at Andrews Air Force Base, Washington, D.C., 1981.

The worst pain of it all was brought on by the length of captivity. Not the boredom, but the fear that grows inside of you over a long period of time. The fear of death. A fear that creeps into the subconscious. That, and just not being able to go outside, to see a bird fly, or to take a walk. The physical cruelty, getting beaten up or being pushed around or being blindfolded, was less of a potent force than the lack of freedom.

There was no other alternative but to live. I spent several months sharing a room with a lieutenant colonel named Dave Roeder. He was a man who knew how to survive. He taught me to get up and exercise and to meet each day with purpose. We learned to make small things beautiful. For example, for whatever weird reason, the Iranians gave me the classifieds from the *Washington Post* boat section. Not great reading, but something. Dave actually knew something about boats, so he would describe the different types, and we would both lie down on the floor and we would take a trip on the Chesapeake Bay. Just escaping in our imaginations like that made life worthwhile.

One morning in January a guard came in and said, "Pack your bags. You're leaving." Just like that. Once again we were bound and blindfolded and then marched to a bus. We traveled on the bus for what seemed like an interminable amount of time. When it finally stopped, they ripped off my blindfold and pushed me out of the bus. I stumbled past this long line of Iranian guards who spat on me. I was just soaking wet from spit. But I saw this light and an arm waving toward me. It turned out to be the entrance of an Air Algiers plane, so I ran toward it.

It seemed so unreal. It was as if we were in another world altogether—very blurred, but once we realized we were free, also very beautiful.

Back in the United States we were greeted as heroes. We were so isolated that we didn't realize that we had become the center of the American news, that we had been their purpose for the last 444 days. In some ways, I think the people were celebrating what they believed was American power. But I honestly think that both countries lost. There was a lot of hate on both sides that didn't need to happen. I don't believe we were winners. I believe it was a period of great sadness.

The hostage crisis continued through the 1980 presidential campaign. Americans were exhausted by disappointment, turmoil, and embarrassment. They wanted to feel good about themselves again. And they elected as president a man who promised to let them do that and to bring the country back to a golden age. That man was Ronald Reagan. In his inaugural address in 1981 Reagan asked Americans to believe once again in their capacity for greatness. And as he spoke the weary hostages were being dragged into the night and pushed aboard an airplane bound for home. The long national nightmare was over.

Americans welcomed the hostages home in January 1981 and looked forward to what the new president, Ronald Reagan, promised would be "an era of national renewal."

11 New Morning
1981–1989

Americans entered the 1980s worn by the events of the previous decade. They longed for a fresh start, and they found it in a new, conservative approach to government. The leader of this conservative "revolution" was the new president, Ronald Reagan.

Ronald Reagan was the most influential president in forty years. Anger over high inflation and the Iranian hostage crisis had pushed Americans to vote President Carter out of office. Reagan, a former actor and governor of California, rallied the nation with nostalgic images of less complicated times. He called upon Americans to return to the values of hard work and self-reliance that had made their country great. To some, Reagan's foreign policy ideas sounded simplistic and extreme, and his economic policies seemed to blame the poor for their own problems. But his message of good feeling and self-confidence seemed to invigorate the nation.

Richard Viguerie, born in 1933, shared the enthusiasm many Americans felt about President Reagan.

The scene at the 1984 Republican National Convention, where Reagan was nominated for a second term.

Ronald Reagan was the epitome of America. He was an optimist and a "can-do" type of leader. He believed that today is great, but tomorrow's going to be better. In times of crisis, Reagan was able to reach out to the American people and put his arms around us and bring us together. He was always recognized as the "Great Communicator." The reason Ronald Reagan was such an effective speaker was because he had a message that resonated with America.

It was no accident that, literally a few minutes after Reagan became president, the hostages were freed. I think that if Carter had been reelected, those hostages would have been there throughout Carter's presidency, because Khomeini knew he had somebody that he could move around like a puppet on a string. But Ronald Reagan had sent a very clear message, which is the old New Hampshire state message—Don't Tread on Me. The Iranians weren't 100 percent sure of Ronald Reagan and they weren't gonna take any chances.

Ronald Reagan moved boldly and decisively. The major world leaders saw that they were dealing with a man of strength and that the rules had been changed from the Nixon-Ford-Carter days. They were now dealing with an administration that was going to stand up for its beliefs and its rights. Mr. Reagan had an agenda, and he knew where he was going.

In the suspicious eighties, much of Reagan's popularity came from his portrayal of himself as a Washington "outsider," which, of course, he was. And he achieved his legislative triumphs by playing more to the public, here at an outdoor market in Philadelphia, than to Congress.

Like Franklin Delano Roosevelt before him, Ronald Reagan was a master communicator. He made people feel that something was getting done. Unlike Roosevelt, however, Reagan did not see the power of the state as a positive tool to help society. He believed that oversize government programs had made people weak and dependent. Where Roosevelt had wanted to save people *with* government, Reagan wanted to save people *from* government.

The essence of Reagan's economic policy was the tax cut. His philosophy was that people who made money should be allowed to keep it. And if the rich had money to spend, it would eventually "trickle down" to the people who had less. This argument allowed him to cut funding for social programs that had been constructed to aid the poor.

At the same time that Reagan cut taxes, he also increased defense spending. His view of the Soviet Union was simple: It was an "evil empire" and must not be coddled. He dramatically enlarged America's supply of nuclear weapons. But with less money coming into the government from taxes and more money going into defense, the federal budget became seriously out of balance.

Nonetheless, the economy seemed to be on the mend. America's standing in international affairs, thanks to Reagan's tough, no-nonsense attitude toward the Soviets, was improving. But all was not rosy. Reagan's trickle-down theory had justified severe cuts in social spending, but the trickling was hard to see. Many people enjoyed the new prosperity, but at the bottom of the ladder, others were falling into deep trouble.

The Reverend Patrick Mahoney, born in 1954, saw a tragedy emerging from President Reagan's economic policies.

What was discouraging to me about President Reagan was that he was the first style-over-substance president. He had great style in front of the public up there, but he was lacking in substance. For example, he talked about church values, but he never went to church. He talked about family values, yet he had an incredibly dysfunctional family and his children didn't talk to him. He spoke out about drugs, but we saw cocaine wars in south Florida. He wanted to reduce government spending, yet the deficit skyrocketed. President Reagan introduced something very detrimental, and that is this photo-op kind of candidacy. It dumbed down the political debate and made everybody more interested in good sound bites and creative commercials than in real issues.

Also Reagan's economic policies made life very difficult for a lot of people. The theory behind Reaganomics was that the rising tide would lift up all the boats. If the already well-to-do started making more money, then it would trickle down to the less well-off and everyone would do better. But in reality that was not the case. I lived in Bristol, Connecticut, in the 1980s. And under Reagan, Bristol experienced this huge boom. I mean, it was great. Everyone was saying, "Aren't things wonderful? Aren't things just spectacular under President Reagan? He's our man. He's lowered interest rates. I'm making money hand over fist." But that was for people who owned property and who were already fairly well off. For people who didn't have money—for the poor—it was a horrible time. Property values in Bristol doubled or tripled, but so did the rents. And as the rents went up, the wages of the working class stayed the same, and suddenly many people couldn't afford to live in their own homes anymore. In Bristol, as in a lot of America, entire families found themselves without a home. These were not lazy people. They were not sluggards or substance abusers. They were committed, dedicated men and women who were trying to make a difference in their own life, and suddenly they couldn't afford a place to live.

So when I hear about the legacy of Mr. Reagan, and I hear of the good times of the Reagan years, I can say that I personally benefited— the value of my home more than tripled—but the same factors that allowed for me to make money turned out to be very hard on the working class. The trickle-down theory just stopped at those who already had money, and many of those who were already struggling to make ends meet were forced out into the streets. It was tragic.

For the poor, life was getting harder. Homelessness was on the rise. So were drug abuse and the crime that came with it. But the Reagan era encouraged many to distance themselves from these social problems. The social consciousness of the sixties and seventies now seemed to have faded, a victim of impatience, cynicism, and, for some, a firm belief that government programs rarely worked. At the top of the ladder of opportunity, some wealthy Americans spent their newly made money more freely and publicly on themselves.

Starting in 1982, more than a hundred thousand new millionaires were created each year, so many that the word *millionaire* lost its significance. Millionaire? Try billionaire. America was throwing itself into conspicuous consumption: big cars, mammoth houses, opulent dinners, and luxurious vacations. The panting pursuit of wealth was now acceptable, even admirable. "Greed is good," claimed a character in *Wall Street,* a movie that defined the times.

These people at a party in New York demonstrated the new dress code for success in the 1980s: jeans were out, tuxes in.

Chris Burke, born in 1958, experienced the excitement of easy money on Wall Street in the 1980s.

Burke in 1989.

In 1979 I was two years out of high school and working in a local bar in Manhasset, Long Island, a bedroom community for people who work in Manhattan. And probably about 80 percent of those people worked on Wall Street. A lot of these Wall Street guys were regulars at the bar and they were always saying things like "What are you doing here? Come on down and work on Wall Street with us. You have what it takes." They made it all seem very glamorous, and I was lured in. In 1980 I went down to work on the floor of the New York Stock Exchange. Wall Street was just heading into a big upswing, so things were pretty exciting down there. Suddenly there I was, a twenty-year-old kid with a high-school education, and I was starting out at $40,000 a year.

I was a clerk for a specialist house that traded in about eighty big stocks like TWA, Delta Air Lines, things like that. I stood behind a counter, and outside the counter was the broker I worked for. Surrounding him were ten to twenty guys just screaming and yelling, buying and selling. And I'd have to record all of these orders. Hectic isn't the word. It was overwhelming. We ripped our hair out of our head for the entire day every day.

When the bell rang in the afternoon, we cleaned up, and then it was cocktail time. I went out every night with the guys that I worked with and our immediate bosses. And we never spent a penny. Everything was on an expense account. We would go to this same restaurant a couple of blocks from the stock exchange. There'd be about fifteen guys. And we'd head right for the bar and just start pounding drinks. Then we'd sit down at the table. And we'd never even see a menu; the food would just start to come out, and it seemed like it would never end. It was obscene. Platters and platters of food and bottles and bottles of wine. We never thought once about what anything cost. Not at all. Just like at the exchange, it was all funny money. Never your money. So you didn't think about it.

In 1982 I switched over to the government bond market. By the mid-1980s the government bond market was booming and I was making good money with a nice bonus every year. I bought a new house, new cars, new clothes, and I became so entrenched in the lifestyle that I was spending tons of money. When your whole life revolves around money, pretty soon your value judgments come into question. My buddies and I would literally be stepping over homeless people on our way to work, and we'd snicker about it. We certainly didn't want to get our shoes scuffed up by their burlap pants. "Get a job" was our attitude.

Wall Street in the 1980s was like nowhere else on this planet. It was a culture of greed and backstabbing and partying. Your best buddy is the one who's gonna stab you in the back tomorrow if it means some more greenbacks in his pocket. It wasn't a good way to live, but it was the only way I knew.

Not since the Roaring Twenties had there been such a culture of money and glitz in America. Yet the new rich were making money differently than their predecessors. A thriving 1920s capitalist might have amassed a fortune building automobiles, while a successful 1950s businessman might have thought up new ways to sell products. In the 1980s millionaires were often lawyers and investment bankers who got rich not by *building* or *selling* anything, but by shifting ownership of companies, by refinancing companies, by making deals. It was all done on paper, and to many it all felt a little unreal.

Looking back, experts would agree that this was a streamlining that American business desperately needed. Still, all this wheeling and dealing, which seemed so abstract, affected the jobs—and the lives—of real people. Sometimes it meant closing factories in the United States and reopening them in places such as Thailand or Mexico. Why should management pay union workers in Ohio or Michigan high wages when they could pay a tenth of that to someone in the Third World? Sometimes it meant buying out local family-owned businesses to break them apart and sell each part.

Whole towns suffered dramatically from this rampage of mergers, acquisitions, and relocations. Communities that had relied on local factories for jobs now found themselves without any source of employment. Increasingly, people could not find new jobs. A new underclass emerged. Most visible were the homeless, people living on the street, whose desperate lives seemed to put the lie to claims that the country was back on its feet. The homeless problem was a complicated one, caused in part by Reagan's welfare cuts, by an inner-city drug epidemic, by a shortage of affordable housing, and by the decline of marriage, which left more people struggling to get by on their own.

A powerful new form of cocaine, called "crack," swept through American cities in the 1980s. Darryl McDaniels, born in 1964, is "DMC" of the rap group Run-DMC. He saw the damage crack did to his community.

I grew up on the tree-lined streets of Hollis, Queens, in New York. Most of the parents in my neighborhood were hardworking people with nine-to-five jobs. You knew everybody's parents, every kid, every uncle, the name of every dog and cat on the block, and the TV repairman, the oil man, and the mailman. Hollis was really a close-knit middle-class community. Almost every Saturday in the summer, the whole neighborhood would come into the park, and a DJ would be there, and the rappers and the emcees from the neighborhood would come on the set and we'd rap and we'd party and we'd DJ and we'd play music and have fun until the police came and said, "Somebody called the cops on y'all. Y'all gotta go home."

In the early eighties I started noticing neighborhood businesses were closing down. Our favorite candy store and deli, where we'd go as kids to read comic books, closed. The supermarket kept closing and reopening under a new name. The crime level was going up a little bit. People, particularly older people and well-educated people, started moving out of Queens, too. Even when we'd DJ in the park, fewer and fewer people were coming.

So the neighborhood was already starting to go downhill when I left to do a tour from 1984 to 1986. My rap group, Run-DMC, had made it big with our first single. Everywhere we went on tour, and especially in the South, people were talking about this new drug called crack. And we'd see crack fiends on the road and we could see how it hooked people. But we didn't realize crack had penetrated so deep into our own neighborhood.

I came off the tour in 1986 and went home to Hollis. I remember walking around and noticing how desolate everything had become. I looked at the playground, and the bleachers were gone. All the signs were ripped off, and there were holes in the fence and glass and rubbish and garbage all through it. The place looked like a war zone.

I was walking around one afternoon when I heard a woman say, "Darryl!" I turned around and I couldn't figure out who this person was. "It's me," she said. She said her name, and I realized she was my good friend's sister. She may as well have pulled out a gun and shot me, I was so stunned. It was obvious she was using crack, but she was trying to hold a regular conversation as if nothing was wrong. How was I supposed to react when she looked like she weighed about ten pounds? She had lost all her teeth and her clothes were dirty. I had held her as a baby. But now to see her like that, it was really scary.

Everyone's sister seemed to be getting addicted to crack. But when I started hearing about people's mothers, I just couldn't believe it. You'd look at the babies and wonder why they were like that. And it was because the parents were cracked out. I never knew that a drug could have such an impact on a community or a society. Every week something happened, whether it was somebody getting killed or arrested or dying. It was as if the whole neighborhood started disappearing. It became like a ghost town.

At the time everything in the neighborhood was falling apart, a lot of billboards saying Say No to Drugs were going up. I remember thinking how much money it cost to put up those signs each week. To me, they were spending money on the wrong thing. I knew perfectly well that people weren't gonna look at a sign like that and say, "All right, I'm gonna just say no to drugs." I found out that just telling people not to do drugs doesn't work. Besides, that saying came a little bit too late. Don't you think, Mr. Reagan?

McDaniels, in center at top, with his mother, left, and a friend; above, the family home in Hollis, Queens.

As the gap between the haves and the have-nots got wider, America sometimes felt like a colder, crueler place. Beneath the glitzy surface ran a chilling current of fear. There was fear of crime, certainly, but also fear of failure, of not "making it" in the rush for riches. The nuclear arms race between the United States and the Soviet Union had intensified, bringing back fears of nuclear devastation. In 1986 an explosion destroyed the nuclear reactor at the Chernobyl power plant in the Soviet Union. A radioactive cloud spread for miles, contaminating the region's soil, crops, and livestock and renewing fears of a nuclear power plant accident in the United States.

The explosion of the space shuttle set back hopes for a revival of the American space program, which had been floundering since Apollo XI landed the first man on the moon in 1969. "More than the *Challenger* exploded in the blue sky over the Atlantic Ocean," wrote *New York Times* science correspondent John Noble Wilford. "We [were] left full of doubts . . . about the very fundamentals of our national space policy."

"We will never forget them nor the last time we saw them this morning as they prepared for their journey and waved goodbye and 'slipped the surly bonds of earth to touch the face of God.'"

—President Reagan,
addressing the nation

But the most paralyzing event of the decade happened in Florida on January 28, 1986. The space shuttle *Challenger* was ready for launch, and it was carrying a very special passenger. Christa McAuliffe, a social studies teacher from Concord, New Hampshire, was about to become the first private citizen in space. Her flight would mark the beginning of a new age of civilian space travel, in which space would be open to everyone. NASA planned to have McAuliffe teach two fifteen-minute classes from the space shuttle, which would be beamed by television to millions of students across America.

It was unusually cold at Cape Canaveral that morning, but not cold enough to cancel the flight. The liftoff seemed to go smoothly, but seventy-three seconds later *Challenger* erupted into a fiery red ball. The space shuttle had exploded, killing everyone on board. For the nation's schoolchildren, it was the end of a dream.

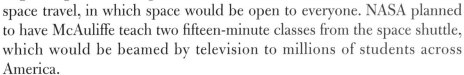

Malcolm McConnell, born in 1939, was at Cape Canaveral to cover the *Challenger* launch for *Reader's Digest.*

Before I witnessed my first shuttle launch, NASA officials escorted several other reporters and me down to the launchpad to see the shuttle up close. I felt like an ant walking around a stepladder. I felt awed and dwarfed by this huge machine. When you're three miles away in the press grandstand and that huge assembly lights itself on fire and takes off, the feeling is overpowering. There is a bright flash from the solid rocket boosters, and then you see an almost volcanic burst of steam from the main engines. Immediately after the flash this huge vehicle begins to rise away, and it's all silent. A second or two later you are literally assailed by the shock waves. The press grandstand has sort of a tin metal roof that begins to bounce up and down, and your chest is hit by this cacophonous pounding. The first time I saw it, I was virtually speechless. I felt proud that my country, my civilization, had put together this wonderful machine which was so powerful, so complex.

By the mid-1980s NASA had pretty well convinced most of the world not only that it could run the space shuttle economically, but that

Above: The astronauts on the morning of their fateful mission. Below: McConnell on assignment at the Kennedy Space Center.

the shuttle could actually pay for itself on a commercial basis. NASA wanted to prove that the shuttle was so safe that even an ordinary person could ride into space. So Christa McAuliffe, a high-school social studies teacher from New Hampshire, was to encourage an interest in space for millions of schoolchildren.

The morning the *Challenger* was launched, very few of us who had covered the space shuttle program thought it was going to fly that day. It was bitterly cold. One reporter pointed up at one of the monitors and said, "Look at the ice." The launch tower looked like a frozen waterfall. But we got our coffee and we sat around and waited. As it got light, the launch control people began saying, "Well, it's looking better and better." NASA had somehow pulled this thing off. And then the countdown reached five, four, three, two, one, and that glare lit up from the solid rocket boosters. I had a sense of great pleasure and satisfaction.

As the shuttle cleared the tower and the first shock waves of sound began to pound the press grandstand, I had my first sense of foreboding. Because the air was so cold and dense, the pounding sound was much louder than I'd ever experienced. I thought, "That does not sound right." But I quickly shrugged it off as the shuttle rose. All of us on the grandstand were screaming our heads off, yelling, "Go! Go!" Any sense of professional composure was lost; we were all caught up in the euphoria of the moment.

The pillar of smoke with the little tiny shuttle had turned to the degree so we could no longer see the shuttle itself. We could just see the rippling cloud of white and orange smoke coming back toward us. From our vantage point, it still looked like a normal flight. Then there was silence. For a long time. I would say ten seconds, which is a long time during a launch. And we began looking around at each other. And then the voice came over the loudspeakers. In a very dry, almost emotionless voice, "Obviously a major malfunction. We have no downlink. . . ." And then there was a pause. "The flight dynamics officer reports that the vehicle has exploded." I felt this terrible cold drenching doom pouring over me. I could almost feel ice water pouring down over my head and chilling me deep into myself. Looking around me, I saw people who had been standing and cheering a moment before sink back down to their benches. Many people put their hands over their faces as if to blot out the sight. Other people put their hands to their throats, as if they themselves were being physically assaulted. One of my colleagues looked at me and asked, "What's happened? Where are they?" I said, "They're dead. We've lost them, God bless them." And she got angry. She kind of pushed me and said, "Stop kidding. What happened? Where are they?" And I said, "They're dead. They're dead." And at that moment we looked up again, and the pieces of the *Challenger* began tumbling out of that pillar of smoke. That massive vehicle had been shredded into tiny little pieces that were falling like confetti out of the sky.

Fear was also stalking America in the form of a new and deadly dis-ease. For years medical science had been scoring one success after another. Its achievements promised to make human life better than ever. Then came the AIDS epidemic. AIDS stands for "acquired immunode-ficiency syndrome." First detected in the early 1980s, it was believed to be a "gay disease." Homosexual men were being struck down by a mys-terious onslaught of unusual infections that their bodies could not fight off. Before long, AIDS was also diagnosed in intravenous drug users, prostitutes, hemophiliacs, and some immigrants from Haiti and Africa. Because there was no clear understanding of what this deadly disease was, how it spread, or how to treat it, fear and hysteria quickly swept much of the nation.

For more than a decade, activists had been struggling for gay rights, and they had made considerable progress. But the arrival of AIDS brought a backlash against the gay community. Some conservative critics went so far as to claim that AIDS was God's revenge against "immoral" people. All the finger-pointing and name-calling often hid the sad fact that real people were dying, including babies who had gotten AIDS from their infected mothers. By the late 1980s the death toll was climbing toward a hundred thousand, and just about everyone in America knew someone whose life had been affected by the disease.

The AIDS quilt is made up of three-by-six-foot panels, each designed by a friend or relative to honor a person who died of AIDS. When all the panels are sewn together, the quilt is the size of a football field. Here a girl studies a panel at a Washington, D.C., showing.

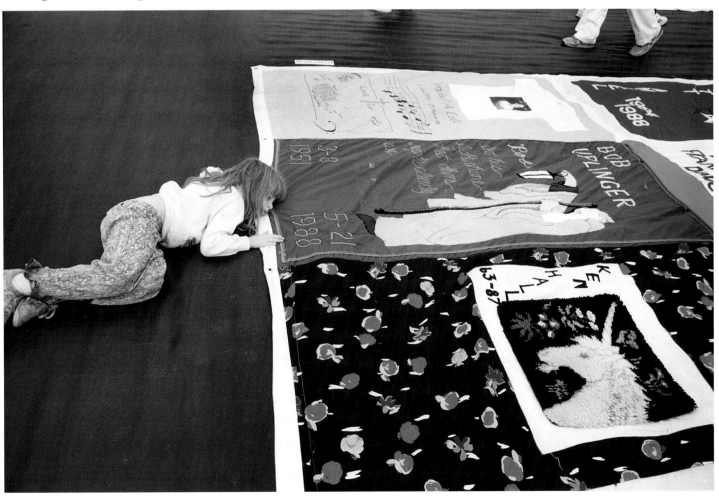

Bruce Woods Patterson, born in 1953, saw the devastating effect of AIDS on the gay community in New York City and pitched in to help.

Patterson, above, in the mid-eighties; below, the GMHC hot line office.

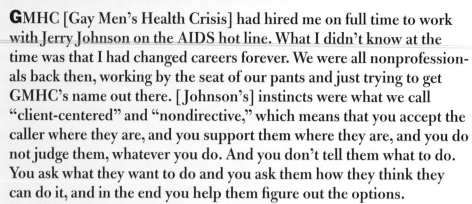

GMHC [Gay Men's Health Crisis] had hired me on full time to work with Jerry Johnson on the AIDS hot line. What I didn't know at the time was that I had changed careers forever. We were all nonprofessionals back then, working by the seat of our pants and just trying to get GMHC's name out there. [Johnson's] instincts were what we call "client-centered" and "nondirective," which means that you accept the caller where they are, and you support them where they are, and you do not judge them, whatever you do. And you don't tell them what to do. You ask what they want to do and you ask them how they think they can do it, and in the end you help them figure out the options.

One of the great challenges of a hot line is that you get one chance to make a difference in the lives of the callers. In our case, we had to do that in under ten minutes, the prescribed time limit on most calls, and you have to maintain your anonymity, another requisite. It's really the only way to stay emotionally distant from the caller, although there are calls I carry around with me to this day. People called who were bed-bound, crying and sad with no hope. They'd start talking about how they used to be young and beautiful and had a future and how they had lost their identity, independence, and pride. A lot of people called and said, "I'm not afraid of death. It's getting there that scares me." Being stripped of all your dignity and losing half your body weight and having friends turn away just because they're in such pain they can't stand to see you that way is just horrible.

The level of ignorance and homophobia from some of the callers was just amazing. And the indifference was overwhelming. When I first started, prank callers would just say, "All you faggots should die!" *Click.* Thank you for sharing. It was bad enough all these people were dying and there was nothing that we could do about it, and then you've got people hating you for being sick or for helping sick people. Of course, you wanted badly to be able to say, "Where's your compassion? Who do you think you are? What's wrong with loving someone?"

My friends and I often talk about the community of infected and affected people. I am HIV-negative but have been affected deeply. We're all living with AIDS. I often wonder why I have been so lucky when so many of my friends and colleagues have died of AIDS. When I look back at the pictures of the early days at GMHC, it hits me every time that the majority of the people in them are no longer living. In the end, I have to be philosophical about it. I guess my job is to be there for everyone else. The best thing that I can do is just stay HIV-negative.

Throughout the 1980s, President Reagan maintained an iron-hard posture toward Communism. And this posture led to yet another government scandal. Nicaragua, a country in Central America, was led by a Communist government. Reagan wanted to help the "contra" rebels, who were fighting a guerrilla war against the government, but Congress had passed a law banning military aid to the contras. In a bizarre scheme to sidestep the law, American ammunition, spare parts for tanks, jet fighters, and missiles were sold to Iran to make money to fund the contra rebels.

Lieutenant Colonel Oliver North ran the secret operation that eventually became known to the country as "Iran-contra." A decorated veteran of the Vietnam War, North was a patriot with an unshakable loyalty to the president. In testimony before Congress, North said that he believed he had acted "with authority from the president" in carrying out illegal operations in Central America and the Middle East. For America to be negotiating with the Ayatollah Khomeini's government was astonishing enough. But for illegal weapons sales to be linked to the White House was shocking. Just as they had during Watergate a decade earlier, Americans now asked, "What did the president know and when did he know it?" Iran-contra suggested one of two possibilities: Either the president himself was involved in an illegal international operation, or else he was a weak leader who did not know what was going on under his own nose. Neither possibility was flattering to the president who had promised a return to America's glory days.

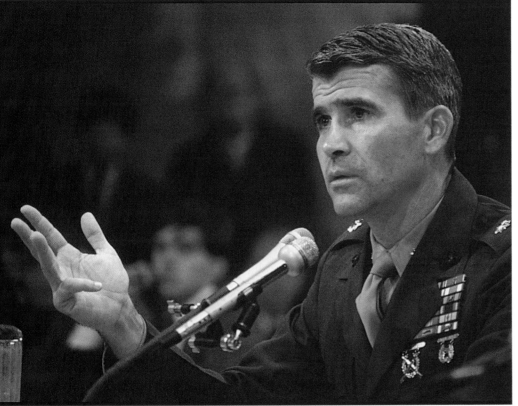

The Iran-contra affair did temporary damage to Ronald Reagan's popularity, for its very deviousness contradicted the essence of his appeal. Said one observer: "[It was] like suddenly discovering that John Wayne had secretly been selling liquor and firearms to the Indians." Here Lieutenant Colonel Oliver North testifies before Congress.

As Americans faced their problems at home and abroad, it was com- forting to know that at least the economy was still booming. That changed dramatically on October 19, 1987, Black Monday, when the stock market crashed. In one day the market lost 508 points, or 22.6 percent of its value—approximately $500 billion, an amount equivalent to the gross national product of France. Black Monday reminded Americans of the stock market crash of 1929. But what really frightened them was the memory of what had followed—the miserable years of the Great Depression. For the next year, people watched and waited, but the depression never came. Slowly the market bounced back, and Americans breathed a sigh of relief.

In spite of—or perhaps because of—President Reagan's hard-line policy toward the Soviet Union and the renewed nuclear arms race, Communism was beginning to crack. In the late 1980s the Soviet Union was going through its most dramatic change since the 1917 revolution. Under the leadership of fifty-four-year-old Mikhail Gorbachev, who came to power in 1985, the Cold War began to thaw.

Even the crusty old members of the Politburo (the Soviet Congress) knew that their country had reached rock bottom. Industrial output was pitiful. Alcoholism was rampant. Workers were absent from their jobs much of the time. Housing shortages forced nearly a quarter of city residents to share bathrooms and kitchens. Food was scarce. Something drastic had to be done.

Gorbachev did not set out to bring an end to Communism in Russia. On the contrary, he saw himself as saving the Communist state. He started a three-part program to revitalize his ailing nation: *glasnost* (openness), *perestroika* (restructuring), and *demokratizatsiya* (democratization). And he presented this program not as a break with Soviet tradition, but as a way of reconnecting to the original principles of Lenin, the founder of the Soviet state.

It wasn't only in the Soviet Union that Communism was teetering. In Poland, a trade union called Solidarity had begun to challenge the Communist government in 1980. Although Solidarity had been shut down by the authorities in 1981, it still fought secretly for greater freedom in Poland. But in the late 1980s the world's attention was riveted on Mikhail Gorbachev. Within the Soviet Union itself, the excitement was building. Newspaper articles revealed corruption and mismanagement. Elections— real elections—were held. People began to talk openly about the past and the terrible things that had happened during Stalin's brutal regime. The truth about their own history had been forbidden to the Russian people. Gorbachev promised that there would be an end to secrecy and deception, the government's strongest weapons against its own people.

The anger that poured forth from the Soviet people after so many years of forced silence was palpable. There were even calls for a public trial of Stalin. As one writer observed, "Had there not been a trial at Nuremberg, Nazi atrocities at Auschwitz and Buchenwald might have been denied by later generations." Here a woman holds a picture of her father, a victim of "the Great Terror."

Marina Goldovskaya, born in 1941, is a filmmaker who took part in the new openness of the Gorbachev years.

In the mid-eighties I was working at the central television station in Moscow, making television programs on politics, on literature, art, social life, public affairs. This took half of my year, and the other half of the year I was a filmmaker for Ekram, a special film studio within the television station. All media in the USSR was heavily censored, and television was probably the most censored of them all. Everything we did was controlled by our administration. Every year we had to submit several proposals for the films for the next year. All of the proposals and concepts had to go through what was known as the "council of editors."

In early 1985 I submitted a proposal for a documentary film version of a book called *At My Mother's,* by Anatoly Streliany. He was a talented writer with independent ideas and a point of view that was not in line with the Communist Party. Because of his views he had a difficult time getting his works published. But this particular book was not overtly political. It described a visit he made to his mother's home in the village he grew up in, and it gave a very interesting portrait of the village. We got this proposal through all the censors, and it was put into the plan for 1986.

Even before we started working on *At My Mother's,* we got a sense that somehow things were changing. For a long time it had seemed as if something just had to change, because the whole country was stagnating. For so many years, the people who had ruled our country were old and outdated. We were so ashamed when we saw these old faces reading their speeches. They were not able to even read them properly, they were so old.

Goldovskaya filming in Moscow in the late 1980s.

When Streliany and I started working on this film, I thought that we could take advantage of the changing atmosphere to do something more useful, more interesting. Something that could somehow help to push this process of change. So instead of making a documentary film based on his book, we decided to make a film about farmers and the struggle between the individual and the communal. We knew that our new idea would never be approved by the censors, but we decided to go ahead and make it anyway. We just acted as if we were still making a film based on our original approved proposal.

We traveled around talking to farmers and doing research, and we ended up in this little village called Ust-Vanga. And there I met this farmer named Nikolai Sivkov, who had been a member of the local collective farm but who had left in order to start his own little farm,

Mikhail Gorbachev discarded the stereotypical mask of a Soviet leader: He actually smiled. And once it became clear that his charm was not some new Soviet ploy, windows all over the East flew open. Here Communism's heroic reformer arrives to a hearty welcome in Prague, where the last big Soviet appearance had been the tanks that crushed the reform movement of 1968.

belonging to him and his family. From the minute I met Sivkov, I understood that he would be a perfect character for a film. He was eloquent. He was witty. He was biting. In him, you could see all the controversy of our system. This man, who only had about two years of education, stood before the camera and talked about the advantages of private property and the inefficiencies of the collective, and how the Soviet farming system was preventing him from succeeding. The story of this man and his little farm was the perfect metaphor for the evils of the Soviet system. As I was shooting, I became so afraid. I understood that this could be the end of my career. The things that he was saying would never be shown on television. You just couldn't attack the collective like that. It was impossible. I was scared to death, but at the same time, I didn't have the strength to say to myself, no.

By the time I finished the film, which I called *Archamgelskiy Mujik,* which roughly translates to *A Real Peasant from Archamgelskiy,* Gorbachev had been in power for about a year, and he was such an inspiration for all of us. He was like fresh air. He was young, brave, and brighter than anybody else. It was something completely new to us; suddenly there was a lot of hope. We were all absolutely euphoric about Gorbachev. We thought that a new time was coming. Finally it seemed that people would stop telling lies. We were fed up with the lies we read in the newspaper. Everything we read was all fake, all lies. And everybody understood it, but nothing could be done. And suddenly there was somebody, Gorbachev.

When he started talking about *glasnost,* "openness," it was exciting. But change came very slowly at first, step by step. And while we were excited by everything, it was a very unsure time. Gorbachev still had a lot of opposition on the Politburo; there were still many of the old rulers around. So it was in this environment that we presented our film to a consultant from the Central Committee of the party. He was one of the members who was behind Gorbachev and who was ready for change, so he decided to take a chance and approve the broadcast of the film.

Archamgelskiy Mujik aired on a Thursday night. The next day the whole country was talking about it—in the buses, on the subway, in classrooms. I became famous in one minute. The television station wanted to repeat the film two weeks later, but suddenly there came an order to stop the broadcast. And the film was banned. Ultimately, because of the new policy of *glasnost,* they decided to air the film again. The fact that this film survived was a sure sign that Gorbachev was winning against the old guard. The feeling that we all had was that now we can start building a new life without lies and with good intentions. We felt that everything would go very quickly in the right direction, that the new life was very close. It took Gorbachev to make the first step, then everyone else just started to push the train.

The Chinese students crowding Tiananmen Square had been inspired by plans for Gorbachev to visit Beijing, which they hoped would cast a negative light on their own nation's leadership. But by the time the Soviet leader arrived in mid-May, his visit had been overshadowed by the plight of thousands of student hunger strikers. On June 4, 1989, the Chinese government crushed their brave protest with troops and tanks.

Poland	10 Years
Hungary	10 Months
East Germany	10 Weeks
Czechoslovakia	10 Days
Romania	10 Hours

—A sign in Prague, describing how long each anti-Communist rebellion took to oust the ruling government

In 1989 life in the Communist countries of Europe was transformed. No one, maybe not even Gorbachev himself, quite knew what he had started. Once reforms began, they took on a life of their own. When Gorbachev announced that the Soviet Union would no longer interfere with the governments of the eastern European countries, the threat of brute force that had kept the Communist regimes in power turned hollow. Poland, East Germany, Czechoslovakia, Bulgaria, Hungary, and Romania overthrew their Communist leaders. Even in China, students began protesting for democracy, although the Chinese government put down the uprising.

For Americans, it was amazing to watch Europe's post–World War II order fall before their eyes. And it wasn't the force of atomic bombs or the threats of a new tyrant that toppled these governments, but the power of an idea: liberty. Was it really possible that the Cold War was ending at last?

There were many heroes of the new times: Gorbachev, of course, and for many Reagan was a hero, too. For even though he was no longer president, many people believed it was Reagan's nuclear arms buildup that had forced Gorbachev to realize that Russia could not keep up and had to change. In Poland, the head of the Solidarity union, Lech Walesa, had never given up the fight for freedom. And in Czechoslovakia, the writer Vaclav Havel had stood up to the Communist authorities, and had stood for justice and truth, since the Prague Spring of 1968.

The Iron Curtain that had divided Europe for so long was coming down. But the most dramatic event of this momentous era came in Berlin. Since 1961 the Berlin Wall had separated West Berlin from East Berlin, and many had died trying to cross it in desperate attempts to escape from East Germany. In 1989, with Communism vanishing like smoke around them, East Berliners marched to the wall shouting, *"Tor auf!* Open the gate!"* The most hated symbol of Communism still separated Germans from each other. On the other side, West Berliners also crowded to the wall, wild with expectation.

Then, while guards put down their rifles, East Berliners climbed over the wall, jumping into the open arms of the West Berliners below. "The wall is gone, the wall is gone," people chanted happily. In a surge of joy, Berliners on both sides began pounding at it with hammers and chisels and pickaxes, turning the terrible wall into a pile of souvenir rocks. Everyone was giddy with excitement, with relief, with hope. The Cold War was over.

"This one's for my mother, [and] this one's for Aunt Frieda. . . ."

—*Woman striking blows at the crumbling Berlin Wall, November 1989, which she declared had "destroyed my family"*

Members of West Germany's environmentally conscious Green Party recommended "the breaking off of the work of breaking [the wall's] stone" until "orderly waste management" could be administered. But their appeals were pointless. No one wanted to wait for the "system," of all things, to tear down this wall.

12 Machine Dreams
1989–1999

Left: The century ended much the way it had started, with people caught up in a whirlwind over the promise of technology. Here a photographer portrayed family life in the high-tech nineties: Mom holding a laptop computer and, along with her child, in the grip of the fantasy environment provided by virtual-reality goggles.

The end of the Cold War brought a new era of world capitalism that was inspired by America, if not led by it. When McDonald's (or, in Chinese, Mai Dan Lau) opened in Beijing in 1992, a record 28,500 customers lined up. By 1998 there were nearly two hundred McDonald's throughout China, inspiring an Americanization of some local customs, among them clean rest rooms and waiting in line.

In the final decade of the twentieth century the new, emerging world felt strangely different. The Cold War had defined so much of Western life for so long that it seemed as though a crippling lifelong pain had finally disappeared, and now it was time to learn how to walk all over again. But where, exactly, was the world headed?

In Europe the collapse of Communism was followed by puzzling questions. Could West Germany absorb East Germany and still remain stable? And if it did, would a unified Germany once again threaten world peace? In Eastern Europe the disappearance of powerful Communist governments brought age-old conflicts to the surface. Yugoslavia was split into warring ethnic groups. Czechoslovakia had broken apart into two states, the Czech Republic and Slovakia. And the Soviet Union had ceased to exist, bringing a handful of newly independent countries into the world. Would all these changes lead to more conflict?

Yet even as these changes shook Europe, there were many signs that democracy and capitalism were uniting the world. For the first time in fifty years the countries of eastern Europe were holding real elections. In places as far away as South Africa, democracy was triumphing. There black citizens were allowed to vote for the first time in 1994. They immediately elected as president Nelson Mandela, a man who had been in captivity for twenty-seven years for his pursuit of black equality.

Capitalism was taking hold in so many countries that a single enormous global marketplace was rapidly emerging. And this new capitalism had a distinctly American style, creating what one historian called "McWorld." As the Internet brought the world closer together, people wondered how this newly linked globe would coexist with the old hatreds that still pitted one ethnic group against another. Would the new technology—and the "global village" it was creating—be enough to bring a new age of world peace?

In the summer of 1990 a conflict erupted in the Persian Gulf that demonstrated what President George Bush called the "new world order." On August 2 Iraq invaded the tiny country of Kuwait, which had large reserves of oil. The United Nations ordered Iraq's leader, Saddam Hussein, to withdraw his troops from Kuwait, but he steadfastly refused. By early 1991 more than two dozen allied nations gathered troops for an invasion of Iraq. Called "Desert Storm," the invasion was quickly successful. In just over forty days Iraq was driven out of Kuwait.

In a clear sign of the changing times, the Soviet Union joined the United States in its attack on Iraq. It was the first time since World War II that Americans and Soviets had fought on the same side. And the two nations fought together in a new role, as a kind of international police force countering acts of raw aggression. But just as important as the Gulf War's new alliance and new purpose was the way the war was fought. Both of the century's world wars had used increasingly destructive technology. Now, with satellites mapping the world and computer-guided bombs that could hit military targets with pinpoint precision, it seemed possible that war could become *less* destructive.

Against a background of hundreds of Kuwaiti oil wells set ablaze by the Iraqis, a group of U.S. soldiers races toward Kuwait City. Desert Storm was mounted for moral purposes—President Bush went so far as to compare Iraq's Saddam Hussein to Hitler—but economics was a driving force, too. Western oil prices depended on a free Kuwait.

Mark Fox, born in 1956, led four major air wing strikes and flew eighteen combat missions during Desert Storm.

Lieutenant Commander Mark Fox in the cockpit, 1991.

When I was a teenager, I really wanted to have a motorcycle, but my father was a doctor and he flatly refused. He said, "I've pronounced too many kids your age dead. You can't have a motorcycle. But if you'd like to do something exciting, I'll help you learn how to fly." So I started flying gliders when I was in seventh grade. I had already known that I wanted to fly airplanes, even then. And when I discovered that there were airplanes that landed on ships, well, that sealed it for me. I entered the Naval Academy in 1974, the year after I graduated from high school.

In 1990 I was assigned to a squadron called VFA-81 in Air Wing 17, or the Sunliners, and we were attached to the USS *Saratoga*. We were scheduled to go in a normal deployment to the Middle East in August, so we were as trained and prepared as anybody when the Iraqis invaded Kuwait on August 2. We made it to the Red Sea, on the western side of the Saudi peninsula, by August 20 or 21. By that time Kuwait had been captured and there was this furious churn to get forces into the region to be able to deter any further aggression. We stayed there for five months before the war actually started. Now, I have a Christian faith, which helped me deal with the possibility of my own death. I felt that if the Lord called me home on this, then that's where I'd want to be. On the other hand, the idea of killing people was distasteful to me. Fortunately, with the technology and tactics at the time, we were far more precise about pinpointing the bad guys who were carrying weapons and driving tanks or airplanes. We could strike our targets with a minimal loss of life.

On January 15 we got word that the diplomatic efforts had failed and that we would soon initiate our opening sequence of strikes against Iraq. We had been training for these strikes for months, so there was a certain level of excitement—and a little bravado—at the anticipation of finally seeing action. At the same time, there was a lot of soul-searching and serious thought given to the fact that, no kidding, we're gonna do this. The opening strikes from the *Saratoga* were designed to suppress the defense around Baghdad. I wasn't on that first mission, but as I was being briefed for the second strike, we learned that one of our pilots was shot down and killed in the central part of Iraq. It was like ashes in our mouths. He was a good buddy of mine, a father of two—our children went to the same preschool together. It really helped bring home the realities of what we were doing.

My first combat mission was the first daylight strike on the seventeenth. From the Red Sea, over Saudi Arabia and into Iraq is somewhere between 650 and 750 nautical miles, one way. And there are no tactical airplanes that can go that distance without refueling, so on each mission we had to hook up with air force tanker planes. Typically there would be a sum total of maybe four or five air force tankers spaced out in a five-mile area in the sky, and there might be five navy airplanes attached to each tanker getting gas. So in that five-mile patch of sky there might be twenty-five to thirty navy jets all gassing up at the same time. It was an amazing sight, especially at night with all of the lights. It looked like the Empire State Building flying on its side through the sky.

We were about thirty miles south of the target and we were just now getting into the heart of the Iraqi surface-to-air missile envelopes.

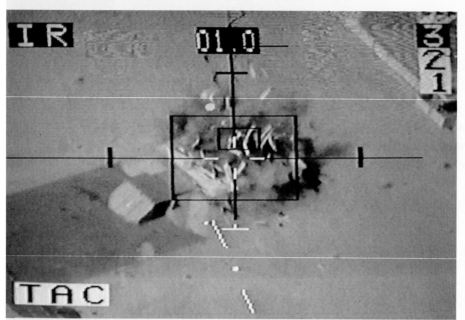

New bombs equipped with "video eyes" allowed pilots to closely monitor the progress of their missions. This image confirmed a successful Allied strike: destruction of an Iraqi munitions depot.

We got a radar lock on another group of airplanes flying very high and very slow just above our target, which is not where fighters defending a target would normally be. I wound up looking behind me for about the next minute, trying to see if this was a trap. These planes then turned and flew away from us. I had to decide whether to run these guys down or just go ahead and complete my mission. I thought to myself, "I came here to drop bombs, not to chase MIGs around." So I let him go and rolled in on the target. I dropped the bombs and did my jinks [erratic evasive maneuvers]. Now, I wasn't gonna come 640 nautical miles and not see my bombs hit their target, so I looked to see my four two-thousand-pound bombs falling together like four little fish in a pond. It was a really nice sight. But I could also see the muzzle flashes and the smoke and the dust coming from all over the field. There were literally dozens and dozens of little corkscrew bottle-rocket-looking things shooting up every which way down below me. It was clear that with all of this anti-aircraft fire, it was no time for me to speculate anymore. So I went back into another series of adrenaline-fed jinks and peeked back at the target just in time to see my four bombs hit their target. And that was the first time I smiled all day. I turned back and headed for the carrier. Less than two hours after I landed, I was being briefed for my next mission.

Peter Arnett traveled to Baghdad to report on the Gulf War for CNN's audience around the world.

Americans followed the progress of the Persian Gulf War on television, both on the three major networks and on the new Cable News Network. CNN offered Americans one of the most dramatic moments ever in television news, a chilling live picture of war as it happened. While the three networks had to decide whether to interrupt other programs to show the news, CNN was a twenty-four-hour window on the world. And CNN was not just broadcasting to American homes. By 1998 its cable links brought the news to 120 million homes overseas, making it the first truly global network. With so many people around the world watching the same images, it was hard not to feel that national boundaries were becoming less and less important.

The Rodney King beating, above, was one memorable video icon in an age of video icons.

"Can we get along?" pleaded Rodney King poignantly, in an attempt to end the Los Angeles riots of 1992, seen below. But much of both white and black America was no longer sure they could. Twenty-seven years earlier the L.A. riots in Watts had helped set in motion well-intentioned efforts to end the misery in America's blighted cities. Now poverty, crime, and racial animosity appeared to be even worse than before.

In March 1991 American television screens were showing graphic footage of violence closer to home. In the early morning hours of March 3, a plumbing parts sales representative named George Holliday used his camcorder to capture the violent beating of Rodney King, a twenty-five-year-old black man, by four white Los Angeles police officers. The videotape was seen on television by millions of people.

Many black citizens asserted that the attack was not an isolated event. They said blacks were routinely treated with greater suspicion than whites and suffered harsher treatment from police officers. Now the whole world became an eyewitness to the kind of police brutality that African Americans claimed to face on a regular basis. It seemed unthinkable that the police officers arrested for the beating of Rodney King would not be convicted. Surely the videotape was proof of a serious crime. But the lawyers for the police officers argued that King had been resisting arrest and was more threatening than the videotape made him look. The jury found the officers not guilty.

When the verdict was announced, Los Angeles erupted like a volcano. Hundreds of fires were set, and looters smashed into stores and ran off with millions of dollars' worth of merchandise. Innocent bystanders were attacked. In three days of unrest, fifty-four people were killed. It was the worst riot in America in this century.

Connie Chang, a daughter of Korean immigrants who was born in 1960, tried to help her parents protect their store from looters.

Chang, far left, with her parents outside the family's store.

I had seen the Rodney King video on television and I did not agree with what the policemen did. I thought they were guilty of overreaction. And I believed that if he was a white guy instead of an African American, then they would not have done what they did to him. But I was not prepared for the riots. It was awful. Since the center of the rioting was in South-Central, I got worried because there are a lot of Korean businesses there, including my family's liquor store. My brother and an employee were in the store when the riots began, and my parents told them to shut the store down and come home.

In the first hours of the rioting, my brother and I watched the coverage on TV and my parents listened to the Korean radio station. Because so many Korean shop owners were affected, Korean radio spent twenty-four hours a day doing nothing except coverage of the riots. Around seven-thirty my parents were listening when the station interviewed this one guy who started announcing the name of our store and saying that people were breaking the door in and taking some stuff out. So my parents went there and I joined them later.

Ours was a small store, a neighborhood store. And the majority of our clients were African American. We had black employees, too, and I treated them like, you know, my brother, and they treated me like their sister. But who starts looting our store? It's not neighborhood people. It's people coming from other areas. And they think it's all right because they don't know us and they think that all Koreans make money from out of their pockets.

When we got to the store, it looked terrible. An African American neighbor helped us get through the mess and into the store. Inside, we found that the lottery machine was gone. The telephones were gone. Even dishes and our rice cooker. The looters took a whole lot of merchandise and when they took it, you know, they dropped it, so the whole place smelled of alcohol. My two brothers and my cousin and my father all got up on the rooftop and stayed all night with guns, protecting the store. And they stayed on the rooftop I think three or four days. We were so worried about them we couldn't sleep. And yet even with my parents around, people were still trying to break the door down and get inside.

In the days after the riots, a lot of people came to the store and said they were sorry about the damages to our store. I think the damage was around $50,000 or $60,000 and insurance only paid half of that. Afterward my parents considered leaving America and going back to Korea. You know, it had hurt our feelings so much after the riot to see what it had done to our store. It's like all our hopes and dreams were gone. But if we went back to Korea, we would have to start all over again there, too.

After the riot I told everybody to put a smile on their face all the time. Just to show that we are human beings, too. When you are nice to people they won't be mean to you. They will be nice to you. Or at least we hope so.

The Bronco chase was a surreal experience on television and in real life. Spectators set up lawn chairs on the San Diego Freeway overpasses to wait for O.J. and wave him on.

In 1994 TV brought another dramatic trial into America's living rooms. O. J. Simpson, a well-known former football player who was now a sports commentator, movie actor, and advertising pitchman, was accused of the brutal murder of his ex-wife, Nicole, and her friend Ronald Goldman. Five days after the killings Americans flocked to their TVs to watch as Simpson fled from the police in a low-speed chase on a Los Angeles freeway. Simpson, in the backseat of a white Ford Bronco, gripped a revolver in one hand and a cellular phone in the other, announcing that he would kill himself if he couldn't see his mother.

By the time Simpson surrendered to the police, Americans were hooked on this tragic story. At first the case seemed to focus the nation's attention on the problem of domestic abuse. Simpson had been arrested before for hitting his wife, and she had once made a frightened 911 call when he had threatened her. But race soon became the dominant issue. Simpson was black, and his ex-wife and her friend were white. When it was discovered that one of the investigating officers had regularly used racist language, many African Americans became convinced that Simpson had been framed.

The decision to ask Simpson to try on the "bloody gloves" was a crucial mistake by the prosecution. "If it doesn't fit, you must acquit," rhymed defense lawyer Johnnie Cochran. But latex undergloves (required to protect the evidence), shrinkage, and Simpson's control over the demonstration (he was said to have crooked his fingers) could have been factors in a scene that led many to see the state's lawyers as incompetent.

The trial was broadcast live on television for eight months and nine days. White Americans tended to believe that Simpson was guilty of two murders, while black Americans tended to believe he was the victim of a racist frame-up. It seemed as though the whole country was watching when, on October 3, 1995, the jury pronounced the verdict of not guilty. You could almost hear the nation split in two as most black Americans cheered and most whites shook their heads in disgust.

The dream of true integration, the kind that would fulfill America's promise of equality and unity, seemed more remote than ever. Two weeks after the Simpson verdict, Nation of Islam leader Louis Farrakhan led the Million Man March in Washington, D.C. Women and whites were excluded. By focusing only on black men, the march appeared to reject the ideal of integration that had inspired Martin Luther King Jr. when he led the famous March on Washington in 1963. The Million Man March did stress some positive values—respect for women, responsibility to families, and a condemnation of violence. Still, it seemed that King's vision of a tolerant, integrated America was now a part of history.

The Million Man March was a bittersweet expression of black community—a "statement that black life is to be rescued from within," wrote African American social critic Gerald Early, "without white help or intervention."

African American men around the nation, including T. Deon Warner, born in 1959, traveled to Washington for the Million Man March.

There is a perception in America that black males are the lowest, dirtiest, most conniving criminal people on this earth. Even black people think that. I know. I'm black and I am male and I have to overcome that image every day of my life. I am an attorney at a Houston law firm. And I'm a pretty good lawyer. I work on the forty-third floor of this modern sixty-four-story building. It's a class building, the kind of place where everybody wears suits every day. One day I was riding the elevator up to my floor when a white woman got on, and as soon as she saw me she

Warner in his Houston law office, 1998.

started clutching her purse, as though to protect it from me. I thought, "This cannot be happening. Surely, I do not look as though I could ever be a threat to this woman or her purse." But, for some reason, to her I did.

So when they announced that there was going to be this Million Man March and that one of the goals of the march was to try to change the negative perception of the black male, I knew that I had to go. I didn't care how I got there or what I had to give up to go. It would be worth it to start changing the perception of black males. They were also trying to make a general statement that there are a lot of black males who don't go to prison, who are not beating their wives and girlfriends, and who are not out to rob everybody they see on the street.

I flew up from Houston and met a friend of mine from Michigan, and we made it down to the march site by about 4:45 A.M. When we got to the grounds things were still pretty empty. And then I started seeing people coming out of the woodwork. I mean, they were coming from all directions. Just thousands and thousands of people. About an hour after I got there, there were people as far as I could see. I was surprised at how many men brought their sons with them. Young kids. I mean, they were ten, twelve, thirteen, fourteen. These men wanted their children to see this event, to be part of it.

There were many speakers throughout the day. And they came from different parts of the community: various religions, various backgrounds. One of the speakers was a twelve-year-old kid. And he gave a speech about how proud he was that he had a black father and that he was there at the march. He said that he represented the sons and daughters of each of the black males that were there. And then he made a demand of the audience. He asked that each person who was at that march go home and, if need be, rearrange their life so that they become a more positive role model in the communities. That they become better husbands to their wives. And a better father to their children. And then he asked everybody at the closing of the speech, "Will you do that for me?" Here's a twelve-year-old kid and in a very eloquent way he made a request that just seemed so simple and so basic and yet so compelling.

Black males have been painted as a subculture in our society. So the point about black pride and black male redemption is that we need to change our image. I don't think we need to change, necessarily, what we do. Because I think we do a pretty good job of being citizens in this community. I think we need to change the image of what people think we do. If we don't take charge to create and mold the perception that we want people to have of us, nobody else will. People need to understand that black males come in all different shapes and sizes just like white males or any other people in America. And if you can't generalize as to the other groups, the white males, the Asian males, et cetera, then you shouldn't generalize as to black males.

233

William H. Gates, founder and chairman of the Microsoft Company, became the richest man in the United States in 1992. Here he appears on a large screen at the 1997 MacWorld convention with a dwarfed Steven Jobs, left, as the two announce Gates's decision to invest $150 million in Apple, his former rival.

In the 1990s it seemed that much of the way life was conducted in the twentieth century was rapidly becoming "history." Technology accelerated the pace of change, rocketing America toward the twenty-first century. Old rules and traditions were out of date, and new ones were not quite established. A revolution was taking place. The Industrial Revolution had brought in the machine age, which was coming to a close. The new revolution was ushering in the information age.

Computers had been around since the 1940s. The very name shows what they were expected to do—to compute, to add numbers. For decades these enormous machines could be found only in government offices and the headquarters of large corporations. What made the information age and the computer revolution possible was miniaturization. With the development of the microchip, the personal computer—a computer so small it could sit on a desk—became possible.

Almost overnight, computers changed play (video games), changed research (access to databases), and changed writing and editing (word processors). Computers even began to change work itself. With a modem, people could communicate through their office networks without leaving home. A scientist sitting in her pajamas in Minneapolis could argue with a colleague in Mozambique. More and more, the question about the computer wasn't "What can it do?" but "What can't it do?" Every day, it seemed, there was something new that this electronic wizard could do better or faster or more efficiently than people could.

By 1995 the computer was beginning to take people into the realm of science fiction—into cyberspace via the Internet. Originally developed by the Pentagon as a communications network that could withstand an atomic attack, the Internet was slow to catch on. But when it moved into mainstream American life, it swept in like a tidal wave. The most popular way to access the Internet was through the World Wide Web. Now people could find information, go shopping, or send electronic mail to the far corners of the world—all at the touch of a key.

Cyberspace pioneers ventured boldly into the virtual world online. Stacy Horn, born in 1956, was one of them.

Above: Horn in 1995. Top: The Echo home page.

When I was in my first semester at NYU, we had to call a place called the Well, and I was an instant addict. The Well is an online service based in California. It's a virtual community, where people get online to pretty much talk about anything under the sun. When I was in my last year of graduate school, I logged into the Well and someone said to me, "Hey, we heard that you were going to start the East Coast version of the Well." I had never said that, but all of a sudden it was like, "Duh, of course I can do that." So I just typed in, "Yes, I am."

In March 1990 Echo opened to the public. I came up with the name Echo because I had some vague idea like you throw your words out into the world and words come back. I couldn't get any investors interested because in 1989 nobody would believe me that the Internet was going to be hot.

I structured Echo so it was made up of different areas—we call them conferences. There's a books conference, a movies conference, an art conference, a New York conference, and within these conferences are conversations that fit under that general heading. The conversations are in what's called non-real time. So I can go into, say, the books conference and type in whatever I have to say. Then you can log in tomorrow, see what I've written, and add whatever you want to say about the subject. So the conversation keeps going on, and you can talk to these people regardless of who's logged in when. It's actually better than a live conversation. In a conversation that's non-real time, you can take your time and really consider your thoughts and say something more substantial.

On the Internet, you get to know someone from the inside out first, whereas in the physical world it's from the outside in. Each way has its pluses and minuses. People are people, and they're no different online than they are anywhere else. We don't sit down at our computers and all of a sudden become unreal. If I say "I love you" to someone on the phone, does that make it not real? So if I say it on a computer, why would that make it not real?

As they waited for the verdict in the 1997 trial of Timothy McVeigh, the families and friends of those who had died in the Oklahoma City bombing turned the fence surrounding the federal building site into a makeshift memorial. McVeigh was found guilty and sentenced to death.

The Internet played a big part in making the world seem smaller. People could now communicate with each other around the world, instantly, without laws or controls or many government restrictions. Many believed that the computer and the fax machine were vital to the collapse of Communism. A system that depended on controlling information simply could not withstand the new technologies. All people needed for ideas and information to flow was a computer and a phone line.

Still, while enthusiasm for the World Wide Web raced around the globe, there was also skepticism. Some intellectuals worried about its impact on society. With technology dominating our lives, would we become slaves to the machines? Would the creation of so many virtual worlds make people care less about the real world?

Michigan's "Gun Stock '95" was just one of the decade's many conventions displaying antigovernment paraphernalia.

Mistrust of technology inspired the "Unabomber." Theodore Kaczynski, a Harvard-educated hermit, had systematically targeted people in the technology industry. His mail bombs killed three people and injured twenty-three in sixteen separate attacks. They were an insane attempt to slow the progress of science and technology.

But Kaczynski's bombs were not as deadly as the work of Timothy McVeigh. On April 19, 1995, a truck bomb exploded outside a federal building in Oklahoma City, collapsing its nine floors. For days rescue workers pawed through the wreckage looking for survivors as outrage and despair gripped the nation. In the end, 168 people were dead, including 19 children who were in the building's day-care center.

How could there be a terrorist bombing in the heartland of the country? At first wild racist rumors placed the blame on "Middle Eastern types." But as federal agents began to investigate, a more disturbing theory arose. April 19 was a date well known to the FBI and other law enforcement agencies of the federal government. Two years previously on that date, the standoff at the Branch Davidian compound in Waco, Texas, had ended in a deadly fire. The Branch Davidians were a religious cult whose members had stockpiled weapons and were resisting investigation by federal authorities into how their children were being treated. On April 19, 1993, a total of eighty-four people died when federal agents attacked the compound.

For those on the political far right, Waco became a symbol of the tyranny of the federal government. The bombing of the federal building in Oklahoma City on April 19 was an act of revenge carried out not by foreign terrorists, but by an American veteran of the Persian Gulf War.

The approaching millennium seemed to focus attention on chaos, destruction, and death. Increasingly the evening news mentioned Dr. Jack Kevorkian, the Michigan physician known as "Dr. Death," who assisted terminally ill people to commit suicide. For decades medical advances had focused on prolonging life even through terrible disease. Medicine seemed unwilling to let the dying die. But by the nineties the "right-to-die" movement was gaining momentum. Advocates of the "right to die" suggested that there were greater concerns for patients and their families than simply being kept alive by machines regardless of the quality of life. The "right to die" with peace and dignity was seen as a humane concern that medical technology was ignoring.

Opponents of the "right to die" argued that doctors would soon be deciding who lived and who died, giving people a power that rightfully belonged to nature or to God. It was an argument that pitted the control of the individual against the power of fate, the quality of life against the sanctity of life. But while the controversy raged, real people still had to cope with agonizing decisions.

Christina Walker Campi, born in 1951, struggled with the best way to care for her dying husband.

Tom Campi, right, and his favorite picture of Christina and their two children, above, in 1980.

In 1996 my husband, Tom, became sick with what we thought was bronchitis. After antibiotics failed, he went through a battery of tests: chest X rays, MRI, CAT scan, bone scan, liver biopsy, ultrasound. It was like Western medicine at its best and its worst. At the end of it all they diagnosed him with metastasized lung cancer. And what was worse was that it had spread to his trachea and his liver. The next day I got our oncologist [cancer specialist] alone. He said, "What do you want to know?" I said, "I want to know how long he has." He said, "Six to nine months." My knees buckled.

For the next several months Tom went through round after round of chemotherapy and treatments, but his cancer continued to spread. The day that I decided to stop treatment on Tom, his most recent MRI showed that the cancer had moved to his brain. He had already started to show some neurological symptoms. He still knew who I was, but he was confused in his thinking. Tom was a brilliant guy who loved to talk, and to see him starting to get confused and losing control of himself was awful. He felt so humiliated. And he was in terrible pain. The cancer had also moved into his bones, which is the most painful cancer of all. I decided to ease his pain with morphine, knowing that this would hasten his death. I knew what I was doing. I was pretty clearheaded at that point. But I'm still tortured by the possibility that he could have had just a short amount of time more, a couple more days. I feel horrible that I was the one with sole control over this decision.

After Tom and I signed the DNR [do not resuscitate] order, he was moved to a private room and he was put on a morphine drip. After he was on the morphine for a while, a friend of mine, who happened to be a doctor on staff at the hospital, came by and said, "You know, he's not going to last more than a couple of hours right now." And I started to cry, because his children were on their way in from California to say good-bye, and I was afraid he would die before they got there. My friend told me to have them turn the morphine pump off, and then he'd come out of it for a little while. He woke up the next morning, and he saw his kids, and he kissed them, he hugged them. He kind of squeezed my hand a little bit, and he went back to sleep. And that was it; he never woke up again. Luckily, because I had them decrease the dosage, he was able to hold on to see his kids. But I had no guidance, no help on this at all except that I happened to have this friend who's on staff there. He would've died that night and not seen his kids had we not turned the morphine pump off.

We had been helped by the doctors with all sorts of treatment, but their help pretty much stopped when the treatment stopped. These were good doctors, with whom my husband was very attached, but they were trained to prolong life, not to deal with the dying process. I was left with this enormous feeling of having been abandoned.

This experience made me realize that birth and death are equally important, but we only pay attention to the birth end of it. Whenever you read anything about death or dying, you inevitably read about Dr. Kevorkian and about physician-assisted suicide. That is just a red herring in the whole discussion of death and dying. It has little to do with ordinary illness and dying. Death is like our dirty little secret. We all come to this world, but we pretend we are all not going to go out of it. I think Americans especially are terrified of death. We're a can-do population, so death seems like a terrible failure to us. We assign blame rather than see death for what it is, which is the way it's going to end for all of us.

"Oppressed by a fatal disease, a severe handicap, a crippling deformity? . . . Show him proper medical evidence that you should die, and Dr. Jack Kevorkian will help you kill yourself free of charge," read advertisements placed by "Dr. Death" in the 1980s. A few years later Kevorkian became a bizarre celebrity, casting the cause of assisted suicide in terms of civil rights.

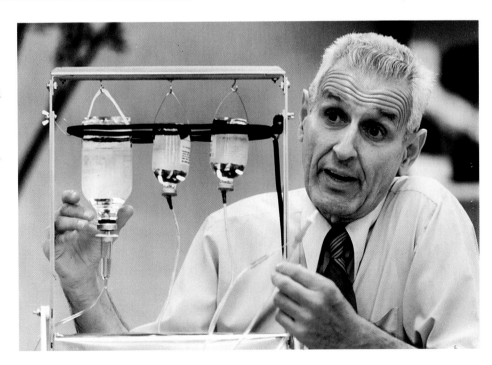

When England's Princess Diana died in a car crash in 1997, the new communications technology spread the news across the globe instantly. Although she and Prince Charles were divorced and Diana never would have been queen, she was known everywhere, and her death caused an enormous outpouring of grief. On the day of her funeral, more than a million people lined the streets of London to watch the coffin pass by. Billions more watched on television. Why did so many people mourn her passing? Diana was beautiful and charming, and she had supported many charities. But her connection to people seemed to go deeper than her outward accomplishments. People felt more loyalty to her than to the royal family she had married into. She was the "people's princess," and the sad story of youth and beauty and promise so tragically cut short moved people around the world to tears.

The funeral of Princess Diana could be seen as a bookend for the century, matching the grand funeral of England's Queen Victoria in 1901, which marked the passing of the 1800s. Life has changed more in the hundred years since Queen Victoria's death than it did in the thousand years that went before. And most of the changes the twentieth century brought were for the better. Think about this: The life expectancy of an American born in 1905 was only forty-nine years; by 1998 it was seventy-six years. Think, too, about the fact that in the late 1800s every other death was that of a baby. And remember how many people at the beginning of the century lived not only without electricity or telephones or TVs or computers, but also without the basic freedoms that democracy now gives them.

When the whole world descended upon Kensington Palace, bearing tokens of mourning for Diana, England's florists declared a shortage. Similar displays piled up around British embassies throughout the world.

It is true that the world completely failed to realize the fantasies of a golden age that many people dreamed of at the start of the twentieth century. Even the sophisticated streets of the new "global community" are still the scene of violence and bloodshed. In the twentieth century people believed that human will could control the forces of existence through science and technology. Yet at the end of the century a new humility seemed to be growing, a sense that there are limits to what people can control.

There is still no communications tool more powerful than the family story, and the family stories handed down from this century have all too often been tales of oppression, of prejudice, of war, of sorrow. In every family's history are ancestors who survived the terror of World War I, the horrors of the Holocaust, the injustices of the Jim Crow laws, or the grim grip of Communism. Both politics and technology made the twentieth century a century of killing. But politics and technology also provide us with hope for the future. And it is hope that carries us forward into the unknown territory we will explore in the next century.

A girl crosses a makeshift bridge connecting the Muslim and Croatian sectors of the Bosnian city of Mostar, 1996. Violence between the rival ethnic factions of the former Yugoslavia had recently destroyed the precious stone bridge that had spanned the spot since 1566. In the fragile peace achieved in 1997, groups on both sides called for the reconstruction of the old bridge as a symbol of reconciliation.

Picture Sources

Picture Sources
CB=Corbis-Bettmann
IWM=Imperial War Museum
LC=Library of Congress
NA=National Archives
UCB=UPI/Corbis-Bettmann
For more than one picture on a page, credits read left to right and top to bottom, unless noted.

Front cover: All credits read left to right and top to bottom. **First row:** UCB; Natural History Museum of Los Angeles; Hulton Getty **Second row:** Mary Ellen Mark; Kenneth Jarecke/Contact; Bob Henriques/Magnum **Third row:** David Scherman/*LIFE* Magazine © TIME Inc., UCB; NASA/Courtesy of Dennis Ivy; NA.

Front pages: Half-title: UCB **Title:** Brown Brothers **Table of contents:** Natural History Museum of Los Angeles **Introduction:** Courtesy of Betty Broyles; Courtesy of Clara Hancox; Milton J. Hinton Photographic Collection; Courtesy of Neal Shine; *The Tennessean*.

Chapter 1: 2: Brown Brothers **4:** Courtesy of Mabel Griep; Wright State University **5:** Culver Pictures; Courtesy of Alfred Levitt **6:** © Collection of The New-York Historical Society **7:** Lewis Hine/New York Public Library **8:** Lewis Hine/NA **9:** Courtesy of Eric Breitbart **10:** Courtesy of Charles Rohleder **11:** Georgia Department of Archives and History **12-13:** Florida State Archives **14:** LC **15:** LC **16:** (both) Courtesy of Lucy Haessler **17:** Brown Brothers **18:** Brown Brothers **19:** (left) Courtesy of Norma Hampson; Courtesy of Carolyn Hicks; Smithsonian Institution/ Political History Collection/ Division of Social History **20:** Culver Pictures **21:** CB.

Chapter 2: 22: IWM **23:** Bildarchiv und Porträtsammlung der Osterreichischen National-bibliothek **24:** CB **25:** Courtesy of Edward Francis **26:** IWM **27:** Collection of Eric Sauder **28-29:** Endeavour Group UK **30:** Courtesy of Alexander Bryansky **31:** David King Collection **32:** Courtesy of Corneal Davis **33:** Courtesy of Leon Despres; New York State Historical Association **34-35:** UCB **36:** Hulton Getty; Courtesy of Laura Frost Smith **37:** Courtesy of Laura Frost Smith **38:** Brown Brothers **39:** Milton J. Hinton Photographic Collection **40:** NA **41:** *San Francisco Chronicle*; National Archives of Canada.

Chapter 3: 42: Brown Brothers **43:** Henry Ford Museum & Greenfield Village **44:** Courtesy of Betty Broyles **45:** Minnesota Historical Society **46:** Courtesy of Albert Sindlinger **47:** CB **48:** Marc Wanamaker/Bison Archives **49:** CB **50-51:** Brown Brothers **51:** National Air & Space Museum **52:** CB **53:** UCB **54-55:** CB **56:** UCB **57:** Schomburg Center/New York Public Library; Courtesy of Howard "Stretch" Johnson **58:** Brown Brothers **59:** UCB; Swift Collection/Ball State University **61:** CB; *Daily News* **62:** Culver Pictures **63:** UCB.

Chapter 4: 64: UCB **65:** Schomburg Center/New York Public Library **66:** Courtesy of Clara Hancox **67:** UCB **68:** CB **69:** Courtesy of Bill Bailey **71:** Franklin D. Roosevelt Library; UCB **72-**

73: UCB **74:** (all three) Bayerische Staatsbibliothek **75:** Courtesy of Margrit Fischer; AKG Photo-London **76-77:** AKG Photo-London **78:** David King Collection **79:** David King Collection **80-81:** Endeavour Group UK **81:** David King Collection.

Chapter 5: 82: Robert Capa/Magnum **84:** The BBC **85:** CB **86:** Archives of Labor and Urban Affairs/Wayne State University **87:** Giraudon/Art Resource, NY, © 1998 Estate of Pablo Picasso/Artist Rights Society, NY; Documentation Center of Austrian Resistance (DÖW) **88:** Courtesy of Karla Stept **89:** Bildarchiv Preussischer Kulturbesitz **90-91:** Documentation Center of Austrian Resistance (DÖW) **92:** David Scherman/*LIFE* Magazine © TIME Inc. **93:** (both) Courtesy of Gilda Snow **94:** Courtesy of Peter Pechel **95:** Ullstein Bilderdienst; Courtesy of Julian Kulski **96:** Ghetto Fighter's House **97:** AP/Wide World Photos **98:** Courtesy of Paule Rogalin **99:** Hulton Getty **100:** Roger-Viollet **101:** Courtesy of Sheila Black; *New York Times* Pictures **102:** UCB **103:** Culver Pictures.

Chapter 6: 104: Yad Vashem **105:** NA **106:** CB; LC **107:** Courtesy of Neal Shine **108:** Marjory Collins/LC; NA **109:** Tsuguichi Koyanagi **110:** NA; Courtesy of Earle Curtis **111:** Sovfoto/Eastfoto **112:** Courtesy of Ernest Michel **113:** Courtesy of Ernest Michel **114:** UCB **115:** Courtesy of Clair Galdonik; Hulton Getty **116-117:** Robert Capa/Magnum **118:** Henri Cartier-Bresson/Magnum **119:** Arthur Leipzig/Courtesy of Howard Greenberg Gallery, NYC **120-121:** Tsuguichi Koyanagi **122:** Shunkichi Kikuchi **123:** Y. Matsushige/Sygma; George Silk/*LIFE* Magazine © Time Inc.

Chapter 7: 124: UCB **126:** AP/Wide World Photos; Joe Scherschel/*LIFE* Magazine © Time Inc. **128:** Courtesy of Sharpe James; Transcendental Graphics **129:** UCB **130:** David Seymour/Magnum **131:** Courtesy of Jack O. Bennett **132:** UCB **133:** UCB; AKG Photo-London **134-135:** UCB **136:** NA; AP/Wide World Photos **137:** Kobal Collection **138:** Michael Barson/Archive **139:** Courtesy of Len Maffioli; UCB.

Chapter 8: 140: Dan Weiner/Courtesy of Sandra Weiner **141:** Dan Weiner/ Courtesy of Sandra Weiner **142:** (both) Courtesy of Harriet Osborn **143:** (both) Culver Pictures **144:** Dan Weiner/ Courtesy of Sandra Weiner; Campbell Soup Company **145:** Personality Photos; Cornell Capa/Magnum **146:** Courtesy of Maxwell Dane; Costa Manos/Magnum **147:** Courtesy of Bunny Gibson; Dick Clark Productions, Inc. **148:** Wayne Miller/Magnum; Photofest **149:** Courtesy of Sam Phillips **150-151:** Jay Leviton-Atlanta; Elvis Presley Enterprises, Inc. **152:** Dan Weiner/Courtesy of Sandra Weiner **153:** AP/Wide World Photos **154:** Dan Weiner/Courtesy of Sandra Weiner; CB **155:** Burt Glinn/Magnum **156:** Courtesy of Anne Thompson; UCB **157:** Reprinted from *Popular Mechanics*, August 1959. © Hearst Corporation; Courtesy of Semyon Reznik **158:** Orlando Suero/The Lowenherz Collection of Kennedy Photographs at the

Peabody Institute of The Johns Hopkins University, Baltimore **159:** Cornell Capa/Magnum.

Chapter 9: 160: Nacio Jan Brown/Black Star **162:** Courtesy of Marnie Mueller **163:** Lee Lockwood © Time Inc. **164-165:** Bruce Davidson/Magnum; UCB **166:** *The Tennessean* **167:** Bob Adelman **168:** UCB; UCB **169:** Dan J. McCoy/Rainbow **170:** Jim Deverman Photo; *LIFE* Magazine, November 29, 1963 © Time Inc. **171:** Jim Murray Film; *Boston Globe* **172-173:** Carl T. Gossett/*New York Times* Pictures **174:** AP/Wide World Photos; Frank Wolfe/LBJ Library Collection **175:** Courtesy of Larry Gwin **176-177:** Larry Burrows Collection **178:** Bob Adelman; Dennis Brack/Black Star **179:** UCB **180:** Burt Glinn/Magnum **181:** Gerald S. Upham; UCB **182-183:** Josef Koudelka/Magnum **184:** NASA/Gamma Liaison **185:** NASA/Courtesy of Dennis Ivy.

Chapter 10: 186: Gilles Peress/Magnum **188:** Robert Azzi/Woodfin Camp **189:** Courtesy of LaNita Gaines; Arthur Grace/Stock, Boston **190:** John Filo **191:** Courtesy of Hugh Sloan **192:** Dirck Halstead ©Time Inc. **193:** Mark Godfrey/The Image Works; Nik Wheeler/Sipa Press **194-195:** Mary Ellen Mark **197:** Courtesy of Jane Adams **198:** J.L. Atlan/Sygma **199:** UCB; UCB **200:** David Burnett/Contact **202:** Sygma; Fred Ward/Black Star **203:** Arnold Zann/Black Star.

Chapter 11: 204: David Turnley/Black Star **205:** J.L. Atlan/Sygma **206:** Owen Franken/Sygma **208:** Arlene Gottfried **209:** Courtesy of Chris Burke **210:** Larry Fink **212:** (both) Courtesy of the McDaniels family **213:** Malcolm Denemark/Gamma Liaison **214:** Bob Sherman/Globe Photos; Courtesy of Malcolm McConnell **215:** Mary Ellen Mark **216:** Arlene Gottfried; Ellen B. Neipris **217:** Arthur Grace/Sygma **218:** David Burnett/Contact **219:** Courtesy of Marina Goldovskaya **220:** T. Orban/Sygma **222:** Kenneth Jarecke/Contact **223:** Raymond Depardon/Magnum.

Chapter 12: 224: William Mercer McLeod **225:** Huang Zeng/Xinhua/Sygma **226:** Bruno Barbey/Magnum **227:** U.S. Navy **228:** J. Witt/Sipa; Sygma **229:** Gamma-Liaison; Michael Schumann/Saba **230:** Ted Landreth **231:** Courtesy of KTLA-TV News, Tribune Broadcasting, Los Angeles; Reuters/Sam Mircovich/Archive Photos **232:** Eli Reed/Magnum **233:** Grady Carter **234:** Jim Bourg/Gamma Liaison **235:** Kevin Walker/Courtesy of Stacy Horn **236:** Ron Haviv/Saba **237:** Jetta Fraser/Impact Visuals **238:** (both) Courtesy of Christina Walker Campi **239:** Gamma Liaison **240:** Peter Turnley/Black Star **241:** Gilles Peress/Magnum.

Back cover: First row: Brown Brothers; NA. **Second row:** Brown Brothers; Orlando Suero/The Lowenherz Collection of Kennedy Photographs at the Peabody Institute of The Johns Hopkins University, Baltimore; Brown Brothers. **Third row:** Peter Turnley/Black Star; LC. **Endpapers: Front:** UCB. **Back:** Carl T. Gossett/*New York Times* Pictures.

INDEX